HOME CARE FAULT LINES

A volume in the series
The Culture and Politics of Health Care Work
Edited by Suzanne Gordon and Sioban Nelson

For a list of books in the series, visit our website
at www.cornellpress.cornell.edu.

HOME CARE FAULT LINES

Understanding Tensions and Creating Alliances

Cynthia J. Cranford

ILR PRESS

AN IMPRINT OF CORNELL UNIVERSITY PRESS

ITHACA AND LONDON

First published 2020 by Cornell University Press

Library of Congress Cataloging-in-Publication Data

Names: Cranford, Cynthia, author.
Title: Home care fault lines : understanding tensions and creating alliances / Cynthia J. Cranford.
Description: Ithaca [New York] : ILR Press, an imprint of Cornell University Press, 2020. | Series: The culture and politics of health care work | Includes bibliographical references and index.
Identifiers: LCCN 2019046918 (print) | LCCN 2019046919 (ebook) | ISBN 9781501749254 (hardcover) | ISBN 9781501749261 (paperback) | ISBN 9781501749278 (epub) | ISBN 9781501749285 (pdf)
Subjects: LCSH: Home care services—California—Los Angeles. | Home health aides—California—Los Angeles. | Older people—Home care—California— Los Angeles. | People with disabilities—Home care—California—Los Angeles.| Home care services—Ontario—Toronto. | Home health aides—Ontario— Toronto. | Older people—Home care—Ontario—Toronto. | People with disabilities—Home care—Ontario—Toronto.
Classification: LCC RA645.36.C2 C73 2020 (print) | LCC RA645.36.C2 (ebook) | DDC 362.1409794/94—dc23
LC record available at https://lccn.loc.gov/2019046918
LC ebook record available at https://lccn.loc.gov/2019046919

For Rob

Contents

Acknowledgments

In this book I analyze tensions between flexibility for mostly poor, disabled, and elderly people who need help with daily activities of life and security for the predominately immigrant women workers who provide this help, alongside the potential for alliances that challenge inequalities in this intimate service and labor. My own biography surely informs this focus on tensions and the hopeful quest for progressive social change. I grew up with a single mother in a working-class, Southern California city but at the formative age of sixteen moved to Kenya, where I came to question much about my Christian, American upbringing. I waitressed my way through university and then found labor activism in graduate school. Later I settled in Canada for both secure employment and for love. My father's stroke and forced retirement in his early sixties, the joys and responsibilities as a mother of two young children, and the coordination of child care and emotional connections with aging parents across Canada, the United States, and the UK have more recently shaped my views on care, labor, and migration. Nevertheless, as an able-bodied, middle-aged, white woman professor with citizenship in two rich countries, my analysis has been mainly forged in the intersection of scholarly debates and interviews with people inside the growing sector of paid elder care and disability support.

I am most indebted to the people my research assistants and I interviewed. I thank especially those directly involved in receiving and providing this intimate service and labor for sharing their personal experiences and for taking the time to explain their worlds. It is their lives that I have put at the center of my analysis. I also thank the government social service representatives, employers, disability and senior advocates, and union and labor activists for sharing their viewpoints on this complex sector from various angles. I must note that my arguments do not necessarily reflect the views of the state organizations from which some of these key informants come, namely the Department of Public Social Services and Public Assistance Services Council in Los Angeles and the Community Care Access Centres in Toronto.

My analysis in this book has been shaped over many years by the invaluable input of several colleagues and community-based interlocutors. The earliest idea for the study of the tensions and possible alliances in intimate labor began through a case study I did as a post-doctoral researcher in 2001–3 at York University. I am grateful to Leah Vosko, Judy Fudge, and Eric Tucker, whose guidance shaped the research that informed chapter 3, and who, along with Pat Armstrong, introduced me to critical, social policy analysis. Our many exchanges enriched my qualitative analysis of inequalities. Conversations around activism challenging precarious employment, especially with Deena Ladd, Mary Gellatly, Tania Das Gupta, and Leah Vosko, influenced my ideas about community unionism featured in the final chapter. These ideas developed further through participatory action research with Asian Immigrant Women Advocates (AIWA) in Oakland and Jennifer Chun. The Pilipinx case study featured in chapter 4 was feasible through collaboration with Jennifer Nazareno and the Filipino American Services Group, Inc., in Los Angeles.

I have benefited greatly from feedback at several conferences and workshops. The audience and other panelists at two Disability Section–sponsored sessions of the Society for the Study of Social Problems, "Care Work in the Home" in 2012 and "Disability, Poverty and Work: Multiple Locations of Disadvantage" in 2014, provided me important critical insights into the analysis of care. I thank Rhacel Parreñas for her invitation to participate in the American Sociological Association (ASA) session "Caring Labor and Citizenship: An International Perspective" in 2010 and for feedback during the event. At this session and a conference organized by Bridget Anderson, Isabel Shutes and Fiona Williams, "Making Connections: Migration, Gender and Care Labour in Transnational Context," at Oxford University's Centre on Migration, Policy and Society in 2011, I received valuable comments on my early comparative framework. Comments from several labor studies colleagues helped me develop my ideas about an intimate community unionism, especially through presentations at McMaster University's Labour Studies Department in 2011 and the Canadian Sociological Association meetings in 2014. I would like to thank Ruth Milkman, whose comments as discussant at the ASA session "Organizing Precarious Workers: Comparative Perspectives on Low-Wage Workers and Labor Movements" in 2013 helped me articulate the complex migration and work histories featured in chapter 1. In 2015 her feedback at the ASA session "Precarious Workers and Professionals" pushed me to articulate an alternative unionism that would fit with the complexities of this labor. The Carework Network has provided intellectual support and fostered many of my ideas in this book, some of which I presented at the Carework Network's 2007 and 2009 conferences and the First Global Carework Summit at University of Massachusetts Lowell in 2017. I also want to recognize the feedback I received in several workshops organized by the Gender, Migration and Work of Care project and the influence of many conversations with colleagues in this project including Monica Boyd, Hae Yeon Choo, Jennifer Fish, André Laliberté, Rianne Mahon, Sonya Michel, Ito Peng, and Rachel Silvey. I thank Deborah Brennan for inviting me to present my work at the Social Policy Research Centre, University of New

South Wales, Sydney, Australia, in 2016. I am grateful to Sara Charlesworth for organizing the Symposium on International Perspectives on Personalised Social Support and Care, at RMIT University, Melbourne, Australia, in 2016, for her insightful comments on chapter 7, and for her encouraging words along the way. The feedback I received from diverse audiences in these venues helped me crystalize the comparative arguments of this book and strengthen its relevance to audiences beyond North America and beyond sociology.

The research that informs this book was possible thanks to assistance from and collaboration with many students at the University of Toronto. Valerie Damasco, Diana Miller, Nicole Freeman, Ingrid Kittlaus, and Jade Vo conducted many of the interviews. These graduate students, along with Athena Engman and Conely DeLeon and undergraduates Jana Borras and Charmaine Lata, assiduously completed the laborious task of verbatim transcription. Valerie, Jana, and Conely also did the crucial creative work of translating the Tagalog interviews into English. My analysis of important pieces of the cases profiled in this book benefited from coauthorship with Diana Miller, Athena Engman, Louise Birdsell Bauer, and Angela Hick and conversations with Yang-Sook Kim about her related dissertation research.

The research that informs this book, formal partnerships with colleagues and community, student research assistance, and the ability to share early ideas at conferences have been supported by several grants and academic institutions. As co-investigator on the Social Sciences and Humanities Research Council of Canada (SSHRC) grant "Community-University Research Alliance on Contingent Work" (2004–6), I was able to begin interviewing key informants, and I thank Leah Vosko for her support. The University of Toronto also provided funding for the early stage of this research through a 2005 Connaught New Staff Matching Grant: "Personal Care-Work in Context: Ontario and California: 1970 to Present." The SSHRC supported the bulk of the research through my 2006–9 grant "Negotiating Quality Care and Quality Work: Personal Care Providers and People with Disabilities in Ontario." The research in chapter 4 and follow-up interviews were supported by the SSHRC-funded Partnership Grant "Gender, Migration and the Work of Care" (2012–19) through the subproject "Understanding and Improving Immigrant Labour Markets for Personal Care Work: A Comparative Analysis of Public Sector Personal Care Work in North America," in collaboration with Jennifer Chun and AIWA. I thank Ito Peng for her support. I also would like to recognize Sherri Klassen in the University of Toronto Graduate Sociology Department for her skill and assistance with grant writing. The Sociology Department at the Mississauga Campus lent crucial support for this project by funding a book workshop and editing, and I would like to thank especially the chair, Anna Korteweg. I also recognize the work of Pamela Armah and Lorna Taylor managing research funds. Finally, I thank the Department of Sociology at the University of Canterbury in New Zealand for providing me with office space in their winter of 2016, when I wrote several chapters.

Several people deserve recognition for helping me to bring this book to publication. Pat Armstrong, Jennifer Chun, and Mary Romero read a draft of the manuscript in a March 2018 workshop. I thank them for their generosity with their time. Their kind and constructive comments shaped this book in significant ways. I especially acknowledge Jennifer Chun for her many discussions with me about this work over the years and her keen analytical comments on the conclusion. I thank Eileen Boris for evaluating the manuscript based on its central analysis and method while encouraging me to pay more attention to the historical context, which helped me to strengthen the argument greatly. Maria Schmeeckle read the entire manuscript and provided helpful editorial suggestions, and her pep talks, goal-setting phone meetings, and overall amazing friendship helped give me the confidence to keep writing this book. Paula Maurutto's friendship and wit also helped sustain me over the years. I am indebted to Jenny Gavacs who, as a freelance editor, helped me tell a complex story in an accessible, engaging way. I thank series editor Sioban Nelson and especially Editorial Director Frances Benson at Cornell's ILR Press for their interest in this book and for their leadership. I am indebted to Chris Tilly for coming up with the *Fault Lines* title. Finally, I want to thank to my mom, Sharon Cranford, and my mother-in-law, Jennifer Wilton, for looking after my children for significant parts of several summers while I worked on this book.

Last, yet anything but least, I want to recognize Rob Wilton for his endless intellectual support and for his care work. Rob listened as I rehearsed and revised, over and over, the ideas that became this book. He read drafts of every chapter multiple times. Our countless discussions were central to helping me elaborate the key arguments. Rob did all this while providing the bulk of care for our children, cooking, and cleaning, especially in the last couple of years. Thank you, Rob, for everything you do for me, the children, and for us.

A Note on Sources

The data I analyze in this book are drawn from interviews with 111 workers and 127 recipients of domestic, or home-based, personal support services and 106 key informants who were knowledgeable about how personal support services were organized. Most of these interviews were done with individuals. The Pilipinx recipients and some of the workers in Los Angeles preferred to be interviewed in groups, however. In the text, in order to protect confidentiality, I refer to individual workers and recipients with pseudonyms that reflect gender, racial, and ethnic identity. In some cases, my research assistants and I interviewed recipient-worker dyads. This was not a feature of the study design but occurred due to dense networks in the sector. Yet my relational approach does not hinge on getting the "truth" from both sides of a dyad. Instead, I analyze recipient and worker positions within intersecting social relations. To protect the identity of the key informants I use the codes described below.

I cite the thirteen union and community-based labor activists interviewed in California as CALabor1–13, and the sixteen Toronto union officials as TOUnion1–16. I cite the four community-based immigrant senior advocates in Los Angeles as CASenior1–4. I cite the ten administrators and social workers from the government body that coordinated the Los Angeles In-Home Supportive Services (IHSS) Program as IHSSA and IHSSS, respectively, and give them a number. I follow the same principle for the eight administrators and social workers from the government body that coordinated the Toronto home care program, the Community Care Access Centres (CCAC). I use "social worker" to refer also to caseworkers who determined hours, even though some did not have a social work degree, because this is how the people we interviewed described them. The Attendant Services program was coordinated by the employing service providers, so I quote them as well as the agency employers in the home care program as E1–30. I quote the eight representatives from the Los Angeles Public Assistance Services Council (PASC), the public authority that represents recipients in Los Angeles, and one representative from a San Francisco Bay Area public authority as P1–P9. Some members of the PASC board were also disability advocates and I describe them as such in the text. I cite the six Los Angeles disability advocates who were not also PASC representatives, all but one of whom was from an independent living center, as D1–D6. I interviewed two people from the same independent living center and label them D5a and D5b. I cite the disability advocates in Toronto, who were all also board members of a non-profit service-providing agency, as B1–B9.

More specific information about the data upon which each case study is based can be found in the unnumbered first note of each of chapters 3 through 6. See Table A1 in the appendix to this book for more information on the key informant interviews.

HOME CARE FAULT LINES

TENSIONS BETWEEN FLEXIBILITY AND SECURITY

Alex is part of the rapidly growing population of people in the United States, Canada, and other countries who need help with intimate daily activities like getting up and dressed, bathing, eating, going to the bathroom, moving around, keeping one's spirits up, and maintaining a clean house. Most elderly and disabled people prefer to remain in their own home, yet unpaid family care is insufficient.[1] After Alex was injured at fifteen, his mother provided the daily support necessary for him to finish school and attend community college. Later his wife facilitated his career as an accountant. For the fifteen years before our interview, Alex had been receiving paid help from mostly immigrant workers. These government-funded services became essential after Alex and his wife each broke a hip. Alex, a white man in his late sixties, described both tension and intimacy with the personal support workers.

> The best part of being confined and my world being turned upside down has, in a funny way, been the people I have met. I mean, I've got attendants from Sweden, Chile, China, Kazakhstan, Nigeria, and, of course, the Caribbean and even a lot of Canadians. I love all of them.... I am able to talk with them. They do seem to understand me. Some of them, they even seem to like me.... Some of them don't, and I'm not sure they like anybody.... The attendants have to have more empathy and understanding. I am not pleased with what happened to my hip and sometimes that frustration, or frustration of living here with my wife, or her frustration boils over, and it comes out sideways. Under the [service-providing agency's]

rules, you could start getting threatening letters about withdrawing services. Or, if you've got an intelligent attendant, they shrug it off and come
back. You can't abuse them in any way. . . . The rule of thumb, you know,
in the real world is "keep it simple, and straighten it out."

Alex's experience living long-term with paraplegia and more recently with
osteoporosis points to the growing requirements for old age and disability
support due to population aging, health care developments that prolong disabled people's lives, and widespread rejection of nursing homes. Alex's case
also illustrates a second pressing issue that intersects with old age and disability
support: immigration.

Kay, a Black woman in her late forties, is among a growing workforce providing intimate support in elderly and disabled people's homes, a workforce mostly
comprising immigrant women.[2] Kay migrated to Toronto in the early 1990s to
join her father and brother, then married another immigrant personal support
worker and had a son. Kay was born and raised in Guyana, where she finished
high school. Upon arrival in Toronto, she did assembly work for several years and
then enrolled in a course for home health aides at a community college. She then
did a series of precarious jobs, often simultaneously, including privately paid
home care and temporary placements in nursing homes and hospitals. At the
time of our interview, she had been working seventeen years for a unionized and
relatively well-paying, government-funded, nonprofit agency focused on services
to people with physical disabilities, like Alex. Similar to Alex, Kay described tensions within this intimate paid relationship.

> My relationship with consumers is very professional, but I sometimes
> break it, you know, just to be lively, because sometimes the consumers
> will put the radio on. . . . I have a very good relationship with them so
> far. . . . I know sometimes they take out their frustration on us. So it's,
> like, a nice sort of word you say, "I would appreciate if you speak to
> me properly." . . . I find the consumers are, like, we don't know about
> anything because we come from another country. It happens all the
> time. . . . That's why I try to be as professional as I can. . . . Sometimes,
> I just ignore them and do what I got to do and get out. And at times,
> "Oh, you think because I come from Guyana I don't know about any-
> thing? You think I don't know what you eating there? My son, the same
> thing I do for my son."

Importantly, Kay also described her efforts to mediate tensions by drawing emotional boundaries and sometimes through direct confrontation.

The relationship between Alex and Kay, and people like them, deserves attention because in this growing sector of in-home elderly and disability support

the worlds of employment and social services come together in complex ways and sometimes collide. Most studies, however, cannot capture these dynamics because they examine just the workers or only the recipients, remain solely at the policy level, or focus on the private sector.[3] Recipients and workers develop close and meaningful work relationships, yet they experience different "faces of oppression," which can bubble up in the relationship and generate tension.[4] Looking closely at the experiences of people like Kay and Alex, in relation to each other and in the social context within which they relate to one another, reveals a tension between *flexibility* for recipients and *security* for workers.

Recipients face marginalization vis-à-vis a state and society that values independence.[5] Many of the people interviewed had been in care institutions that cast them wholly as dependents; others experienced lack of adequately funded support at home, requiring reliance on insufficient unpaid family help, as was the case for Alex. This marginalization fuels recipients' quest for *flexibility* in their current services.[6]

Workers experience different axes of oppression, namely devaluation and lack of recognition within class and gender inequalities, which shapes their pursuit of *security*. Like Kay, the majority of personal support workers in the urban areas of industrialized nations are immigrant women from less industrialized countries, and their economic insecurity is infused with racialization through nation of origin, language, accent, religion, culture, or skin color.[7]

Crucially, paying close attention to the relationship between workers and recipients not only allows us to understand tensions but also to chart the potential for flexibility with security. Alex's and Kay's quotes include traces of hope for working through tensions—in Alex's claim that he "loves" the workers who hail from all over the world and in Kay's feeling that she has crafted a "very good relationship" with the "consumers" by keeping it "professional." Yet such assertions can be problematic if recipients and workers do not have collective backing and instead negotiate tensions as atomized individuals.

What exacerbates tensions or encourages solidarity between recipients and workers? In this book, I answer this question with a multilevel comparative study of in-home, old age, and disability support programs in Los Angeles and Toronto. I call this sector "domestic personal support." The United States and Canada are both white settler nations of immigrants, and both face expanding domestic personal support needs, thus providing ideal locales for this study. Yet understanding tensions, and the possibilities to mitigate them, requires not comparative analysis of large entities like nations but rather multiple levels of comparative analysis.

Flexibility-security tensions between people like Alex and Kay are shaped not only by clashes between distinct locations in a matrix of oppression but also by the government policies and service agency rules that structure domestic personal support. In recent years, scholars have analyzed how care, migration, and employment policies work together to shape inequality within domestic personal support, yet within this integrative framework the analysis of employment policy is least developed.[8] Recent policy initiatives in Australia, Canada, New Zealand, the United States, and within Europe, beginning with disability support and more recently extending to the elderly, aim to give recipients the labor market flexibility of employers, by allowing them to hire and fire their own workers.[9] However, employment scholars document that this labor market flexibility generally results in precarity for workers through temporary contracts and insecure income.[10] Here we see the relationship between the state and the labor market, through social policies defining the employer. This raises a question: is it possible to achieve security for workers even when recipients have labor market flexibility? Policies that seek to combine labor market flexibility and labor market security have operated in Europe under the umbrella of "flexicurity."[11] A labor-disability-senior alliance won a version of labor market security with flexibility in California.[12] Yet the level at which social movements engage with their members to bring security with flexibility requires much further analysis, the complexity of which I delineate in figure 1. Indeed, flexibility with security will require more than policy reform at the state and labor market levels.

State funding and labor market policies, while important, are only partial solutions because they do not address tensions at the more intimate level of the labor process. The workers and recipients interviewed for this book emphasized everyday concerns at length. Workers complained of not only insufficient employment and of income inequality in the labor market but also of deeper

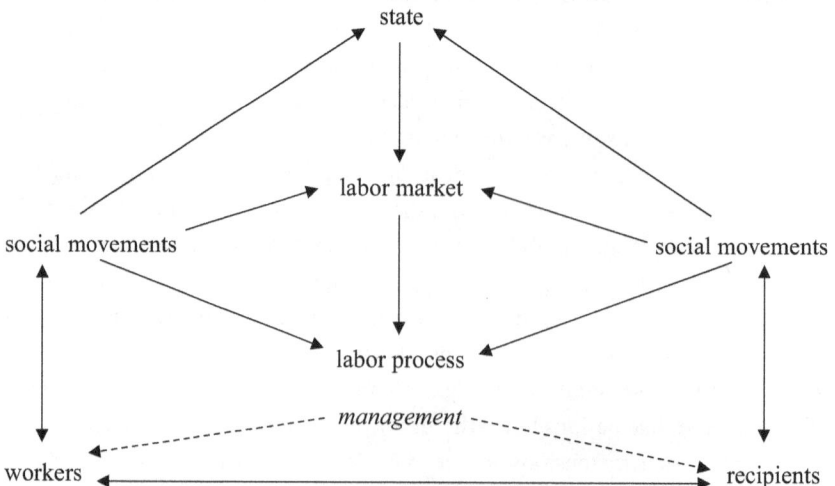

FIGURE 1. Levels of analysis in the study of domestic personal support

sources of insecurity—like the racialized indignities linked to assumptions that connect place of birth in a less industrialized country to inferior knowledge, as mentioned by Kay. Nonetheless, the importance of flexibility at this intimate level is clear in the views of Alex, who feels workers should adapt to his and to his wife's moods because they come not from a place of privilege but from the marginalizing experiences of disability and age. Flexicurity and policies like it cast recipients like Alex as "employers" of workers like Kay, presumably so they can change what, when, where, and how their support is provided. However, there might be other ways to give recipients the sought-after flexibility at this labor process level that do not result in workers' insecurity. In some domestic personal support programs but not all, there are agencies whose managers mediate the relationship between workers and recipients. Here we see the relationship between the labor market policy (that defines who is the employer in a program) and the labor process.

An agency's rules regarding how workers and recipients should engage one another is another aspect that can shape flexibility and security at the intimate level. Agency rules can support workers' efforts toward, in Kay's words, "keeping it professional" or not. They can also require recipients to control their frustration, as alluded to by Alex. How do workers and recipients negotiate tensions within agency rules or lack thereof? Domestic personal support programs vary in terms of whom legislation deems the official employer but also in the level and type of rules that managers set and enforce, rules that shape worker and recipient relationships in the labor process. As such, comparative analysis at the program level is essential to understanding the flexibility-security trade-off and untangling the potential for flexibility with security in domestic personal support.

Looking closely at the experiences of people like Alex and Kay across domestic personal support programs that have different labor market policies and different labor process rules, I am able to ask original questions. In settings where the recipient is the employer, how do workers negotiate their relationship with recipients in order to keep their jobs and to garner respect? What kinds of relational work do recipients do in various settings to keep good workers and their dignity?[13] In settings where an agency is the employer, do agency rules encourage recipients and workers to compromise, or do they pit them against one another? How much do workers and recipients negotiate their relationship under the agency's radar? Finally, how do workers and recipients' collective backing, through labor, disability, or other social movements, shape their ability to negotiate flexibility with security?

In this book I compare Toronto and Los Angeles domestic personal support programs that provide assistance to adults with physical disabilities and to elderly people across and within class and racial lines, inside and outside of families, and provided to and by both women and men. Given dynamic politics that have ushered in distinct programs over time and place, as well as diverse theoretical frameworks, different actors use different terms to refer to recipients and workers in this sector. Disability advocates and some scholars reject the terms "client" and especially "patient" and embrace the terms "consumer" (in the United States and sometimes Canada) or "service user" (in the UK) to emphasize recipients' efforts to gain more influence over these nonmedical social services. Some reject the term "care" as denoting medicalized professional expertise or paternalistic charity and pity and instead use "support" or "help."[14] Yet the use of the term "consumer" suggests choice in a market that is not evident, despite creeping marketization.[15] The frontline, in-home personal support workers in this study are referred to in the literature and in various programs as "personal support workers," "personal attendants," "home health aides," "home care aides," "home care workers," "caregivers," and sometimes "domestic workers." Following work and employment scholars and labor organizers, I use "worker" rather than "caregiver" to emphasize this care as labor. I analyze, rather than assume, the meaning of the relationship between those directly receiving and providing domestic personal support. I thus use the most generic, if somewhat objectifying terms "worker" and "recipient" to refer to their structural location as paid frontline workers and as beneficiaries of state-funded services. However, when I cite study participants or discuss the particular programs under analysis, I use the terms used by the actors in question to recognize how program language and identities embed a politics situated in time and place.

By comparing flexibility and security across domestic personal support programs I address the biggest question of this book: how do workers' and recipients' distinct locations in multiple systems of inequality, social policies defining the program and its labor market, rules about the labor process, and social movement strategies combine to shape tension between flexibility and security (or, alternatively, cooperation)? In order to answer this question, we need not only a multilevel analysis, as shown in figure 1. We also need conceptual tools that better bridge the scholarly silos of gender, labor, and migration on the one hand and disability and aging studies on the other.

Flexibility and Security at the Labor Market Level

Gender and labor scholars link the growth of precarious labor markets, representing insecure employment, to employers' advancing labor market flexibility to hire and fire, pay lower wages, and provide fewer benefits.[16] Women, migrants,

and indigenous and racialized peoples have long experienced labor market insecurity in sectors like farm labor and domestic work, but since the 1970s precarious
conditions have spread to more occupations, including public or government-
funded ones.[17] Employers gain labor market flexibility in large part through their
use of part-time and temporary employment contracts. In personal support,
governments contract out employer responsibilities to nonprofit or for-profit
agencies and increasingly to individuals, even though they still control the funding. There is growing evidence that this contracting out is meant not only, or
even primarily, to respond to recipients' desire for flexibility but also to generate flexibility for the government to cut welfare costs.[18] In the United States and
Canada, labor policy based on the post--World War II factory links labor market
flexibility for governments and employers on the one hand to workers' labor
market insecurity on the other. This policy assumes a standard employment
relationship—that is, a direct and continuous relationship between an employee
and a firm. It imagines that a single employer pays, hires, fires, and supervises
the worker, as in a factory, but this does not protect workers with multiple,
flexible employment contracts. As a result, such workers are highly precarious
in that they have insecure employment and earnings and limited social security
coverage. Key to the analysis of insecurity in labor markets, then, is answering
this question: who are the actors in the employment relationship?[19]

Making its study complex but also opening up space to analyze the potentials for flexibility with security, the state rarely provides services directly and
arranges support in multiple ways. Sometimes an agency is the legal employer,
but the recipient gives direction and acts as a de facto employer. This agency
model is common in in the UK, Canada, and parts of the United States, including
two of the cases profiled in this book.[20] Sometimes the person using the services
receives funding directly from the government to hire a worker, and legislation
thus defines them as the sole employer; this is becoming increasingly common
in English-speaking countries and Europe and is included in a third case profiled
in this book.[21] Legislation defines workers in this situation as either domestic
servants or self-employed.[22] In both agency and direct models, the government
acts as a de facto employer through its influence on funding, but it accepts little
to no employer responsibility. Given this complexity, examining the degree of
influence of both the legal and de facto employers is a major pillar of my analysis.

Workers' immigrant status, nationality, and race also contribute to labor market
insecurity, but it is unclear how recipients fit into this dynamic. The government-
funded services of focus in this book are neither the most flexible nor the most
insecure forms of domestic personal support. Many migration and labor scholars focus on private-sector systems that recruit temporary migrants whose stay
in the country is contingent on living with their employer, or undocumented

migrants working in a highly unregulated economy.[23] Some of the workers in my studies started out in these extremely insecure systems with highly precarious citizenship status but had achieved legal immigration status by the time they entered the government-funded sector of focus here. Yet their quest for security continued well beyond gaining formal, permanent status, as found in other studies.[24] Furthermore, immigrants who arrived with permanent status face labor market disadvantages through the racialization of their national origin.[25] When recipients are white and governments deem them the employer, as is true in one of the cases profiled in this book, any deeply held prejudices can take the form of direct hiring bias against workers of color, but anti-discrimination policy does not extend to individual household employers or to de facto employers. When recipients are white and an agency contracted by the government is the employer, as is common in another case I studied, these employers may appease recipients' racialized preferences yet still get around anti–employment discrimination legislation by classifying the worker as casual or self-employed.[26] Yet, while preferences for white workers could mean exclusion from employment or fewer hours for workers of color, studies of sectors rejected by native-born workers document employer preferences for immigrant workers of color because their limited labor market choice gives them little power to demand fair conditions.[27] Immigrant recipients, who are the subject of a third case in this book, also use "ethnic logics" in order to recruit workers like themselves, but how this might shape workers' security is unclear because few studies examine co-ethnic personal support.[28] Comparing cases where workers and recipients have varying social locations allows me to consider how labor market flexibility gets tangled up with racialized preferences in multiple ways, and the implications for worker security.

The other side of potential labor market flexibility for recipients, employers, and governments, on the one hand, and insecurity for workers, on the other, is the possibility of labor market security for workers at the expense of flexibility for recipients. Labor market security for workers is most easily and commonly achieved in North America by limiting labor market flexibility, since labor protections are based on the rigid, factory workplace. In personal support, the closest we come to this type of workplace is the nursing home or long-term residential care. Studies find that recipients have little, if any, ability to influence who enters one's living area to provide intimate support in these institutional settings.[29] Some direct a similar critique at the agency model, even though it provides support to people in their own homes, because, like care institutions, agencies rarely allow recipients to hire and fire.[30]

Insights into precarious employment from gender, work, and migration scholarship can help unravel the implications of recipient flexibility for worker insecurity and vice versa, but there are some unique features of domestic personal support that require modified questions. Similar to broad trends in precarious employment, actors beyond the one defined as the employer in labor policy shape the security of personal support workers. In personal support, however, there are usually more actors with influence over worker security, and their influence as legal or de facto employers is more varied than in other cases of precarious employment. This reality requires moving beyond the common analysis of precarious employment at the policy level by asking instead which actor or actors— the government, the agency, the recipient, or all of the above—influence workers' employment and income security and in what ways. Marking an even greater distinction of the domestic personal support sector: even when policy deems the recipient the employer, they are not really a traditional employer because their requests for flexibility are based not on cost-cutting but rather on intermittent, bodily needs. This fact requires a second question inspired by (but moving beyond) matters addressed by most precarious employment scholars and integrating concerns raised by aging and disability studies: does workers' labor market security hinge on limiting recipient flexibility? Tackling this question requires also analyzing the possibilities of imaginative social movement organizing.

Returning to Alex and Kay: Alex is an advocate for better funding, while Kay is an active union member, suggesting that the collective backing of social movements boosts both of their calls, one for flexibility and the other for security. Kay tries to speak nicely even when recipients "take out their frustration" out on her, but when faced with racializing assumptions about her country of birth she directly confronts them. Kay at times feels empowered to challenge recipients' racialization because her union seeks to address workplace tensions, but not all unions are attuned to the intimate labor process of domestic personal support, and many of these workers have no collective voice at all. Recipients also have varying levels of collective backing from social movements. Some programs are closely linked to an independent living movement—a section of the disability rights movement that pushes for flexibility and quality in disability support services. However, what kinds of worker protections are compatible with recipient flexibility? Policy studies too often stop short of examining whether social movement strategies address flexibility with security. Drawing on a vibrant field of labor studies, I ask: how do social movements, including unions, community-based labor organizations, and labor-disability or labor-senior alliances, organize for flexibility with security? Historically, unions have had more power in Canada than in the United States, given better legislation, less employer and state opposition, and a larger public sector. Yet both labor movements have suffered and are rethinking their strategies in light of growing labor market precarity and neoliberal policies.[31] There are also connections between labor and disability movements' strategies across Canada and the United States.

Flexibility and Security at the Intimate, Labor Process Level

Uncovering how social movements might push for flexibility with security in domestic personal support requires attention to the intimate relationships so central in this sector. Recipients and workers, like Alex and Kay, seek flexibility and security not only in the labor market but also in the daily labor process of giving and receiving personal support. A long tradition of studies in the sociology of work analyzes the labor process, meaning how employers organize work in an effort to control which tasks workers perform, when, where, and how, and workers' strategies of resistance.[32] In domestic personal support, employer control is often indirect. Recipients' pursuit of control could objectify workers as extensions of themselves.[33] Yet workers' resistance could result in power over other people's bodies and homes.[34] Although the labor process tradition directs us to important social relations between employers, consumers, and workers, the majority of recipients and workers interviewed describe a desire not for control but rather for a respectful relationship where workers show empathy and recipients speak nicely, to paraphrase Alex and Kay. Workers and recipients want respectful negotiations over what is done and when, where and how it is done, and this is what I mean by "flexibility and security at the intimate level." Intimate labor—labor that requires particular knowledge about and attention to another—is a useful concept for my study of flexibility and security in personal support.[35] Scholars have examined the daily practice of intimacy in sectors ranging from domestic work to sex work.[36] What does the daily practice of intimacy look like in domestic personal support, which is high on intimacy due to the centrality of direct contact with other people's bodies in their home? The most common ideas used to understand the intimate labor process come from scholarship on "emotional labor," from theories of "relational care," or from studies of domestic work. These bodies of scholarship alone provide only partial understanding of flexibility and security in domestic personal support, but each contributes important insights.

Emotions are the oil that greases the wheels in this intimate body labor—for example, through efforts like Kay's to stay "professional," but the dominant concept of emotional labor is insufficient for understanding flexibility and security within domestic personal support. In her pathbreaking book *The Managed Heart*, Arlie Hochschild argues that women always did difficult, skilled emotion work to manage their feelings while caring for their families but that when employers tried to control workers' emotions in order to please customers and turn a profit, like in the airline industry, they transformed skilled emotion work into alienating "emotional labor." Since its first publication in 1983, this book has spurred many studies of emotions in different types of service work.[37] Yet scholars argue that the use of emotions and their effects in elder care and disability support are different from the same in commercial services, because workers and recipients develop long-term relationships, the work requires more skill, and recipients of state-subsidized support have less power than paying customers.[38] In particular, academics have spilled much ink debating how much ability workers (especially health and personal-support workers) have to develop and express authentic emotions outside of employer control.[39] At one extreme, Bolton argues that health care workers, ranging from nurses to aides, have significant autonomy over how to perform their job since they, not an employer, own their emotions, but several have questioned this argument.[40] We still have insufficient understanding of the use and effects of emotions in personal support due to two entangled issues. The first is the complex power dynamic between recipients and workers who encounter different axes of oppression. The second is the muddling of distinct rules guiding appropriate emotions in the public and private realms as governments shift services from institutions to homes and contract their management to for-profit agencies or individual recipients.[41] In a later edition of the *Managed Heart*, Hochschild recognizes this marketization and calls for analyses of how people manage the crisscrossing of emotional rules from the realms of home and employment in different sectors.[42] In line with this recent approach to intimate labor processes, I ask how personal support workers manage their own and others' emotions to gain security at the intimate level, meaning being respected and having a say in which tasks they do and when, where, and how they do them. However, this question and the emotional labor studies that inspire it address only part of the complex puzzle of how recipients and workers negotiate flexibility and security because it leaves out the other half of the relationship: the recipients.

The recipients my assistants and I interviewed discussed emotions as extensively as did the workers, as is evident in Alex's mention of the accepted "rule" to "keep it simple, and straighten it out." There are studies that examine customer influence in the commercial service sector, but few probe recipient expectations in the government-funded sector, and most rely on workers' and employers' beliefs about what recipients or customers desire.[43] Aging and disability scholars, by contrast, start from the experience of recipients, including recipients of state-subsidized support. Aging studies find that some older recipients seek relationships with workers resembling genuine friendship or family, yet others value empathetic relationships with clear boundaries.[44] Disability studies help elaborate on recipients' emotion work due to their attention to complex power relations between workers and non-elderly adults with long-term experience living with physical disabilities. As Julia Twigg argues, recipients gain some power from the ideology of privacy, which gives them a degree of influence over what happens in their home. At the same time, this hands-on tending to vulnerable bodies can become a source of power for able-bodied workers.[45] Within this context, disability scholars write about people's expectations for service with respect tailored to their individual needs, as opposed to a paternalistic caring.[46] Taking these insights from aging and disability studies, I consider not only how workers manage emotions but also ask how recipients manage their own and others' emotions in their attempts to gain flexibility at the intimate level, meaning being respected and having a say in which services are provided and when, where, and how.

Aging and disability studies suggest a range of emotional expectations and actions from recipients, but, as in early studies of "emotional labor," they lack a relational perspective. Since aging and disability studies rarely include the workers, they prevent us from fully understanding the potential for flexibility with security. The relational turn in care theory provides some additional tools in this regard because it considers emotion work on both sides of the relationship—that is, *relational* work.[47] Relational care theory is useful for analyzing how recipients and workers negotiate flexibility and security at the intimate level because it emphasizes interdependence within relationships. This interdependence is historically and still today associated with women and contrasts to traditionally masculine practices and values of individualism.[48] Another important insight from this body of work is how it marks the difference between the practice of providing help and the feelings surrounding it. This theory reminds us that just because one cares *about* someone does not mean she should have to do the hands-on work of caregiving or the work of managing the care, the caring *for*; and even if one does the work of caregiver and caring for, this does not automatically denote a deep caring *about*.[49] This decoupling of the practice and emotions of relational work is essential, but theoretical attention to both sides of the relationship does not mean that the perspectives of recipients are included. In her recent book *Caring Democracy*, Joan Tronto comes close to capturing the experiences of disability and age by calling for an analysis of "caring *with*," meaning a probing of trust and respect in the relationship.[50] Drawing on these insights into relational, intimate labor, I ask: how do workers and recipients negotiate mutual respect in the daily relations over what is done and when, where, and how it is done? Relational care theory, however, insufficiently addresses power and inequality, whether stemming from marginalization through disability and age or from racialized class inequalities.[51] In contrast, the concept of intimate labor decouples intimacy from a paternalistic notion of care.[52] What does caring personal support look like from the perspective of recipients? It is important to examine empirically how, and under which conditions, the practice of intimate labor is caring or controlling or both.

One of the levers that might move the intimate relationship toward care or control, especially from the perspective of workers, is racialized labor market inequalities. Domestic work scholarship pushes us to analyze how personal support workers' racialized labor market insecurity connects to their struggles for respect in the labor process.[53] These studies draw attention to racialization in the "realm of indignities," like the disrespect linked to assumptions about one's culture underscored by Kay.[54] Parreñas argues that Pilipina domestic workers across the globe try to get and keep a "good employer" (who, for example, will not order them around) and that this quest might even lead them to put up with poor extrinsic rewards, like low wages.[55] Racialization also occurs at the intimate level through the drawing of boundaries between emotion work and menial work, like the work of teaching a child to read versus cleaning up soiled bodies.[56] Labor markets structured by race, nation, migration, citizenship, and gender inequalities and ideologies assign women of color or immigrant women to the bodywork considered menial and limit alternatives.[57]

Domestic work scholarship connects racialization at the intimate and labor market levels, yet the analysis of domestic personal support requires modified questions. Studies of domestic work focus on the relationship between racially privileged and class-privileged women who employ women of color or immigrant household workers (or both), but labor process struggles between racialized women and employers also marginalized by disability or age are likely different. Not only are assumptions linking Global South origins to "backward" cultures potentially brought into the relationship, as alluded to by Kay, but so is marginalization due to the "confinement" of disability articulated by Alex. Furthermore, most studies of domestic work focus on the direct, dyadic relationship "between women," yet this arrangement is only sometimes evident in personal support.[58] Respectful interactions may be the oil that greases the wheels in negotiations over what is done, when, where, and how, but different labor markets for personal support likely require different amounts and types of oil. Under what conditions might domestic personal support represent flexible care and secure work at both labor market and intimate labor process levels? Answering this pressing question requires comparative analysis.

A Comparative Study of Domestic Personal Support Programs

Guided by studies of precarious employment and labor documenting the link between labor market flexibility and worker insecurity, we asked employers whether recipients could choose their worker, under which circumstances, and its implications for workers. We also asked labor and disability advocates about the possibilities of coalitions for flexibility with security. Versed in labor process theory, I expected tensions in the daily work, especially in contexts where recipients were unable to displace them through firing. Interview guides thus included a series of scenarios to prompt in-depth conversation on the degree and kind of conflict over what was done, when, where, and how. We asked workers questions like: "Are you ever asked to do something you feel is not part of the official job? How do you respond?" We asked recipients questions such as: "Can you change what the worker does? Do they ever refuse to do something?" One recipient criticized this focus on tension: "With this study," Gord said, "you're going through scenarios that I might deal with only once a year. It would be like you watching CSI all the time and thinking there are a lot of extreme crimes in Las Vegas. You're just looking at one angle." In analyzing the interviews comparatively, I have attempted to bring in other angles by looking at how recipients and workers navigate tensions in different contexts. It is my hope that Gord and others interviewed for this book will find the analysis valid—that is, that they will see their experiences reflected in it—even if they do not agree with my emphasis or my conclusions. My conclusions stem not just from a presentation of people's experiences but also from an analysis of their experiences as they are related to flexibility and security within scholarly debates. As a sociological analysis, it locates people's experiences within workplace, policy, and social contexts, and it is thus my hope that the comparative approach provides insight to people inside the sector, either now or in the future, as much as it gives scholars new ideas.

This is a large comparative study based on qualitative interviews with over three hundred people in two countries over many years.[59] In the first phase of the research, in 2005–6, I interviewed key informants who were knowledgeable about how state policy and agency rules shaped the structure of domestic personal support programs. I interviewed twenty-nine key informants in Los Angeles and fifty-five in Toronto, including government program administrators and social workers, employers, disability advocates, and labor organizers. The second phase of research began in 2007, first by using employers and unions to contact recipients and workers. In Toronto, where most employers were agencies, I asked the organizational contact from phase one to give a letter to its workers and clients describing the study and requesting that they contact us if they wished to participate; most organizations agreed to do so. In order to ensure we did not end up with a sample of workers uncritical of their employers, I also asked union informants to refer us to active members. In addition, once my research assistants and I began to interview workers and recipients we asked them to refer people they knew.[60] In Toronto we interviewed ninety-six recipients and ninety-six workers across three different models and multiple immigrant groups in 2007–8. In Los

Angeles, where the employers were also recipients, recruitment through formal organizations was more difficult. We formed a partnership with an immigrant service organization that recruited workers and recipients through their work in the community.[61] Here we focused on a case study of one immigrant group, Pilipinx, and the dominant California model of service, interviewing thirty-one recipients and fifteen workers in 2015–6.[62] All these respondents were sampled within the metropolitan areas of Los Angeles County and the Greater Toronto Area, although government and movement informants also spoke about state-level and sometimes international strategies and policies. We gave pseudonyms to all the workers and recipients reflecting their social location.

This spatial and temporal breadth allowed for the collection of in-depth data on a range of contexts, thus allowing me to make arguments at a higher analytical level than a single ethnography while providing deeper insight than a policy-level comparison reliant only on official documents and key informants. However, the time between interviews with workers and recipients and publication, especially in the Toronto cases, required a third stage of select data collection. From 2015 to 2019 I did select key informant interviews with fifteen labor organizers and community advocates in Ontario and California to learn of a few important shifts in state policy and developments in labor movement strategy. I also reviewed official program websites in 2017–19 to determine any key changes. The time gap between interviews with workers and recipients and publication also required a contextualization of the findings that recognized case studies as a moment in time. This required me to be clear about the time period of reference for a particular piece of data, such as a quote, and to distinguish it from my analysis, which both considered the context under question and any important changes up until May 2019.

We interviewed all but a few people face-to-face. I interviewed key informants individually in English. I also conducted several of the interviews with recipients and workers, but the skilled interviewing of several graduate students and a postdoctoral researcher assisted me greatly.[63] We conducted all the interviews with recipients and workers in Toronto in English. We did the interviews with recipients and workers in Los Angeles in Tagalog, English, or Taglish, depending on the person's preference. We completed the Toronto interviews with individual respondents over a period of several months, while the interviews with Pilipinx recipients and workers in Los Angeles required shorter, more intense interviewing that included some group interviews. Pilipinx elderly recipients preferred group interviews, and we gained additional insight from listening to their collective reflections. Student research assistants transcribed interviews verbatim and translated them into English where necessary. These research assistants assisted in some of the early coding of the data, especially in terms of participants' background and objective indicators of labor market security, such as their hours of work and pay. I derived the majority of the analysis, however, from my own focused coding, which developed significantly over time through dialogue with the scholarship discussed above.

The Voyage of the Book

The central methodological and conceptual contribution of this book is an in-depth analysis of how recipients and workers in domestic personal support craft flexibility and security in relation to one another within constraints defined by intersecting social inequalities, state funding, labor market policies, and managerial rules. The programs I studied allow me to compare four distinct recipient-worker social locations: white men and women citizens working for white, largely middle-class, non-elderly, disabled men and women citizens; Pilipina immigrant workers assisting poor, elderly, Pilipinx immigrant men and women; immigrant men of color assisting white, working-class men; and immigrant women of color assisting white women of varying class backgrounds, both immigrants and citizens. In chapters 1 and 2, I underscore what these diverse workers have in common given their location in precarious employment and note similarities among recipients due to their marginalization vis-à-vis the state. Chapter 1 traces the making of domestic personal support workers out of women (and some men) with diverse migration and occupational histories. Chapter 2 shows how different groups of people, of varying age and impairment type, become disabled recipients through their need for state-provided support. By placing people's biographies within social, economic, and political configurations, these chapters elaborate the distinct axes of oppression that recipients and workers bring into their relational encounters.[64]

Chapters 3–6 each address a different program of domestic personal support, one in California and the other three in Ontario, allowing for an analysis of the state policy features that exacerbate or mitigate flexibility-security tensions. In chapter 3, I analyze the Direct Funding (DF) Program in Toronto. This is a small program providing funding to approximately one thousand people with physical disabilities.[65] Though small, this program has wide significance: individualized direct funding is also available in several U.S. jurisdictions as well as in Australia, New Zealand, the UK, and parts of continental Europe.[66] Shaped by both the independent living movement and neoliberal state policies to cut costs, the DF program is aimed to give people labor market flexibility through hiring and firing and management responsibilities. The workers are employees of individual "self-managers," so they are called "personal attendants" and considered domestic servants under labor legislation, with no ability to organize a union and with limited labor protections. The funding is universal in that it is not means-tested, although the Federal Canada Health Act does not guarantee personal support at home but leaves it up to provincial discretion. Can disabled people translate the labor market flexibility given to them by this program into the sought-after intimate flexibility to influence and change what is provided, when, where, and how? And what does that mean for workers? This chapter introduces the importance of analyzing flexibility and security at both labor market and intimate levels, which becomes more complicated in the next chapter when government actors are more present.

In chapter 4, I examine the In-Home Supportive Services (IHSS) program in Los Angeles, which is means-tested. The State of California serves approximately 443,000 low-income elderly and disabled people in their homes.[67] Like Ontario's Direct Funding Program, both the independent living movement and a neoliberal state shapes IHSS, as reflected in the terms "consumer" and "provider" to refer to recipients and workers. Yet a family model also shapes IHSS, in that people can pay even close family members, usually their children, to be their providers. California's IHSS is unique in the United States in several ways: it serves and pays more immigrants than other states; the population qualifying for this program is larger; the elderly population is growing faster; and service recipients have more labor market flexibility.[68] Here legislation recognizes both

TABLE 1 Comparative Study of Domestic Personal Support

	SERVICE DELIVERY MODEL			
FUNDING MODEL	**INDIVIDUALIZED AND DIRECT FUNDING**	**FOR-PROFIT CONTRACT AGENCY**	**NONPROFIT CONTRACT AGENCY**	**INDIVIDUALIZED, STATE HYBRID**
• Means-tested • Independent living, family hybrid				In-Home Supportive Services, Los Angeles: consumers & providers; parents & children
• Some means testing • Medical (implicit family) • Provincially universal • Independent living	Direct Funding, Toronto: self-managers & personal attendants	Home care, Toronto: clients & personal support workers	Attendant services, Toronto: consumers & attendants	

recipients and the government as employers, allowing workers to unionize and achieve more labor market security.[69] Yet how do workers and recipients negotiate flexibility and security at the intimate level? In this chapter, I focus on one long-standing, large immigrant community in L.A.: Pilipinx. This particular case allows me to illuminate how people negotiate flexibility and security within rarely studied yet increasingly significant ethnic and family care economies. Pilipinx are similar to other racialized communities within IHSS in that most recipients prefer to hire people from their own race or ethnicity. Sometimes this is due to language barriers of both recipients and workers, as is the case with other immigrants, but it is also related to unique cultural preferences for how care is provided and trust that comes with community, which is a preference also evident among Latinx and African American IHSS recipients.[70] Compared to other immigrant workers, Pilipinx in the United States have relatively more options in the labor market because they speak more English, given the impact of U.S. colonialism on education in the Philippines. As a result, most Pilipinx have entered IHSS work to care for family members and combined this work with privately paid care work for English-speaking recipients. This makes them similar to African Americans. In addition, roughly half of recipients hire family members through IHSS, so the Pilipinx case sheds light on the unique subset of paid family providers.

In chapter 5, I analyze the Home Care program in Toronto. This provincial program provides long-term support to all elderly and chronically ill people in Ontario as well as home health care for those with acute illnesses.[71] Yet Ontario government funding is based on a medical model that prioritizes acute over long-term needs. Like in the United States, a model that equates this work with family care is evident, although it does not allow people to hire their family. Some services are means-tested in this program, while others are not. The government contracts with mostly for-profit agencies, which has increased workers' labor market insecurity through de-unionization and employers' use of casual employment contracts. Despite this marketization, recipients are not guaranteed labor market flexibility like customers, nor do they have collective voice. How do "clients" and "personal-support workers," as they are called here, negotiate flexibility and security in this privatized context? This chapter allows me to examine whether the employing agencies' rules support or undermine flexibility and security. The final case study chapter probes this question in a less competitive milieu.

In chapter 6, I examine the provincial Attendant Services program within supportive housing environments in Toronto. In this program, approximately fifty-one hundred physically disabled, non-elderly people direct workers to help them with routine daily living activities, through just over a dozen nonprofit agencies funded by the Ontario government.[72] The recipients here are usually called consumers, reflecting the independent living philosophy, but sometimes they are called clients, reflecting the formalization of that philosophy in social services. They live in low-income buildings that include some accessible apartments, in a number that reflects the proportion of people with disabilities in the community; they are tenants, not residents; and there is no collective eating or shared living spaces. These services are not means-tested and are guided by the independent living model, like Ontario's Direct Funding (DF) program. Yet, unlike DF, here labor market security for workers coincides with limited labor market flexibility for recipients, in that the agency, not the recipient, hires, fires, and assigns workers. Here I ask: does this lack of labor market flexibility result in rigid, poor quality in the labor process? Both workers and recipients have collective voice in Attendant Services. This chapter thus allows me to examine how workers' and recipients' collective backing might help them craft flexibility with security.

By comparing these cases in the concluding chapter 7, I can answer the major analytical questions posed in this book. How do the workers' and recipients' social locations—defined by inequalities of disability, age, gender, class, race, and immigrant status—combine with social policies, managerial rules, and social movement strategies to undermine or support recipient and worker negotiations of flexibility and security? The conclusion does the comparative work necessary to identify the dynamics that exacerbate flexibility-security tensions and to chart the potential for flexibility with security.

More broadly, my comparative analysis of domestic personal support programs, from the viewpoint of multiple actors, allows me to provide a unique angle on some of the most important sociological questions today, given growing precarity in labor and migration and the aging of the population. What does caring personal support look like? Existing studies suggest that flexibility in which services are provided, when, where, how, and by whom, are important. What does security in the labor of providing personal support entail? Studies based on interviews with workers in this sector underscore the importance of both labor market security of employment and income and security at a more intimate level through respect and recognition. Drawing on previous studies on each side of the relationship and extending their frameworks to include both workers and recipients as key actors alongside managers, state officials, and social movement activists, I ask an utterly pressing conceptual question given the multiple inequalities that crisscross this sector. Under what conditions might domestic personal support represent both flexible care and secure work? We begin with a look at workers' quest for security.

GENDER, MIGRATION, AND THE PURSUIT OF SECURITY

Jovelyn is a fifty-four-year-old mother and wife with a four-year university degree who had worked in accounting before leaving the Philippines. She migrated to the United States in the early 2000s when her husband got a job there in his profession. In addition to this common form of gendered migration—led by husbands—the aging of immigrant populations in this country of long-standing settler immigration also fueled Jovelyn's move. She officially entered through her husband's temporary work visa, but Jovelyn's own close family ties in the country, initiated by U.S. political and economic intervention in the Asia-Pacific region, shaped her migration just as much.[1] Indeed, Pilipinx are the third largest group of Asians in the United States (after Chinese and Indians), with the greatest concentrations in California.[2] Jovelyn's father helped the American effort to gather intelligence on the Japanese during World War II from the Philippines, granting him U.S. citizenship. The U.S. government shaped Jovelyn's security in a second way when a social worker told her she could receive money to look after her mother who qualified for personal support as a poor, elderly U.S. citizen. Jovelyn said, "That started all my in-home support." When her mother passed away, Jovelyn began to provide personal support to other elderly within the dense Pilipinx community in Los Angeles. By the time of our interview, thirteen years after she arrived in the United States, Jovelyn had permanent residency status, and her daughters were attending university. Still, settlement did not deliver security. Jovelyn pieced together a living by working with multiple elderly Pilipinx clients. She experienced this not only as temporary, low-paid work but also as potentially rewarding, working with "seniors living alone," since, she explained, "they're helpless without someone."

With little hope of returning to her accounting profession, Jovelyn did her best to navigate the precarious personal support labor market and, at the intimate level, sought recognition for the skill of helping people.

Parvati is a woman of East Indian descent born in Trinidad, where she raised four children. As she explained, "I didn't have to work when I had all my kids because my husband had a good job back home." After her children grew up, she trained and worked as a seamstress, making wedding dresses and other garments from complex patterns. She migrated to Canada with the "whole family" in the early 1990s, when her youngest was in her twenties, facilitated by the support of her brother. Parvati's migration was part of a significant movement of people from former British colonies in the Caribbean to Canada through family ties, which flourished after Britain closed its doors to prior colonial subjects.[3] In Toronto, Parvati had a series of personal support jobs. She worked nights in long-term residential care (LTRC) but quit because of a heavy workload that limited the job to bodily tasks. In her words: "So you have to do all the clients. This is a lot! How could you do proper caring? You can't!" When she got her health care aid certificate she applied to "all the agencies" and worked through two in order to make a living. By time of our interview, seven years after arriving in Toronto, Parvati was a Canadian citizen and was able to make do with only one job. Despite increased labor market security, she still sought security at the intimate level by negotiating with agencies and recipients over the tasks that make up "proper caring."

How is it that two people with such different histories can both end up in the personal support sector of North America? Some women, like Jovelyn, were professionals who had fallen into this low-paid, insecure job through migration. Others, like Parvati, were industrial workers who had taken a step sideways into this more meaningful yet still low-paid, casual job. In this chapter I show how dynamic processes of gendering, racialization, and precarization make diverse people into personal support workers who lack security at the labor market and intimate levels. I do so first by demonstrating the gendering process in a simplified form, contrasting the work histories of Canada-born women and men, and then by successively weaving in dynamics driven by migration, class, and race. I then show how various groups wound up in the most precarious sectors of the personal support labor market and end by analyzing how their work history shapes their quest for security at the intimate level.

Gender and the Pursuit of Security

The great majority of personal support workers in North America are women, and women comprised 87 percent of the workers in my case studies. Enduring gendered inequalities that relegate more women than men to unpaid domestic work serve to structure and justify the concentration of women in this paid domestic work and its devaluation.[4]

How women's gendered location in unpaid domestic work shaped their location in domestic personal support, and their pursuit of security, was clear in the work histories of the white, Canada-born, married mothers in my sample. These women achieved lower-middle-class or stable working-class status for a time, in large part through marriage to a permanently employed man. They either left the labor force for a significant time or were in and out of it frequently, in order to care for dependent children. For example, Kelly was a white, Canada-born mother of two in her mid-fifties. She was a "stay-at-home mom" until her children went to school. She then worked a series of part-time jobs that allowed her to juggle unpaid and paid work—as a laborer in a factory, a school crossing guard, and in retail jobs—before entering personal support services upon separating from her husband. The draw of Kelly, and others, to this work was its contrast to boring, difficult, or alienating labor processes in previous jobs and the search for a more intimate connection through work. As Kelly said, "I think if you're a people person you're not really into factory work." Women also compared the labor processes of available paid work to their unpaid care work in terms of intimacy. For example, Dawn is a white, Canada-born, forty-five-year-old woman who earned an early childhood education diploma and worked in day cares. She left the labor force when she had children because she "didn't think it was right" to put her children into day care while she took care of other people's children. At first glance, Dawn seemed to have a caring orientation linked to an acceptance of the private sphere ideology of women looking after their own children without pay first and foremost. However, the conditions in her unpaid domestic work, compared to her former day care job, also shaped her decision, as was evident in her comment that "when you're looking after like twenty-four screaming kids versus the one child at home, . . . that looks a little bit better." Many of the women compared paid and unpaid labor processes, but the men we interviewed did not.

How gendered social location shaped workers' quest for security in paid personal support also was evident in the different meaning of this work to white, Canada-born men. Like Kelly and Dawn, white, Canada-born, forty-two-year-old Chris sought meaning through this work. He said he did this job to "give back" and characterized most people who did it as the "do-gooder" or "church" type. Yet, unlike Kelly and Dawn, Chris did not connect this work to previous unpaid or paid relational work. He distinguished himself from the "nursing types who do this as a full-time job." Instead he did this work to "make some money on the side," which was necessary because stable work was hard to come by in his occupation: technical work in the creative industries. He was also clear that he only planned to stay in this job a little while longer. Mike, a white, Canada-born, thirty-two year-old man, did not plan to stay in this line of work either. He lamented, "It's been a great experience, but it's a huge sacrifice. If you want to have a family or whatever, it's impossible on fifteen dollars an hour." These men's temporary orientation to personal support work contrasted not only with white Canada-born women but also with more marginalized men, thus necessitating an analysis of how gender intersects with migration and class.

Gender, Class, and Migration

The quest for security for many personal support workers was part of a long journey that started with migration. The majority of personal support workers in the cities of the United States, Canada, and many other countries are immigrants.[5] Similarly, 79 percent of the workers in my sample were immigrants—defined as those residing in a nation in which they were not born—from a range of countries. Immigration policy shaped their insecurity but did not fully determine it. Canada and the United States are both white settler nations that combined cultural genocide against indigenous populations with permanent settlement of those of British and other European heritage.[6] At the same time in the 1960s, both countries abandoned explicit racial quotas and allowed migration for family reunification.[7] At this time both countries were also increasingly tying permanent settlement to skills, which they would later require even for temporary migrants.[8] A much higher proportion of immigrants have entered and lived without legal status in the United States, but Canada has not been immune to the phenomenon.[9] Neither country had an explicit immigration policy to recruit workers to do the publicly funded elderly or disability support work that is the focus of this study, yet both had small temporary migrant labor programs that allowed for recruitment into private paid elderly and disability support.[10] The great majority of the immigrants in this study entered as permanent residents; most of these came through family sponsorship, fewer as permanent refugees, and even fewer based on their education, investments, or other human capital. The rest of the sample is split between those who entered on a temporary visa and those who had no immigration status on entry but instead entered as visitors, as tourists, or under the radar. People who wound up in this sector did not necessarily have a past doing this type of work or enter the country specifically to do this work. In fact, many of them first worked in other sectors in their countries of origin, in North America, or in both. It is thus important to understand these workers' quest for security as starting with migration but also continuing through their jobs in the United States or Canada.

Understanding these workers' lives requires first understanding how gender intersects with migration and class to shape the depth and duration of their insecurity. One way gender, migration, and class shaped workers' insecurity was through women's entry as dependents of men. For example, both the U.S. and Canadian government granted permanent status to southern Europeans from working-class or peasant backgrounds, primarily Italians, Portuguese, and Greeks, by the 1960s. Many entered through family reunification policies, resulting in a large number of dependents (women, children, and sometimes elderly kin) accompanying or following male laborers.[11] Paola was one of three such working-class, dependent immigrant women in my sample. Paola's search for labor market security began with male-led, extended family emigration from Italy. She came to Canada in the late 1950s to join her just-wed husband, who had come via sponsorship by his brother. Paola was nineteen when she arrived and did not enter the labor force. Two years later, she had her first child, and over the course of her twenties, thirties, and forties she raised seven children. In 1980, at the age of forty-two, she entered privately paid elder care. By the time of our interview, she was a seventy-year-old widow still working ten to fifteen hours a week to supplement her late husband's pension. Like white, Canada-born Kelly, Paola had entered the labor force due to insufficient male wages, with caring skills gleaned from years of unpaid domestic work. Unlike Kelly, Paola never worked in another industry before she entered personal support; her entry into private elder care was shaped significantly by her greater volume of mother work but also by her status as a dependent immigrant in a country with a different language and culture, which further limited her job options.[12]

Highly educated women also migrated as dependents. Gender intersected with migration and class to shape educated women's insecurity in a different way since these women had much to lose professionally with migration. For example, Aneta was an accountant in Poland who moved to Canada in 1992 in her late twenties, with her daughter. Her husband had come three years earlier, just after the fall of communism. Her description of why she came to Canada combined political, economic, and gendered reasons. Referencing gendered struggles within families, Aneta said, laughing, "He came to Poland, and he pushed me to go. I said I am not going, because I have job!" Her husband went back to Canada with the goal of making enough money to live securely in Poland, but when he could not achieve such security he again "pushed" Aneta to come to Canada and see what it was like. She consented in part due to her desire for gendered intimacy, telling herself, "it's no sense, he is in Canada." The changing political context also prompted Aneta to go since "everything [was] bad in Poland, so I said better maybe I come here." In Canada, she and her husband had another child, with whom Aneta stayed at home until first grade. This exit from the labor force, coupled with her lack of English fluency and accounting requirements in Canada, limited Aneta's ability to practice her profession. Instead, after attending English school, she got a job in personal support, doing "mostly homemaking."

Several professional women in my sample experienced downward mobility through migration from a variety of countries experiencing political upheaval and economic difficulties. Some professionals were downwardly mobile into personal support work or equivalent mid-level, care-related jobs but some fell much lower, especially single women without access to male wages or family sponsorship. For example, Valeria fled Colombia after her husband was killed in the conflict there between government, leftist guerrillas, paramilitary groups, and crime syndicates that had been occurring since the mid-1960s, with U.S. anticommunist intervention. She first went to the United States because she had a sister there, but when the U.S. government denied Valeria and her son asylum they came to Canada, even though they had only seen the country on the map and knew no one there other than a sibling of an acquaintance. Yet permanent status did not grant Valeria security in the labor market. She had a university education in Colombia where she had worked as an accountant. Yet, unlike Aneta, the Polish former accountant, without male wages Valeria went on social assistance to support herself and her son while learning English. Unable to practice accounting, she worked nights and weekends in food services while she studied to obtain a personal support certificate.

Women who worked in feminized yet stable sectors in their countries, like banking, retail, or administrative support, also ended up in North American personal support work. Like some professionals, many experienced a period of more severe downward movement before climbing back up the occupational ladder to personal support. For example, Lilia was a married woman in her late seventies. She had earned a university education in a business-related field in the Philippines, where she worked as an administrative assistant for high-level political figures, and then took care of her elderly mother. She arrived in the United States in the late 1990s with her husband. When asked why she came to the United States, she attributed the decision to her sister: "My sister sponsored me. I didn't want to come here, but she insisted. Okay, since we're sixty years old now." Lilia illustrated how migration decisions and their meaning were embedded not only in husband-wife relations but also in extended family relations. Lilia's first job in California was at the extended family's convenience store, where she worked for five years until the store closed; it paid very little. She also had an informal home day care—Pilipinx neighbors would bring their children to her house. These migration and work histories reveal how class intersects with gender to shape labor market opportunities. So does citizenship, nationality, and race.

Gender, Citizenship, and Racialization

Publicly funded personal support workers, the focus of this book, generally have secure immigration status, yet some of these workers entered Canada or the United States in more precarious situations. Migration to Toronto from English-speaking Caribbean nations is extensive.[13] Several of the women in my sample from Caribbean nations migrated in a context of racialized immigration policy meant to limit their settlement. One early way that women came to Canada was through the Canadian government's Caribbean domestic schemes, beginning with immigrants from Barbados and Jamaica in 1955 and then expanding to other nations up to 1967. Initially the state granted these domestic workers permanent residency after a period of live-in employment with an assigned employer. Over time, immigration officials became concerned that Caribbean domestic workers were sponsoring relatives, resulting in settlement, and they discontinued the schemes and introduced a skills-based system in 1967.[14] However, in 1973 Canada introduced a more general temporary migration program, the Non-Immigrant Employment Authorization Program (NEAP). Domestic workers from the Caribbean continued to migrate under this program, and this time it did not allow for conversion to permanent status. For example, Tina came from Guyana in her early twenties in the mid-1970s as a temporary domestic worker during the NEAP. After returning to Guyana she reentered Canada a year later, this time on a student visa. She also had a brother here and some cousins. Tina had a high school diploma and some additional home economics courses in Guyana, where she worked in hospital housekeeping. She came to Canada, she said, "I guess to make a better life for myself . . . go to school and . . . get a life." In this period of circular migration, she had her oldest child in Guyana, but this daughter did not join Tina in Canada until she was a preteen. After leaving "domestic babysitting," and after a period on social assistance as a single mother of two children born in Canada, Tina could only find factory work.

In the 1990s, Pilipinas became the preferred domestic workers in Canada, like in other parts of the world, and many of these workers have found their way to personal support.[15] In my sample, there are three Pilipina professionals who came under a temporary domestic worker program, although a key informant and recent research indicate that their presence in the personal support sector is significant.[16] Maribel came to Canada in 1992 under the government's temporary migrant Live-in Caregiver Program in her mid-thirties. She earned a university education from the Philippines where she was a teacher, but, like other professionals from countries in the Global South, the wages were too low so she migrated for "financial" reasons. Maribel "had lots of struggle" with the live-in requirement. She recounts being fired by many employers and having to search for another sponsor in order to stay in the country. "I had I think nine, nine employers or eleven employers . . . releasing me, releasing me from one employer to another. Would you believe that? . . . The problem is that I live in." In 2014, the government discontinued this program, once again folding it into the general temporary migration program and making conversion to permanent status difficult.[17]

Professional Pilipinas ended up in private-pay domestic work in the United States as well, some through clandestine entry.[18] There are a few such women in my Los Angeles sample. For example, Myla had some college education and worked in a grocery store as a "promo girl" for various food products in the Philippines. Nevertheless, she too experienced significant downward mobility into live-in domestic servitude, linked in part to her entry on a tourist visa and lack of family ties. She explained: "Before, I had a hard time because I'm not even legal. So, that's the first job I have, caregiving." These examples show how gender intersects with citizenship and race to shape the depth of workers' insecurity.

Racialization works through citizenship status but extends beyond it too. Those from what immigration scholars call "the 1.5 generation"—children who migrated with their families and were largely raised or educated in the receiving society—are another source of personal support work in North America, and there are several in my sample. Like their parents, they can experience a period in highly insecure work before personal support. For example, Zoe is a thirty-two-year-old Black woman. She migrated from Guyana at the age of nine in the mid-1980s with a family friend to join her mother Tina, whom we met above. Since her mother left Guyana when Zoe was two she "didn't know her that well," but her grandmother, who had been looking after her, was getting older, so it "made sense" for her to come to Canada too. Zoe finished high school in Toronto, yet she worked as a nanny like her mother for "three years or four years, ever since I finished high school," because she "needed a job." Continuity across generations in paid domestic work points to the meeting of global and local racialized inequalities.[19] These inequalities shape not only the depth but also the duration of workers' insecurity by funneling them into the most insecure sectors of elderly and disability support.

Insecurity in the Personal Support Labor Market

How do inequalities in gender and migration more specifically funnel workers into the personal support labor market? Do they draw women to choose this work? Or do they close off other options, making precarious personal support a residual, constrained "choice"? Many of the women in my sample revealed how their gendered family duties shaped their decision to enter this predominantly part-time and temporary sector. For example, Adi, who migrated from Nigeria to Canada as a baby with her family in the late 1970s, started in this sector with "privates who were supplementing their nursing" by doing in-home care. After doing this "private duty" for some time, she enrolled in a BA nursing program at a university, but she had to drop out because she could not find a sitter for her child. So instead she opted for a personal support certificate, which was a much shorter course. This was a familiar story of women in my sample. Better-paid and recognized care professions, like nursing, were not open to women, in part due to family duties.

Elder care responsibilities also fell to women. In Canada and the United States, governments expect women to look after their parents as well as their children, while the practice of families taking care of their parents is predominant in some Asian, Latin American, and African countries, including several from which the immigrant women in my sample migrated.[20] Gendered elder care duty shapes the other jobs one is able to take, as is the case with child care. For example, Leizel cut back her job to part time in order to take care of her elderly mother. Leizel's mother was part of a unique program in Los Angeles that paid family to look after their kin. The women in this program spoke of how gendered duty shaped their entry into this hybrid form of paid family work. For example, as part of a discussion of why she became a personal support worker, Lilia, who was in her late seventies, emphasized gendered duty. Laughing, she said: "This is my sibling-in-law, so it's okay. If I can take care of others, then I should take care of family too." In addition to this cultural pull, however, Lilia also said: "I don't have any money if I don't have a client, so that's one of the reasons. . . . I won't have any other job, eh, since I'm old." As this example suggests, gendered family responsibilities intersect not just with immigrant cultural practices of elder care but also age-related labor market barriers.

What role do inequalities connected to immigrant status and racialization within the receiving countries play in pulling immigrant women into personal support? Vera's experience is insightful. Vera migrated to Canada in 1994 in her early forties with her husband from Russia, where she was a nurse. Similar to others, Vera noted the impact of gendered child care duties on her ability to train for a better job, but for Vera gendered duty combined with systemic lack of recognition of her foreign credentials to channel her into personal support. A conversation Vera had with an immigration officer shows how constrained her choices were. When the officer saw her nursing background, he told her she could look for employment in personal support, but "the worst part," Vera explained, was that he also told her it was a "dead end job." At the time she did not understand this expression, but she came to learn it meant "a job without any future

because it's temporary." Vera generalized from her experience to make a connection between precarious employment and immigrant labor, noting that her
personal support employer hired "mostly foreigners." She considered this a "sad
story" because, "for some reason, some believe that it's a second-class job, but it's
not." Several of the professionals in my sample explained how the lack of recognition of their credentials shaped their entry into this job. Others emphasized how
language barriers exacerbated devaluation. For example, Leah, a Jewish woman
who in 1990 migrated to Canada from Poland, where she had been a nurse, said:
"Nobody wants to give you the job because basically the barrier of language and,
you know, they ask for your [Canadian] experience. . . . So I went to [a personal
support agency] at the time." Inequalities of gender, age, and immigrant status
coincided with broader industrial change that was also driving precarity.

Broader trends toward precarious employment also make people available for
personal support work.[21] Several people in my sample entered personal support
after losing long-term factory or administrative jobs with stable pay and benefits.
For example, Danique was a teacher's assistant in Jamaica but could not afford
to get a teaching credential in Toronto. Instead, she went to a community college
to study quality control, in which she worked for a couple of years, until the factory for which she worked moved to the United States, prompting her to enter
personal support. Aaliyah was a forty-year-old married mother of Arabic background who worked as a flight attendant in Trinidad before coming to Canada
in her late twenties. In Toronto, after having a child and working in office administration for three years, she got an administrative job at an airline, but after it
merged with another airline and then 9/11 happened, the company laid her off.
That is when Aaliyah decided to go earn her nurse's assistant certificate, while on
maternity leave with her second child. This disappearance of secure employment
is even more troubling for older immigrants. My sample includes workers who
arrived in the United States or Canada in their fifties or older as well as those who
aged after migration before entering the personal support sector, so that some
workers are in their sixties and seventies. For example, Leizel was in her early forties when she migrated to the United States and entered personal support eight
years later at age fifty. When asked what the most important thing of the interview for us to remember was, she said: "We all need jobs." She elaborated, "It's
not like before"—in that there was no longer "equal opportunity employment."
Instead, employers look for younger people, prompting Leizel to conclude: "Age
discrimination is a big issue." While opportunities for secure manufacturing and
administration jobs were closing, openings in less secure personal support were
proliferating.

The majority of immigrant workers in this sample entered the corners of
personal support with the most labor market insecurity—that is, jobs with

individualized or casual employment arrangements, very low pay, and little to no benefits. For example, Abby, a Black woman of Caribbean origin, migrated from England to Canada as a child with her family in the mid-1970s. After getting a personal support certificate, she got a job at a nursing home in the early 2000s but only as a temporary worker, as she described. "I was picking up hours, and then my hours got dropped because they hired students for the summer." Others found work in care facilities through temporary agencies. For example, Marites's first job in L.A. was at a hospice, which she got through a temporary agency months after arriving from the Philippines. Marites was not employed in "hospice nursing, actually taking care of the clients" but rather as the "eyes and ears of the family" to supplement the overworked nursing staff. In Marites's case, the employer here was not the hospice but rather the agency, which a family paid privately. Sometimes the family hired the worker directly, often called "private duty." Wenna, who came to Canada from Trinidad in the early 1970s as a teenager, said she had been working through an agency in a hospital, visiting one elderly woman, when the woman's daughter approached her and offered her a private-duty job with her aunt for two hours an evening to "make sure she eat, because sometime she doesn't eat." Similarly, Chejtel, a Jewish woman, migrated to Canada from Russia in the early 1990s at the age of thirty-eight. She earned personal support certification a year after arrival but could only initially find work with privately paying clients "sitting" in a hospital. Then she got a job with a private agency that sent her to work at a retirement home. After several years of this, she landed a relatively more stable job with an agency that had a contract with the government to provide elder support services; here she worked for nine years until the company lost its government contract. Chejtel's experience and others' underscore the range of precarious arrangements under which people work in this sector.

Some highly insecure personal support work has resembled domestic servitude. One common form of live-in personal support work in Los Angeles was boarding care, where a few women shared the night and day shifts to look after what they termed "non-ambulant," or largely bedridden, elderly people in need of twenty-four-hour care. For example, Evelyn came to the United States in the late 2000s. She had a university degree from the Philippines and owned a computer store there, but in L.A. she worked for a small Pilipinx-owned boarding care business, living in and coming home twice a week. Anjali started as a nanny and housekeeper in Toronto, but when her employer's mother acquired Alzheimer's and the father developed diabetes, she asked Anjali to look after her parents on the weekends, to give the weekday workers a break. And when the father was hospitalized, the employer sent Anjali to supplement the limited nursing care there. In other words, Anjali's duties changed with the aging of the extended family of her employer, harking back to feudalistic relations of servitude. At the same time, however, this work in the hospital, outside a private home, expanded Anjali's skills and her networks. One day a doctor noticed how well she had changed the father's dressing and told her she should train to be a personal support worker. The next weekend she responded to a flyer she saw about such training, passed the English test, and enrolled. After some struggle, her employer allowed her two nights off a week to take the course, but the employer continued to call on her for elder care. Anjali had gained permanent immigration status through a period of temporary live-in work, but, as for so many others, it did not provide her with labor market security. She continued to work as a live-in, all-around domestic for eleven years in Toronto. Not only did formal citizenship fail to translate into labor market security, another part of the state, employment and settlement services, were funneling women, many of them immigrants, into the most precarious corners of personal support.

Many of the women interviewed spoke of the influence of government programs and actors on their entry into personal support. Several people in Toronto linked their entry into personal support to welfare-to-work policies.[22] For example, Tanice was a hairstylist in Toronto but could no longer do this work due to an injury, so, as a divorced mother, she went on social assistance, which helped pay for her to get a personal support certificate. However, she was also required to "volunteer" in order to continue to receive social assistance. Tanice explained how if she earned over a certain amount, her welfare check was cut back. "I was workin' on call as a health care aide . . . sendin' me over here, over there. I used to go on to my one hour, one hour, one hour. And then welfare would dock it from my check. It was paid back to the $350." While not all workers who were on social assistance entered this job through this sort of "workfare," as it is called in Ontario, where wages are deducted from one's welfare check, Tanice was one of many workers who had been on social assistance before working in personal support. Several mentioned that social assistance provided subsidies to pay for personal support training, even though we did not specifically ask participants about this. Others spoke of different ways social assistance was instrumental to their becoming a personal support worker. For example, social assistance required Leah to do a year-long course made up of half a day of school, mostly focused on English, and half a day of work at a nursing home.

The U.S. government also directed poor women to personal support work but it drew the women in my L.A. sample into it in a different way. In Los Angeles, unlike Toronto, people must be poor to qualify for publicly funded personal support services. This reality generated connections across the private and public personal support sectors in several ways. First, as recipients entered poverty due to the combination of aging and growing personal support needs, they sometimes brought workers with them to the public sector. For example, one Pilipina, Myla, explained that she started with a private agency, but the family of the elderly person she was assisting could no longer afford to pay the agency so they applied for the state-funded support and hired Myla as the worker. Second, as poor people aged, they qualified for a unique service in Los Angeles, where a family member could be one's personal support worker, paid by the state. This included the aging of poor immigrants who recruited family and friends within a co-ethnic care economy. Fourteen of the thirty-one personal support recipients interviewed in LA hired family, while seven of the fifteen workers worked with family members. The remainder of recipients and workers hired other Pilipinx they knew. Angelica, whom the state pays to look after her mother-in-law, gave a typical response when asked how she found out about this work. Referring to one co-ethnic friend, she said, "She's the one who told us about it, she was like 'Oh, you qualify for this . . . they can pay you too.'" As this example suggests, formal state programs intersected with social networks to facilitate workers' entry into precarious personal support.

Understanding how people entered personal support also sheds light on why they did so. In addition to limited alternatives in the labor market and state directives to enter personal support, most immigrants had a connection to the work through people they knew. All of the immigrant participants in my L.A. Pilipinx sample got their job through ties to other Pilipinx, and over half of the immigrants in my Toronto sample got the job through someone they knew, often co-ethnics as well, while a little over a third described a combination of informal networks and formal actors shaping their entry into this job. Some immigrant men also entered disability support through ethnic networks, underscoring how economic and migration-related drivers could trump previous work experiences. For example, Jon migrated from Jamaica to Canada in 1990, in his early twenties with his siblings, sponsored by their mother, who had been living in Toronto for over ten years. Jon had a high school diploma from Jamaica, where he was a truck driver, but he got a disability support job through the suggestion of a friend. "When I first come to Canada," Jon recalled, "I hooked up with [agency] because I had a friend there." Indeed, many longtime workers entered primarily through informal means. Network recruitment facilitated the entry of other Caribbean workers into personal support throughout the 1990s and into the 2000s. Evan was convinced to enter in the mid-1990s by his wife, who was already in the sector; Selina was recommended by her cousin in the late 1990s; and Zoe was recommended by her mother in the early 2000s. Similar dynamics were happening in other communities. For example, Ray, from a South American country, reported: "My wife actually forced me to get into [personal support]." This was in the mid-1990s, when he had a telemarketing job that was not secure; Ray's wife had worked in the sector for fifteen years. Bao, who was from Fiji and had worked in a Canadian factory until it moved to Mexico, got a job in personal support through a Fijian woman who worked in the factory with him. By the mid-2000s, the hiring process in Toronto was not as network-driven because the state was encouraging employers to require personal support worker certificates, yet network recruitment remained the dominant form of entry in Los Angeles, where certification was not required.

Given the labor market insecurity of these personal support jobs, characterized by casual arrangements, insufficient hours, and low wages, many workers took multiple jobs in an effort to make a living. Individualized employment relationships bring insecurity due to recipients' intermittent or temporary needs. As one Pilipina, Riza, said about her elderly clients: "The first one died, and even too the second one." One common coupling of jobs in my sample was in-home personal support with either permanent or temporary work in long-term residential care. While also attending to individual clients in their homes, Imelda, Angelica, and Nenita worked in food services in a hospital, a "convalescent" facility, and a jail, respectively. Another common combination of jobs, in both Los Angeles and Toronto, was working both state-funded positions and "private duty" (paid in cash) for in-home clients. For example, Evelyn was the state-paid, personal support worker for her mother-in-law during the week but supplemented this small income by working as a "reliever" for the weekday worker with a twenty-four-hour private-duty client. Others had a second job outside the personal support sector, in positions ranging from fitness instructor to factory worker. When asked why she had multiple jobs, Marites said simply "because of money" and explained the situation well. "If you only rely on one job, your money will be gone immediately. It's not enough. How are we going to survive? We won't be able to eat ... The most expensive expense here is the rent." In short, inequalities of class, gender, age, race, and immigrant status intersected to close off options, leaving personal support a real but constrained choice, and both formal state directives and informal social networks funneled workers into the most precarious corners of personal support. Yet labor market precarity was not the only form of insecurity these workers experienced.

The Meaning of Insecurity at the Intimate Level

The meaning of this work is deeper than that conveyed by the notion of precarious employment. Workers experience insecurity at a more intimate level through the extent to which their skills are recognized and through the value attached to the types of tasks that make up the job.[23]

Tasks

All workers are deeply invested in their ability to influence which tasks they perform, when and how.[24] But in what ways do the nature of tasks figure in the meaning of work with people? Studies of service and domestic work emphasize how employers seek to control not only the physical tasks done by workers but also the emotional work essential to service labor.[25] In this context, Mary Romero shows how Mexican American women transformed domestic work into "job work," where they sold not their whole self to a master (as in pre-industrial, live-in work) or their time to an employer (as in industrial work) but rather specific tasks to multiple clients as contractors. The workers in Romero's study sought to limit their job to specific cleaning tasks and to exclude caring for children.[26] This conceptual contrast of servitude, industrial labor, and contract service work is useful for my analysis, given the range of past jobs held by the women in my sample.

The meaning of personal support work varied for former factory workers, domestic workers, service workers, and professionals. A small but not insignificant number of people in my sample had worked in factories, either in their country of origin or in Canada. Former factory workers emphasized the reward of emotional over physical tasks. For example, Liling focused on factory work's impact on her body. "Even now if I have to run fast, my knees will give in, because [of] the standing eight hours in a cold place. . . . I need to think about my health, so I quit that job." Similarly, referring to the monotony of physical labor, Tina said, "I couldn't cope with working [in the factory] anymore . . . I knew I wanted to get into the health care field." Former factory workers sought more meaningful work with people than they had experienced in monotonous and unhealthy work with things. Yet not all work with people was rewarding.

Former private-pay domestic workers, who comprised over half of my sample, carried not the alienation of working with things but rather the scars of degrading relationships with people. For example, Myla described her live-in job in Los Angeles, when she was undocumented, as having been a "prison." Contrasting economic rewards to these confining conditions, Myla said: "They paid me, but . . . I keep crying, and I said, 'Bring me back to the Philippines.'" Here she emphasized precarity at an intimate level, linking it to feudalistic control over people's lives. Former domestic workers spoke both about degrading treatment from the household employer and sometimes the way the children in their charge treated them. Anjali lamented how the employer did not provide her with a separate room but just a bed in the basement, with no bathroom. The last straw, however, was when the children played a cruel trick on her one night upon arriving home late. "I had no bedside lights because I was in the corner of the basement where the kids play. So I had to turn the lights off at the door, feel my way through to my bed," Anjali began. Then she conveyed with dismay, "I went into my bed, I felt something cold, and I screamed. Nobody can hear me." When she turned on the light, she saw a big rubber snake on her bed. This disrespect from the children prompted her to say, "That's it" and to quit the job, even though a more secure citizenship status in Canada hinged on staying in this sector. Indeed, studies of domestic work point to the importance of analyzing insecurity at the intimate level, in that, for example, domestic workers seek "good employers . . . defined by relations of mutual respect," who treat them not as servants but as people with families and lives outside of work.[27] Some former domestic workers had less explicitly degrading experiences, yet they too hoped the move into personal support work would allow them to have respectful relationships with elderly and disabled people.

A significant number of people in my sample had worked in long-term residential care (LTRC), and they preferred in-home personal support work, given the limits to emotional connections with people in LTRC. Kelly equated work in LTRC with factory work, which she had also done. "I felt the poor people were treated like in a factory. You were inclined to get in [and] get out; you didn't have time to hear what they had to say or listen to their stories. You were rushing them all the time and rushing off to someone else." Adi linked such conditions to working on call. She said she was called at the "last minute" when someone did not show up for a shift and felt pressure not to "bother washing or anything like that, just hurry up, put everybody in their chair." Alissa said: "We had to cut corners, and it bothered my conscience, so I couldn't do it. And I quit." Chronic understaffing in LTRC was a reason given by many we interviewed for seeking in-home work instead.[28] In these descriptions, we hear people who sought a job where they would have the time to do the emotional work that allows for a meaningful relationship with people. Former professionals, of which there were many in my sample, also drew meaning from emotional connections with people. For immigrant professionals, the lack of recognition of their skills significantly shaped their views of personal support work, and skill played a part in the meaning of work for others too.

Skills

Workers informally learn many of the skills required to do this job well, during years of practice, usually through relationships between women engaged in unpaid work in domestic spaces.[29] These are the skills of relating to people, like listening, being patient, and developing trust. For example, when we asked Lilia how much training she had, she said: "From children to elders, I took care of them, my grandma and grandpa, mom and dad. Why do I need more training?" Speaking of her mother, whom she looked after in the Philippines, Lilia said: "She's very formal and snobby." Lilia explained that her mother did not want to get undressed in front of her, so, to coax her into accepting her help bathing, Lilia would "joke around with her." Lilia referred to this classic example of emotion work in unpaid settings, joking, a skill she continued to use when she entered paid personal support.

Women develop skills that help them do this job well through unpaid work, yet many of the workers we interviewed also had some formal personal support training. Some workers had done a course at a private school or a community college, while others were caring professionals in their countries of origin. Personal support workers are "neither nurses nor maids."[30] The hybrid nature of this domestic, nurse-like job is evident particularly when it comes to a discussion of skills. There are credentials associated with this work in some settings, yet the extent to which the state or employers require and recognize formal skills has varied over time and varies across different parts of the elderly and disability support sector. In contrast, workers we interviewed valued both credentials and informal relational skills, although the meaning of "skill" varied based on one's work history.

Many former factory, domestic, and service workers shared how they deliberately sought personal support training in an effort to move into work they considered to be higher-skilled. For example, Zoe said about her nanny job, "I wanted to leave, but I didn't really want to go to a grocery store or a factory. I needed to decide, okay, what do I want to do? So when I left, I decided to go to school." For Zoe going to school to earn a personal support certificate was a conscious effort to move out of privately paid domestic work, yet it was also a way for her to enter something more meaningful than the other available options for a high school graduate, namely low-wage service or factory work. Donna also emphasized her agency in seeking personal support training to move into a career more skilled than retail work: "I really put a lot of thought into it, and, you know, I was at an age where, do I really wanna be folding shirts for the rest of my life? And when I really thought about what I wanted to do, personal support was it." Several workers in my sample had worked in non-relational service work, such as retail or hotel or office cleaning, and for them too personal support work was more meaningful because working with people required more skill. For example, Maria is a forty-nine-year-old divorced mother of two, with a high school education. In Toronto, after working as a nanny, she worked as an office cleaner, but she was not satisfied with this work. "When I was cleaning the offices," Maria explained, "I saw some people taking care of disabled and [thought], 'I'd really like to do that.' I went to the school, and I find out where I can go to do that course." Many others, like Maria, spoke specifically of the recipients of personal support having drawn them to this work.

Workers crafted the meaning of personal support work as a skilled job of helping people in need in reference to their long-term labor market insecurity resulting in multiple jobs and periods out of work. For example, Amoya held a series of low-paid insecure jobs in Toronto, as a "cleaning lady," nanny, and restaurant server. Upon having children and splitting up with the father, she went on social assistance [welfare], which she described as "very demeaning, and very low, and you feel like you're garbage, because they pry into your private life." The state encouraged Amoya to enter personal support work, which she described very differently. "I always liked to work with people, especially needy people like that, like clients that we do take care of, you know, like children or disabled people or elderly people that can't help themselves." The meaning of personal support as skilled work with people derives from a different type of labor market insecurity for former professionals. Immigrants who were professionals in their countries of origin were de-skilled in Canada and the United States, but they spoke of personal support as a way to use some of their skills, especially those who were formerly in the caring professions. For example, Vera, who had been a nurse in Russia, not only spoke of financial and gendered barriers to retraining in Canada, as noted above, but also revealed a more intimate security she was hoping to find through personal support work. Vera said she was "a little bit shocked" at how elderly people were not looked after by their families in Canada, claiming that in Russia people "have a different mentality," in that they are "more family-oriented, so it's our full obligation to take care for our parents." This cultural viewpoint coupled with Vera's training as a nurse drew her to personal support, as she explained. "Oh, my god, I saw so many different lonely people. . . . And I feel for a few. . . . I could make their life better, easier, and, of course, my education and then my experience—I use it every day regardless." Vera sought intimate security through helping others, in a context of limited labor market security, given the financial, gendered, and migration-related barriers that pushed her out of her profession. Tala, who had been a nurse in the Philippines, said she did not want to work in LTRC, not only because the work entailed mostly heavy, body-related tasks rather than emotional ones, but also because of the way this affected the clients. Tala felt the LTRC clients were not happy and elaborated: "With seniors especially and with those who are disabled . . . mentally and physically, [they] wanted attention." Similarly, Imelda linked her location in this job to wanting to help lonely people. "It's been years that this is my job 'cause I really pity old women who are living alone." The people we interviewed derived meaning from this work in part through their valuation of the skill of helping people, who they sometimes constructed as helpless. Given their migration and work history, whether as domestic workers, factory workers, service workers, or de-skilled professionals, and most as unpaid caregivers to some degree at some point in their lives, it is perhaps not surprising that they wanted to gain or reclaim a job defined by the physical and emotional skills of helping people.

For most women we interviewed, entry into domestic personal support was a step in a long trajectory in search of security at the labor market and intimate levels, starting with migration. The policy under which people entered Canada or the United States shaped their degree of security, but formal citizenship status was not the only driver of insecurity. The majority of people in both my Canadian and U.S. samples entered with permanent status. Those who did not had become either permanent residents or citizens of the United States or Canada by the time we interviewed them. Although this was a difficult road for some, they continued to search for security as former domestic workers, factory workers, service workers, and professionals alike entered precarious employment in Los Angeles and Toronto, including the most insecure corners of the elderly and disability support sector.

What immigrant women from professional and working-class backgrounds had in common that shaped their eventual location in personal support was the marginal place of their nation of origin in the global economy vis-à-vis the United States, Canada, and by extension Britain. Gendered and racialized migration shaped the location of immigrant workers in North America, but their entry into personal support had as much to do with dynamics in the local labor markets of Toronto and Los Angeles, namely the intersection of racialization, gendering, ageism, and precarious employment, supported by the state. Social networks certainly opened up jobs to immigrant workers with few other options, but these jobs were precarious.[31]

Whether they were former professionals, factory workers, or domestic workers, all these women were searching for security, not only in the labor market but also at the more intimate level, although class background shaped the meaning of intimate security. Workers' reflection on past jobs illuminated the importance of analyzing security at the intimate level. The meaning of work constructed by the people we interviewed was similar to what Clare Stacey characterized as "finding dignity in dirty work," by emphasizing the intrinsic rewards of the job.[32] We saw this focus on intrinsic rewards in how the workers' profiled here contrasted factory or non-relational service work with the presumed greater purpose of personal support work. Yet what I am calling insecurity at the intimate level is both more broadly linked to the labor market insecurity of personal support work, hence the use of the term "insecurity," and goes deeper into the relationship with the person receiving support, hence the label "intimate." It is concerned not just with rejecting alienating work made up of tasks with things or bodies and gaining more dignity through emotional connections with people. It is also about resisting dehumanizing work, most starkly inherent in past experiences of privately paid, live-in domestic work but also found in other types of precarious jobs they have done. The workers we interviewed sought humanity in personal support work also by constructing a narrative of it as the skilled job of helping people crafted through their experiences in unpaid work, past jobs, or formal training. This construction sometimes involved casting recipients as needy, and this was done not only among those with professional care backgrounds but also among those with working-class or poor backgrounds. I use the term "intimate insecurity" to conceptualize this deeply relational dynamic.

It is important not to overemphasize the importance of security at the intimate level over labor market security, even if the workers do so themselves.[33] This is particularly vital for immigrant women, whose ethnicity or culture can too simply be associated with a supposedly natural caring orientation, glossing over how work orientation links to gendered and racialized inequalities. Instead, the experience of personal support work depends on the way the work is set up and how this setup shapes the relationship between workers and recipients. These workers' pursuit of security continues but also changes as it meets recipients' quest for flexibility.

DISABILITY AND THE QUEST FOR FLEXIBILITY

Migration and work histories reveal workers' long-standing quest for security. Yet to understand the other side of the personal support relationship, we need to delve into the histories and biographies of elderly and disabled people. Ella, a single, white Canada-born woman in her thirties, has needed help with daily activities since childhood. Her parents and sister provided this support in the family home until her late twenties when Ella obtained paid, personal support and moved into a subsidized, accessible apartment in Toronto. Ella had a college diploma in business administration, but she did not have paid employment. She survived on $8,000 a year from the Ontario Disability Support Program (ODSP). Ella felt that paid personal support services in her own apartment allowed her to live a full life despite her bodily limitations. "I know I'm in this body, [with] which I can't help do for myself," Ella said, "but you want to be treated just like everybody else." Ella contrasted support in one's own home to institutional care. "My biggest fear," Ella said, "is the government cutting back and, you know, sending people to other types of more institutional [places], like where you just get a room. I'll fight tooth and nail." Many people contrasted in-home support with group homes, rehabilitation hospitals, nursing homes, or other types of long-term residential care, viewing the latter as constraining, and they explained the need for flexible, home-based support that did not simply mirror rigid forms of institutional care.

Ella and others valued paid personal support in their own home because they felt it offered them the potential to make decisions on how to live their lives to the fullest. I call this a desire for "flexibility" in the first instance because it contrasts with the typical, rigid institutional care and with care by only unpaid family members. More specifically, it is important to recipients to have flexible services at two levels. First, they desire the ability to influence the type of worker who helps them with personal daily activities, what I call flexibility at the labor market level. Speaking of the workers, Ella said: "When the good ones come in and . . . they don't make you feel bad for having to take a shower, it's stress-free." In contrast, others—perhaps because "they're tired and maybe they don't want to, or it's a lot of work"—reinforced exclusion of different bodies and thus stymied Ella's effort to be "treated like everyone else." Thus, secondly, Ella stressed the importance of a worker with an empathetic attitude toward her needs and linked it to a "stress-free" experience at a more intimate level, given the experiences of living with bodily limitations. Yet the importance of empathetic workers for recipients stemmed from more than bodily impairment. Marginalization also drove the quest for flexibility.[1] "Sometimes I think to myself, 'Really? Is it really that difficult to deal with me, like physically?' And then I feel bad. I feel like I'm a burden on society." Ella mentioned a key way that bodily impairment becomes disabling marginalization—through ideas that people who cannot help themselves are burdens on their families, on the state, and on society.

Elderly people also sought flexibility in the face of disability. Rosa, who was ninety years old and had arthritis and diabetes, recounted a "funny story," involving overhearing her daughter, who was also her state-paid personal support worker as well as a full time nurse, talking to her son. "She keeps calling her brother in the Philippines [saying] 'I can't handle it anymore.'" Her son, a nonpracticing nurse in the Philippines, "is a bit silly," said Rosa, "so he replies, 'Why don't you send her to a nursing home instead?'" In addition to her recounting this story as "funny" and her son's suggestion as "silly," indicating a rejection of institutional care, Rosa directly expressed this view to her children. She told them, "Hey! I'm still strong! I'm not yet dying." Rosa, like many elderly people, associated long-term residential care not only with rigid care out of her control but also with death. The return of immigrant seniors to their countries of origin is one option transnational families may consider to manage the elder care time bind. Rosa was contemplating such a return, noting that her son kept asking her to do so and that she had a nephew who would look after her, but she also worried about her ability to cover health care expenses there. A university-educated teacher, Rosa had left the Philippines after retirement and widowhood, through the sponsorship of her children, nearly twenty years prior to our interview.

Rosa received paid personal support services through a unique program for poor and elderly people that allowed them choose which workers would help them, including their own family members. Rosa chose her daughter, yet she lamented the loss of influence over who helped her with her daily activities, given her daughter's main job as a nurse. "My daughter . . . she doesn't have time. . . . She leaves early in the morning. Her husband comes home in the morning. He will change my wet sheets, as if he is the one taking care of me." In addition to this quest for labor market flexibility, Rosa also resented losing influence at the more intimate level—for example, over her grooming and diet. Rosa bemoaned the daughter's "bland" cooking to reduce her salt intake. "I told her to at least let me smell the fish sauce," recalled Rosa. She also complained that her daughter told her to wait to curl her hair until they visited the Philippines because it was too expensive in Los Angeles. "That's why she's the boss," Rosa concluded.

What do people as different as Ella and Rosa have in common as recipients of state-funded personal support? How does their common experience as personal support recipients shape their desire for flexible services? Whether one acquired an impairment through birth, an accident as a teen or young adult, chronic illness, or gradual aging, a disabling institution weighed heavily on their minds. In addition, whether they had experienced it directly or, like Ella and Rosa, had a more abstract fear of being sent to a group home or nursing home one day, they sought flexible services in contrast to rigid institutional care.[2] People with a range of backgrounds talked about the type of person they felt would be a good personal support worker. That is, they spoke about their desire for flexibility at the labor market level. They also spoke at length about flexibility at a more intimate level, meaning their ability to influence and change what they needed help with, when, where, and how. In order to grasp the quest for flexibility among personal support recipients, we first must understand their experiences of impairment and old age and how these bodily realities clash with the value that North American culture places on independence and youth. Second, a brief foray into the study participants' varied race and class backgrounds presents a more holistic account of who they are in addition to being beneficiaries of state services. Finally, I illustrate the flexibility that people seek to limit the disabling effects of aging and impairment, at the labor market and intimate labor process levels.

Age, Impairment, and the Marginalization of Disability

In order to understand why recipients want flexible services, we first need to appreciate their experiences of impairment and aging, and their bodily support needs. The recipients in my cases were split between nearly equal numbers of elderly (sixty-five and over) and non-elderly disabled people. Age intersected with impairment to shape one's experiences at a given point in time and in terms of when people acquired impairment.

One group of people using personal support services are non-elderly disabled people injured as teens or young adults. For example, thirty-year-old Jordon had no use of his arms or legs due to an accident in twelfth grade. He described his services as a series of intermittent segments. In the morning, workers helped with "bathing, grooming, just getting me basically dressed and in the chair and ready to go for the day." Then he did not need help until lunchtime, he explained, "just getting food shoved in my mouth," and setting him up to work at his home office by "getting the mugs filled up" for a warm drink. A worker came back "close to five p.m." to help him "get stuff ready for dinner or other little things." Someone came back later at night to help him with a bedtime routine. Although not all people talked about it, people with spinal cord injuries lose function of their bowels so they require complex help involving suppositories and sometimes manual stimulation.[3] Thirty-year-old Albert, who had burned himself ten years prior to our interview, summed up the sentiments of many when he said he needed support with "all the usual daily stuff." In general, people in this study who were partially or fully paralyzed had high levels of services, ranging from twenty-eight to seventy hours a week. The majority had more than forty hours a week, with some receiving services at night.

A growing number of people who experience disabling effects of disease since birth or early childhood also require personal support. This includes people with cerebral palsy, polio, or various muscular diseases. Abilities within this broad category varied. For example, Doug was a university student in his thirties who described himself as "fairly independent" and used crutches to get around but needed help with issues requiring fine motor skills, like tying shoelaces. In contrast, Charlotte, who was in her twenties, said, "I can't even get myself a drink out of the fridge," and she required considerable hours of support at home and at school. These two were at the low end and high end of service hours, but most people in this group received between twenty and forty hours of service a week, help with daily activities throughout the day but rarely at night like the first group. For example, Pamela described her services like most in this group: "assistance with ADLs [activities of daily living], getting out of bed, showering, um, going to the washroom, getting dressed, getting undressed, cooking. . . . I have a housekeeper." "Assistance with ADLs" did not mean that the recipient did not assist the worker in these activities. As Jane explained: "I have enough muscle control to help but not really to do it on my own. They do all of my cooking, toileting, et cetera."

Another group of non-elderly disabled people requiring personal support had met with progressively debilitating illnesses in adulthood, such as fibromyalgia or multiple sclerosis. Most people in this group did not need help with daily activities multiple times a day but did need support in some activities every day. Given progressive impairment, their hours ranged from less than one hour to thirty hours a week, with more toward the lower range. For example, Olivia, who was in her late fifties and had lived with MS for eleven years, was able to get her groceries in the neighborhood on her own using her power wheelchair but received twenty-four and a half hours a week for "light housekeeping, showering, bathing, helping to get dressed and undressed." In contrast, Melissa, who was in her early sixties and had fibromyalgia and osteoarthritis, received half an hour a week for help washing her hair.

Some people had acquired physical impairments due to chronic illness, such as diabetes, obesity, stroke, HIV, or cancer, whether they were elderly or younger. Services to this group ranged from two and a half to fourteen hours a week. For example, Luciano, who was in his forties and had suffered a stroke, received two and a half hours a week. The worker helped him get undressed and transfer from a wheelchair to a shower bench. Often the bench hit the curtains and water spilled out on the floor, so the worker also mopped up the water. "So it's safe for me," Luciano explained. Then the worker helped to transfer him back onto the wheelchair and to get dressed. Luciano was on the lower range of hours in this group, but others too in this group described getting in and out of the shower or bath and ensuring the floor was dry (for safety purposes) as the main activity with which they needed support, rather than hands-on help with washing. This was also the case for elderly people. For example, Julia, who was in her seventies, described how blood clots and other health conditions combined to limit her mobility. Pointing to her knees, she said, "There was an injury here. Now arthritis has set in and also because of my overweight, my bones are rubbing. . . . So the minute I get up, with all this heavy weight, it's just agony to walk." Julia received two hours a week for help getting in and out of the bath. Various degrees of help with showering or bathing was the most common type of support needed by the people profiled in this book.

Finally, there are people who need personal support due to age-related physical impairments such as osteoporosis or health problems that had resulted in a fall. For example, ninety-two-year-old Delano had high blood pressure, which caused him to fall, injuring his hip. He said, "I had a surgery for my eyes . . . hip surgery. . . . I feel ill. I feel weak. I can't do anything due to my surgery. I cannot walk on my own." He thus needed help getting in and out of the shower safety. Alma, who was in her early nineties, fell and hit her head, which combined with incontinence to require significant hours of support. She described, "I'm still able to stand, but when I have to go to the bathroom, I have my worker with me in the bathroom to assist me there. You have to be careful because you will fall." Others had illnesses earlier in life that became worse with age. For example, seventy-year-old Gloria was a diabetic and cancer survivor and felt depressed and anxious. The doctor told her that her earlier radiation therapy had damaged her digestive system, but it only emerged as a problem with aging. Elderly people in my sample received hours ranging from one for Eleanor, who was in her seventies and needed help in and out of bath, to thirty-two for Alma, with the majority receiving less than fifteen hours a week. In short, the amount of help people required and the number of hours they received varied greatly.[4]

For elderly people, or people who acquired impairment late in life, needing daily assistance made them feel different not only from young, able-bodied people but also from the people they once were.[5] Consider the conversation, among people with a variety of routes to impairment, which followed a discussion of the difficulties of going up and down stairs in the house of one of the study's participants. Marisol, a sixty-seven-year-old woman who had been in a car accident and had seizures, vertigo, and frequent falls, started the conversation: "This is difficult because you're not who you once were. You always have to have a companion, since you cannot be by yourself anymore. Before you can dance and dance but now not anymore." Sonia, who was eighty-two and used a cane, chipped in, saying, "Just a few shakes and you feel sleepy." Ernesto, who was seventy-two and used a walker, said: "That's right. Before you were young but now we are all old." Ligaya, who was seventy-seven and frequently got dizzy, agreed with the general sentiment of the group that "it's not like before. It is different now." Age met up with impairment in different ways, but all agreed that their activities had become more limited.

All of these personal support recipients, despite the variation in their type of impairment and age, experienced disabling exclusion and marginalization in our able-bodied, youth-oriented society. Limitations imposed by their bodies are only one type of restriction that recipients faced. Most people also mentioned a built environment premised on able bodies as a key barrier to their full participation in society. This included inaccessible housing. For example, Jeff had to live in a rehabilitation hospital for two years after his accident in the late 1980s due to the lack of wheelchair-accessible apartments. "Back then," he explained, "I had no choice." Viviana gave an example of housing that had been made less accessible and that had amplified disablement. She needed services not due to the polio that she had lived with since childhood but rather a recent fall when she was approaching seventy years old, a fall that could have been prevented. In the building she lived in, carpeting by the elevator had been replaced with tiles, on which she had slipped and fractured her leg. Viviana criticized the property manager, the assistant superintendent, and the president of the condo board, saying, "I warned them. I said, 'Please don't.' 'Oh, no, everything's fine, it's perfectly safe, they're not slippery.' And I thought, 'they're not listening to me.'" Another barrier in the built environment most people mentioned was transportation. Those who lived in urban areas emphasized the importance of sidewalks for wheelchairs and both public and specialized, subsidized transportation. Those in more suburban areas noted the need for someone to drive them to appointments or errands. For example, Roberto, who was sixty-six years old and had had a stroke thirty years prior, was paralyzed on his left side so that his weaker right hand easily tired. As a result, he needed help carrying groceries and running other errands, noting that the worker "always gives me a ride." The built environment was not the only barrier.

Cultural barriers were also significant. Put simply, in the words of Kerri, this entailed "society's attitudes towards people with disabilities." Some, like Kerri, emphasized that these problematic attitudes stemmed from "ignorance, not having the knowledge or experience," influenced by cultural institutions like media and education. Others underscored the root of able-bodied people's ignorance in a deep-seated fear of "different" bodies that cannot be "normalized" or cured. Owen, who had lived with a muscular disease for many years, touched on a number of deep-seated cultural barriers.

> There's lots of discrimination. . . . People think you're either a freak—some people, if you're physically disabled you're mentally disabled, that's a typical one. . . . And because you're disabled you're dirty, you don't keep clean, . . . you actually smell or something. . . . They don't wanna be reminded that they could get sick like you or that they could . . . get into an accident and then, you know, end up like you.

Others also mentioned these issues. Emily explained how some of these ideas about people with physical disabilities being less intelligent were perpetuated by institutionalization of disabled children. She had gone to a school for disabled children from age four to fourteen but left with a fifth-grade education. Her parents had to fight with the board of education to get her a teacher's aide in an integrated school. Given this parental commitment and a supportive principal, Emily "found out I had a brain because I was being asked to use it" once she left the "sheltered environment" of the separate school. Emily was able to do four years of school in two and started an integrated high school at age sixteen. As Emily's story illustrates, the state—here through social policies encouraging separate education—can reinforce the simplistic association between physical and intellectual disability, while state officials, like Emily's principal, can help to undermine this problematic coupling.

Cultural barriers are not just out there in society. They permeate interactions with state officials or quasi-officials, including police, teachers, doctors, social workers, and sometimes personal support workers. Cultural barriers are reinforced considerably by the pervasive medical model—the notion that different bodies must be cured or made to match a "normal" body or otherwise contained and managed in institutions.[6] For example, Nathan had a university degree, worked part-time, played wheelchair hockey, was a disability advocate, and described himself as "fairly independent," in large part due to personal support services. This was a far cry from the medical assessment of him as a child. "The doctors told my parents that I'd be a vegetable, like, to put me in an institution and forget about me," he explained. Nathan was born in the early 1970s but said he knew others with the same impairment as him but born in the 1980s whose doctors had given the same dismal assessment. Pamela also explained how the medical model devalued people with different bodies, giving examples of disabled people being denied kidney transplants, and parents of a child with a disability being allowed to stunt her growth so she was easier to look after.

Related to the medical model of either cure or containment is the widespread cultural value placed on independence in the United States and Canada. In such a context, receiving state-funded services is stigmatizing and shameful or, at best, even when it helps people be more engaged in society, something people want to minimize or de-emphasize. One key way people articulated this desire to be independent was in their effort to limit the amount of services they received and to do as much as they could on their own. Some people resented having to resort to receiving help. Carol, who was in her late fifties and lived with chronic pain due to several falls and broken bones, said it had taken her years to accept services. She contrasted her former life as a labor activist with her limited activity and said, "Psychologically it was very much about shame," especially, she said, since "the wounds don't show." When she finally accepted personal support she had not been able to have "a proper bath" for five years, which was "very demoralizing." Tearing up, she recounted that the first day the worker came and helped her bathe and washed her clothes and linens she was "full of gratitude and joy and peace. . . . I felt like a woman again." Carol underscored how state services could bring dignity to people, but this is not always the case.

The shame of receiving services was sometimes perpetuated by state officials—including the social workers who assessed people in the first place. This was particularly evident for difficulties that were themselves stigmatized. Darlene was in her forties and described herself as "quite overweight," a condition that contributed to physical difficulties including arthritis in the knees and feet, osteoporosis, and deteriorating spinal discs. She said she "should have gotten someone sooner, but pride and everything . . . I was embarrassed. But it got to where I couldn't even take care of myself." Once she mustered up the courage to ask for state support, an interaction with a social worker set her back. The first time she spoke with her on the phone to set up an appointment, she mentioned that she had gained weight. The social worker had asked how much she weighed, and when

Darlene told her she weighed well over four hundred pounds, the social worker had asked, "How do you get through your apartment door?" Darlene characterized herself as assertive, with a "pretty thick skin," saying, "I heard every rotten comment about fat over the years, including from my own mother." But she was concerned with how this social worker might affect others, who might be "totally devastated" by such insensitivity, so Darlene called her supervisor and complained. Indeed, others were less assertive. Younger people with disabilities emphasized the need for assessments to be specific to their often extensive needs. As one advocate said: "You can't give a quadriplegic a bath in ten minutes."[7] Marisol, a sixty-seven-year-old woman who had seizures, vertigo, and frequent falls, felt she did not receive sufficient hours. She elaborated on how this limit on her hours made her feel the need to play a pathetic part: "I am just not sure, but when the social worker comes to your house it's almost as if you should act in a way to be pitied and that you're so weak." Even if it is not explicit, state officials often play a role in translating impairment into marginalization. Inequalities of gender, class, and race assist this process of marginalization.

The Intersection of Disability with Gender, Class, and Race

Inequalities of gender, race, and immigrant status shape the disabling effects of bodily need, impairment, and age. There are many more elderly women than men needing personal support, and this reality is reflected in the demographics of the people we interviewed. Differential aging by sex combines with the gendered reality that unpaid care is still relegated largely to wives and daughters, meaning that elderly men are more likely than elderly women to have unpaid support.[8] For example, in our interview with Paul, his wife Elsa frequently interjected to describe her unpaid personal support work and the work of managing Paul's care. Paul was in his eighties, and Elsa had been taking care of him by herself all but one of the seventeen years since he'd had a stroke. She felt the state-funded services were not sufficient and said, "It's getting more difficult all the time. . . . And it's just more than I can handle. I'm getting old, you know?" Suggesting enduring gendered power relations in the family, despite Paul's bodily dependence, Elsa continued, "I would have liked him to get into a nursing home, but he wouldn't sign the papers. . . . Last year he signed . . ., but when [a spot] came up he wouldn't go." The underfunding of in-home support pits Paul's effort to maintain his unpaid family care against Elsa's own support needs. Indeed, many people, especially women, could not rely on family support. For example, Sarah detailed how her partner was "supposed to help, but that was an issue" with which they "had been struggling for a very long time." Her mom, she said, "always tried to be there, but that has been a little tense too," so she tried not to involve her any more than she had to.

Race modifies the effects of gender inequality in this process of marginalization. When recipients are people of color, underfunding can be racializing. Denise, who was in her seventies, felt the social worker's questioning of her need was linked to the fact that she was an immigrant woman of color who lived in a poor neighborhood. When at the house visit the social worker suggested Denise could walk, Denise felt she had to defend herself. She said to the social worker, "Definitely, I walk with a cane. And then I go on WheelTrans, you see?" Showing her arm, she continued: "And I'm asthmatic. . . . I just went for a test now. You see? And a basket of medication I took." Our group discussions with Pilipinx recipients were full of unprompted comments between them about social workers' power in the assessment process along lines of race, gender, and class as well as age and disability. For example, one group characterized the process of determining hours as discriminatory. Delia said: "Sometimes, they will give you less hours even if you really need it." Saturino elaborated: "Sometimes, if they don't know you, they will give you less hours. But if they know you, they will give you more." Adelaida agreed: "Yeah, if you become friends." Saturino then rhetorically asked: "Isn't that discrimination? Because sometimes others have worse sickness, but they won't increase it yet." These discussions gave a glimpse into widespread feelings of state power in the lives of immigrant recipients. Fifty-four percent of the recipients in this study were white and native-born, while 15 percent were European immigrants, 29 percent were immigrants of color, and 2 percent were native-born people of color. Social class also varied among those we interviewed.

Class intersected with impairment and age to marginalize people in different ways. For example, class contoured the lack of choice for Jeff, discussed above, who had resided in a rehabilitation hospital for years after his accident. High school–educated, Jeff was living off a state disability pension with some contributions from his former employer in a job as a skilled trade worker, which nevertheless put him below the poverty line. In contrast, as a university-educated professional working full-time, Diana was buying an accessible condominium. Elderly people with financial means can consider options for collective living where they retain some decision-making influence. For example, Richard was in his eighties, had had hip and knee surgeries, and had fallen several times. He was only given two hours a week of personal support, and when his wife, Gladys, could no longer provide most of Richard's care, the plan was for Richard to go to an assisted living apartment, which Gladys distinguished from "a nursing home, where you don't get out of bed." The gender dynamics between Richard and Gladys contrasted from the less well-off Paul and Elsa, whom we met above. Class resources would help Elsa limit gendered obligation but Elsa does not have access to such wealth. Abigail, who was in her eighties, had damaged her ribs and hips through falls and has seizures, but she said, "I guess I'm kind of independent and thankful that I, so far, can manage to pay the bills. You know? Because I really want to stay here. This has been my home forever, for fifty-eight years." More broadly, freedom to make choices about one's life, especially in the United States but also in Canada, is tied to one's degree of economic security.[9]

Many non-elderly people experience exclusion from employment, which contributes to the disabling effect of impaired bodies. As Owen said, "Some people—I believe, anyway—they resent you because you're living off their tax dollar." Doug, who had lived with a disability since childhood, was one of the many disabled men who had never entered the labor force.[10] Others spoke of insecure income due to chronic illness. Referring to private insurance companies and state disability agents, Monica said, "You wouldn't believe what they put people through to prove they are sick."[11] Pamela, who had lived with a disability since childhood, had worked for the government, but she and others lost their jobs and could not find secure employment when employment reforms rendered "completely useless" the Ontarians with Disability Act that mandated equal treatment.[12] Most elderly recipients were not working due to retirement rather than because of exclusion, but many elderly women were mothers who had never been in the labor force or had had only short periods of paid employment before having children, which limited their income in old age.

People with disabilities also work in precarious employment, and this was also true for the people we interviewed.[13] Several of the elderly people had been in precarious jobs in their working years, including jobs as cleaner, common laborer, and casual construction worker, and some were even former personal support workers, while others had been managers and professionals and still others had worked in feminized jobs as dieticians and receptionists. Several of those under sixty-five were still working in precarious employment. For example, Cameron, who breathed through a tracheostomy, worked at home on a part-time basis with personal support but lamented that he could not get a job in his field as a graphic designer. "I went to art school and all that. There never seems to be any occupations for people with a disability in the arts. . . . So I am basically just kind of reduced to doing little freelance jobs or volunteering." Discrimination and inaccessible workplaces resulted in limited hours and earnings, so Cameron and others relied on the Ontario Disability Support Program for non-elderly people, which put them below the poverty level. Some people had fallen into poverty with aging or disability (or both) and a few with migration and thus had a contradictory class location, like many immigrant workers who have experienced downward mobility.[14] Intersecting social inequalities translate diverse forms of impairment into marginalizing disability, but how does the experience of marginalization shape a desire and need for flexible services?

The Meaning of Flexibility at the Intimate Level

The people we interviewed valued the ability to receive flexible services in their own homes so they could live their lives to the fullest. More specifically, they desired two types of flexibility at the intimate level. One dimension of flexibility was the ability to influence and change the tasks that were done in a given time period. Another was the ability to influence and change how workers helped them with daily activities, which related to recognition of their knowledge and not just the workers' skill.

Knowledge versus Skill

Recipients resisted the idea that support with their daily activities should be only or primarily directed by skilled experts, rather than self-directed and based on their own embodied knowledge. Those who had lived with impairment for many years most strongly emphasized their knowledge of how their bodies worked and the importance, therefore, of having the ability to influence and change how services were provided. This viewpoint was articulated strongly by a disability advocate with quadriplegia: "What happens is: your aide thinks that they're the boss." She explained that although she usually hired aides directly, sometimes she had to use a temporary support worker from an agency who hired certified nursing assistants (CNAs). Providing a vivid account of an explicit knowledge-versus-skill tension, the advocate recounted how, when she tried to direct one worker's services, the worker kept saying, "I'm a CNA," prompting the advocate to say: "I don't give a darn what you learned. You need to do what I would like done, not the way you want it done." She added that the nursing assistant's resistance to thinking that she, the advocate, was the boss was because of medical model training where they, for example, "want you to wear diapers." She felt infantilized by the very idea of this: "It's a whole reversal."[15] Another advocate emphasized: "One size does not fit all. . . . If a person says they have the skills, the consumer still has to judge whether they are at a level satisfactory for them or not."[16] Others also mentioned training the worker themselves, even if one already had a certificate. As another advocate said: "If you were a quadriplegic, and you used a catheter, and you need somebody to change that on a regular basis, how you change it . . . is maybe vastly different than how a medical professional would insist upon changing it. And the issue can be accomplished just as effectively one way as another way."[17] These disability advocates are rejecting the notion of standardized skills based on disembodied medical expertise. They are also asserting that the recipient is the one who should judge the applicability of the worker's skills for the recipient's particular needs. For many, flexibility was about influence at this most intimate level of the body.

Elderly recipients, who generally had not lived with impairment as long, did not have such an articulated critique of medical expertise, yet they too talked about the importance of influencing how things were done. They often spoke about influence over the home environment as much as about how their bodies were handled. For example, Joel, who was in his seventies and had diabetes, gave an example of the specific ways people often wanted things done in their own homes. "Ah, for example . . . the bed, the bed is easy to fix. Sometimes, I want to rearrange it, like put the pillow on this side, something like that." Then a senior advocate sitting in on the interview and helping to translate raised the following scenario: "How about if your provider is disrespectful and says, 'No, do this, this is better"?[18] Joel said the workers had not been disrespectful like this but admitted that it could happen to other people. "Yeah, they take advantage too, especially if you're old." As this conversation suggests, flexibility in how things are done is not just about influencing and changing the ordering of tasks but also about whether workers take over or people are able to decide how their homes and bodies are managed.

It is also important to recognize gendered experience through which women learn the emotional skills of relating to people, largely gleaned from other women through unpaid work in families.[19] This does not mean that family care always provides flexibility. Instead, tensions related to marginalization through dependence emerge here too. Several recipients spoke of wanting more influence than they had when receiving support from unpaid family. For example, Doug, who was born with an impaired body and received unpaid help from his mother for many years, sought flexibility in paid personal support in his own apartment in contrast to "the mothering instinct. . . . You know, your mother comes in and wants to whip everything up?" Elizabeth valued paid in-home services for providing her some degree of independence from her family, who provided most of her care unpaid. She underscored how she did not want her husband helping her with the shower, not only because he was "not the most organized" but also because she was less able to direct him. Contrasting unpaid family support with the services of paid workers, she said:

> They get me ready for the day; they get me dressed; they cheer me up. It gives me an independence that, oh, I don't know what I would do without.

> My feeling of self-worth would be absolutely devastated if I didn't have that.... I am not relying on [family] 24/7 because I have this hour a day that I can direct.

Elizabeth articulated the value of not just help with physical tasks but also the workers' emotional skills of cheering her up. She also explained that her self-worth was tied to the ability to direct the workers, which mitigated her feelings of dependence on unpaid family care. In this sense, the workers' skill was connected to Elizabeth's embodied knowledge. More broadly, whether in reference to unpaid care in families or paid care in institutional settings, the translation of impairment into marginalization through relations of dependence underpinned people's desire for flexible services. This was also evident in their desire to influence and change which tasks workers provided and when.

Time versus Tasks

Recipients also considered flexibility in which service tasks were provided and when as essential to a meaningful life. Their experiences are in line with what feminist disability scholars call "crip time," which "bends the clock to meet disabled bodies and minds" instead of molding "disabled bodies and minds to meet the clock."[20] For example, Jane, who was born with cerebral palsy, admitted that it was easier to "sit in your apartment and do nothing and wait for whoever it is to come and help you." Yet, she claimed, "this is not a nursing home environment; it's an independent living environment." Again, flexibility was often contrasted with the idea of controlling institutions. Key to Jane's notion of an independent living versus a nursing home environment was the question of *when* services were provided, as she elaborated. "It's not 'When will you come and see me?' It's: 'I need this at this time because I am going here'.... Each person is an individual and should be treated that way." Related to flexibility in *which* tasks and *when*, was *where*. Many emphasized the importance of personal support for grocery shopping and other related social reproductive activities outside the home. Others emphasized the need for help in the community in order to participate more fully in society. Some underscored the importance through a critique of the degree of flexibility of their current services, even though they were home-based. For example, Suzy, who was in her seventies and often used a wheelchair or a cane due to osteoporosis, lamented having to be in for the evening in order to meet the agency scheduled worker: "I could go out to meetings at night, but I have to be here at six o'clock or something. I can go out after that, but then I have to get my leg bag off and put a bed bag on." This lack of scheduling flexibility on certain days limited her ability to participate in the community, as she explained.

"I was doing some volunteer work at the church before. . . . Now I can't do it." Others described how paid help in the community minimized their isolation. For example, Marisol had a worker who drove her to an adult day care center, and Marisol said: "I have been in the center for seven years, and, before, I was not able to walk, laugh, or move, but now I am stronger." Given the connection between aging and one's sense of self, discussed above, such sites are important for living a full life. Influence over when and where services were provided allowed others to work or go to school. For example, Jacob, a twenty-year-old man who was paralyzed in high school, was able to attend university with mobile personal support.

The quest for flexibility also arose from the unpredictability of one's needs. This is behind much of the desire to not just initially set out but also to change which tasks were done when and where. One disability advocate felt that the way social workers assessed people was "almost like putting you into a straitjacket" because "you might not exactly know how long it would take to do certain things."[21] As Elizabeth, who was in her late fifties, said: "Rheumatoid arthritis is a very energy-limiting thing. So I can't say every Wednesday morning I will be fine." Similarly, Abel, who was in his seventies and had lived with MS for over thirty years, said, "With MS you never know what you get tomorrow; you know, sometimes you're all right, sometimes you're not." Thomas, who was in his early sixties and had been in a serious car accident twenty years prior, described his body as three-quarters "plastic and steel" and said: "A lot of times I don't feel well, like today . . . because of this weather. Apparently with the way they're talking about the humidex for next week, that's going to be even worse." Lauren explained that she was only *para*plegic, so she usually did her own shopping, but said that getting three bags of milk was "sometimes cumbersome, that's all." Lauren emphasized the importance of flexibility in getting help outside the home when she needed it. These experiences show how "crip time" is not just an accommodation to people who need more time than a hypothetical normal person but also flexibility in time that could be "a challenge to normative and normalizing expectations of pace and scheduling."[22]

People needed flexibility to manage the ups and downs not only of their bodies but also their homes. They expressed their need, not just want, for support with some housekeeping some of the time, although how often and how much varied and changed over time for a given individual. For example, Edwin, who was in his fifties and had had a heart attack ten years prior, had long received help with a shower once a week. This worked for a time because his wife joined him from their birth country, Trinidad, and was "keeping things together." But when his wife died, Edwin "went into a depression, thinking about all the problems." Edwin explained how the social worker "came to a home visit to see the condition it was. And it was not looking too good." So the social worker recommended help with housekeeping, and the paid workers did "almost every house cleaning." Not only men without wives needed help with housework. This was evident in a group discussion among four women in their eighties and nineties in response to a question about the strengths and weaknesses of their services. Patricia said: "One of its advantages is the elder or disabled have someone to help them do the things they cannot do themselves." Amihan said: "Especially when it comes to doing the house chores, like cleaning the house, since we get tired too easily. My balance is not as good as before so even going down to the van I need assistance. It's different now." Normie chipped in: "Yes, just like when I gained weight all of a sudden. That's why I cannot stand for a while." Rosario agreed, "Yes, you really need the help." This conversation illustrated how the support these women needed with housework varied over time, with age, with a change in physical health, like weight gain, and in a given day when one got tired. People emphasized how they could not physically do some of the cleaning tasks, or if they did they would not be able to do other important things. For example, Aldo, a middle-aged man with a bone disease requiring several surgeries, said: "I can make my own bed, but once I've done it I have to get back in it." He contrasted his life with his parents, when he was "big out of society," to the present and told how personal support in his own apartment had allowed him to earn B.A. and M.A. degrees, work as a substitute teacher, and do his own grocery shopping. Again, unpaid family care was not always the best way to gain flexibility in regard to what was done, when, where, or how. This is one reason people want influence over who provides services, what I call flexibility at the labor market level.

Flexibility at the Labor Market Level

People articulated a desire for flexibility in determining who provided services, because the services were so personal. For some recipients, this flexibility seemed best achieved through a strong form of labor market flexibility—the ability to hire and fire the workers. One disability advocate in his sixties, who got polio as a child and had had personal support services for many years, expressed this viewpoint well. "You cannot have an attendant that you don't have the ability to hire and fire. I think that's crucial. That has to stay with the individual disabled person. And I couldn't imagine another kind of model because eventually it would become like a nursing home."[23] Another disability advocate, a person with quadriplegia, said hiring and firing was "very important" because through hiring the right person you seek "some measure of control of how things are done, what needs to be done" and otherwise "you're kind of at that person's mercy."[24] In Los Angeles, people can request that their family member be their paid provider. The

Pilipinx elderly IHSS recipients we interviewed expressed a strong preference for having family assist them, in line with the notion of children's filial duty to their parents. Some people used ethnicity and race as a proxy for a familial level of trust. For example, Alma, a ninety-one-year-old Pilipina who received paid help from a Pilipina who was not family, said: "As much as possible, you have to know the person. . . . At least you want to know if she's Pilipina, right? . . . You have to know the integrity of the person. . . . So you get information from friends whom they know." Networks were key to recruitment when recipients hired and fired, but in some programs they did not.

Some did not want to hire or fire but still wanted a say over who an agency sent to provide their intimate support, thus desiring a softer form of labor market flexibility. For example, one disability advocate who was on the board of directors of a personal support–providing organization and also received personal support services, described how he once sat in on an interview where the job applicant spoke of wanting the job because of feelings of "pity for these people." He explained that, for him, the interview stopped at that point, and he just went through the motions. He did not "have the time or the strength or enough penicillin to try and train someone, to say: 'You know what? I am someone with a mind and a heart and intelligence,' that 'I do need this help, yes, but that doesn't mean that you have to feel bad for me.'"[25] Others also felt that a certain type of worker, one that recognized individual differences, was essential in this type of service, given varied experiences of impairment. Sarah, who was in her thirties, said that in this field, working with people with illnesses or physical limitations, "you have to have some sort of understanding to the fact that everybody's different. . . . So one person might have a lot of pain, another person may have no pain." Sarah emphasized the pain of her rheumatoid arthritis coupled with exhaustion of MS. Others also discussed how the pain and exhaustion of impairment drove their desire for flexibility in who provides services.

Many connected intimacy with physical vulnerability, and this was another reason why people wanted a say over who provided support. People with stigmatized impairments or illnesses, like mental health difficulties or those who were overweight, spoke extensively of the vulnerability that came with intimate services. For example, Jean, who was sixty-five and described herself as "morbidly obese," said: "If somebody's going to make me feel uncomfortable being naked in front of them, then why on earth would I have that person in my bathroom helping me take a shower? No, I'll not put myself into that kind of a situation." Similarly, Julia said it was important to be able to build a relationship of trust with the workers providing services "because you are in a vulnerable position. I mean, I'm helpless, and I am undressed, and they are helping me shower! You never get used to it because everybody wants to be independent." Julia and others emphasized the importance of continuity in the worker sent by the agency so they could develop the trust that made them feel less vulnerable. Justine, who was in her early sixties and had back and neck problems as well as depression, said: "It was a little disconcerting when I was having a changeover of workers. Like, I wanted somebody permanent." Julia, Justine, and others sought a soft form of labor market flexibility, while others wanted to be employers with hiring and firing power, but both groups linked their quest for some degree of labor market flexibility to the intimacy of bodily services.

The personal support recipients in this study—whether born with an impaired body, injured as a teenager, debilitated through ill health in mid-adulthood, or more gradually limited through aging—desired flexibility because they felt it facilitated equal participation in society. Bodily impairments were not inherently disabling but rather became disabling through an environment built for people who walk without assistance, cultural barriers that stigmatize, and, most important for this study, relations of dependence vis-à-vis the state and the family. For example, while people's individual experiences were unique, most respondents recounted a stressful period of interacting with state officials or quasi-officials who had control over their eligibility for personal support benefits, interactions that reinforced the shame of dependence already widely circulating in U.S. and Canadian society.

If the goal is to decouple impairment and old age from disabling exclusion and marginalization, understanding recipients' quest for flexibility is an important first step. Recipients sought flexibility in the labor market, which was a continuum ranging from hiring and firing power to a degree of say on who came into one's home to provide intimate support. Recipients also sought flexibility at the intimate level along two dimensions. The first was their ability to use their own knowledge to direct how their bodies were handled and their homes managed. The second dimension was their ability to influence and change which service tasks were provided, when, and where.

This deep understanding of recipients' quest for flexibility, together with the account of workers' long-standing pursuit of security in the preceding chapter, begins to reveal tensions between the two groups. Because of the gendered and racialized class inequalities that shape workers' lives and the emphasis on independence that, along with other disabling forces, transforms old and impaired bodies into marginalized people, each group has different interests—yet they must work together. Recipients' desire for flexibility in service tasks can be in tension with workers' efforts to gain security by defining the parameters of their job. Recipients' aspiration for flexibility in how the work is directed and accomplished, based on their embodied knowledge, could be in tension with workers' quest for security through a job that includes some formal training and also recognition of their often invisible emotional skills. At the labor market level, recipient flexibility to choose the worker can be in tension with worker's employment and income security. It is important to understand how these tensions are embedded in the reality that workers and recipients are located within different axes of oppression.[26] Still, these are complex social ties that could also provide openings for change.

The disabling forces that turn impairment and old age into marginalization are central to the experience of personal support recipients, but the people described in this chapter are more than state beneficiaries. They are also sons and grandmothers, often providing as well as receiving support; some are or have been workers in precarious employment; and some are immigrants. Some people have experienced downward mobility with disability, not unlike the downward mobility of professionals with migration. Given the overwhelmingly immigrant background of the worker sample, and the mostly white, native-born background of the recipient sample, which reflects broader trends, interactions between many workers and recipients must cross racial and national divides. At the same time, other recipients in my sample have a similar racialized background or are part of the same ethnic community as the workers. Some of the recipients had fallen into poverty with migration, like many workers. To the extent that these other social locations are in line with those of the workers, there might be more potential for the two groups to negotiate flexibility with security. Furthermore, sameness is not equivalent to solidarity. For example, when Gord was asked about whether communication with workers from different countries was ever an issue, he responded, "My CP [cerebral palsy] accent is not that bad." His answer reveals a potential line of solidarity between people with speech impairments and people with (non-Canadian and non-American) accents, both of whom have to work to be understood by the dominant culture. Intersecting inequalities that result in workers and recipients having something in common, along class or race or other lines, could support interdependence at the intimate level. Yet the social organization of the services also shapes the ability of recipients and workers to negotiate flexibility and security. How this happens is the focus of the next four chapters, starting with the case of Ontario's Direct Funding Program, in which service provision is individualized and collective supports are limited.

MANAGING FLEXIBILITY WITHOUT SECURITY IN TORONTO'S DIRECT FUNDING

Robert, a forty-year-old white, Canada-born man who had become impaired ten years prior, managed Pilar and a couple other personal attendants through the Direct Funding Program (DF) of Ontario's Self-Managed Attendant Services. As a self-manager, Robert received funding from the Ontario government to recruit, hire, manage, and fire the workers who assisted him in daily living activities. Contrasting DF with previous services he had received, Robert said: "[N]ow I hire and fire whoever I want. Within limits, they do anything that I ask them to do . . . if I'm nice enough." Robert linked a strong form of labor market flexibility, hiring and firing, to a labor process marked by flexibility in tasks. Robert hired immigrant women from Latin America and Asia who had been care professionals in their countries. One of these workers, Pilar, married with no children and in her mid-twenties, arrived in Toronto a year before our interview. With a university degree and two years working as a nurse in Latin America, Pilar was one of the many immigrant professionals in Canada whose credentials Canadian employers did not recognize, people who were thus working well below their formal skill level.[1] Robert was paying Pilar fourteen dollars an hour, which was well above the minimum wage at the time, but her hours were few. The support Robert needed was intermittent, so he hired two other workers in addition to Pilar, while Pilar supplemented this job with one in long-term residential care, for which she earned only ten dollars and fifty cents an hour. Pilar had left a janitorial job for this work that she considered more meaningful, yet she resented being asked to do tasks she considered in the realm of nursing without the protection of a credential. Despite an otherwise good working relationship with Robert, which included reciprocal acts like his helping Pilar with English on her résumé, Pilar was looking for employment that would be more secure.

How do self-managers seek to translate the labor market flexibility given to them by this program, through hiring and firing, into their sought flexibility at the intimate level, meaning the ability to use their embodied knowledge to influence how the support is given and to determine what kinds of support they get and when? How do personal attendants attempt to obtain security at the intimate level, meaning the ability to use their skills and influence the types of tasks they do, in this highly insecure labor market? Much depends on the willingness of the self-managers to build and sustain a respectful working relationship with personal attendants, yet gendered and racialized inequalities and the program design matter too.

Context: Independent Living through Direct Funding

In her book on Ontario's Direct Funding Program, Christine Kelly described it as "a quintessential manifestation of the Independent Living movement."[2] The key principles of the IL philosophy are that people with disabilities should have self-determination and be full members of society, through organizations of and for all people with disabilities.[3] The IL philosophy redefines independence to focus on decision-making rather than doing everything for one's self, and decisions over personal support are seen as key precursors to a fulfilling life. Like the overall social model of disability of which it is a part, the IL philosophy criticizes the medical model that defines rehabilitation programs, which locate the problem in physical impairment or a disabled individual's lack of knowledge and views the solution as cure or professional expertise. Instead, the IL paradigm sees the problem as environmental barriers, including dependence on professionals or family, and views the solution as disabled people's control over their lives, including their personal supports, through self-help, peers, and removal of barriers.[4]

The IL movement started in the United States, where student disability activists influenced by the 1960s civil rights movement and "radical consumerism" first organized independent living centers in the early 1970s to support disabled people living in the community.[5] In line with dominant social reform philosophies in the United States and strong values of self-reliance and individualism, the movement embraced the term "consumer" to replace "patient" or "client." The U.S. IL movement influenced the Canadian IL movement, but, emerging ten years later, the Canadian movement was also influenced by the international disability movement as well as key alliances with the government and the Mennonite

Church. Independent living activism took off in Canada in the early 1980s, and throughout the 1980s and 1990s independent living centers were established.[6] The leaders of both movements were mostly young, white men with physical disabilities. Whereas the U.S. movement drew on antistate ideas, the Canadian IL movement has been more connected with Canada's more developed welfare state. As a result, while Canadian IL activists also refer to themselves as "consumers," the meaning of the term in Canada places greater emphasis on the ability to have choice and control in government-funded support and service processes than on individual purchasing power in a free market.[7] Direct funding, however, is a move toward individualization.

Direct funding in Ontario began in the early 1990s when the government allocated money to the Centre for Independent Living Toronto (CILT) to run a pilot. In 1998, the pilot became a program, run by CILT in partnership with the Ontario Network of Independent Living Centres (ONILC).[8] In line with the casting of recipients as consumers of state-funded services, former CILT director Vic Willi described the program like this: "In return for taking on more risk and responsibility, Direct Funding participants gain greater choice, flexibility and control."[9] Reflecting the social model of disability, as opposed to the medical model of rehabilitation, the Direct Funding Program website stated: "this Program is not for everybody; especially persons who are quite ill, or who need 'looking after.'"[10] Like in the United States, Ontario politicians became interested in direct funding as a way to contain costs.[11] Indeed, there has consistently been a waiting list for direct funding, indicating unmet need.

Ontario's Ministry of Health and Long-Term Care funded the program through the Toronto Central Local Health Integration Network (LHIN). It was not means-tested, yet if one received an insurance settlement, insurance payments, private health coverage reimbursement, or Workplace Safety and Insurance Board (WSIB) payments due to an injury at work, DF was the last payer, topping up services covered by these alternatives.[12] Those eligible needed to be sixteen years old or over, residents of Ontario with an Ontario Health Insurance Plan (OHIP) card, and require attendant services at home due to a permanent physical disability, with stable needs for at least one year. The program defined "attendant services" as neither just help with housework nor professional medical care but broadly as help with activities of daily living (like transferring from place to place and bowel routines) and related services (like food preparation, laundry, and shopping). Funding was based on individual needs, but the government defined a maximum of seven hours a day.[13]

The program based funding on a maximum wage defined by the provincial average, but there is also a minimum wage.[14] One self-manager and key informant characterized the min-max wage as an "equity framework" that CILT worked hard to build into the program, as CILT argued that wages "couldn't be too low" while the government said they "couldn't be too high."[15] Self-managers generally had more than one personal attendant, and the program suggested paying different rates to reflect experience, but program policy directed self-managers to pay the rate defined by the provincial average after a three-month probation period.[16] Self-managers also received a percentage of the workers' wages to cover statutory benefits, such as Canada Pension Plan (CPP), Employment Insurance (EI), Workplace Safety and Insurance Board contributions, vacation pay, and holiday pay under the Employment Standards Act. Prospective self-managers could apply for funding to cover one-way travel to work if shifts were short, very early in morning, or late at night, if workers lived far away from them, and/or there was no public transportation but travel in between clients or for errands was not covered. They could apply for funding for support at night, for a nearby agency to provide regular night turns, for the attendant to "sleep over," or for emergency help. However, application guidelines suggested that the self-manager plan for emergencies by having a personal attendant available by phone between certain hours, maintaining a list of "casual part-timers to call on short notice," asking personal attendants to arrange temporary replacements if they were unable to work, or planning to call family, friends, or neighbors.[17] Self-managers could also request funding for a bookkeeper, advertising costs, home insurance, bank charges, and other miscellaneous costs. CILT retained a "contingency fund" for unforeseen events, such as a surgery or broken limb that would require additional hours.[18]

CILT determined the level of funding allocated to each self-manager, within the parameters of government funding. Applicants to the program submitted proposals to CILT stating the frequency of their needs. Self-managers had to be capable of knowing one's needs sufficiently to complete an application in one's own words and meet with a selection panel to discuss them. Selection panels—made up of a CILT staff member, an elected representative of the applicant's regional independent living resource center (if not CILT), and a peer consumer of attendant services from the same region—reviewed the application, interviewed the applicant, determined eligibility, and negotiated a budget.[19] Participants entered into a contract with CILT that set out their obligations, including "sole responsibilities for their attendant service arrangements and full legal liability as the employer of their attendants."[20]

The DF Program gave self-managers labor market flexibility in that they chose whom to hire, with the ability also to fire. Self-managers had to be capable of "self-directing" (including scheduling, training, instructing, and supervising attendants) and "managing" (hiring, firing, meeting all the legal requirements of an employer, accounting for the funding, evaluating one's services, and assuming the responsibilities and risks of the above). Detailed regulations also stipulated that they register with Revenue Canada for a business number, sign paychecks, and keep records of employee hours and level of pay for tax purposes.[21] One exception to the self-manager's hiring flexibility was that they could not hire "immediate family members," defined as "any parent, child, sibling, person to whom the Participant is married, or person, other than a blood relative, with whom the Participant has lived for at least one year, and with whom the Participant has a personal relationship of primary importance." The program also advised against employing more distant family members, like nieces or daughters-in-law, because "mixing family with employer/employee relationships is fraught," especially in the case of dismissal.[22]

As employees of the individual self-manager, these workers have limited labor protections because several laws consider them domestic servants. For example, they are excluded from the Ontario Labour Relations Act that protects workers' rights to bargain collectively through a union. They are thus covered by the basic fair labor standards law, the Ontario Employment Standards Act (ESA). CILT instructed self-managers to comply with the ESA, which regulated the minimum wage, hours of work, vacation pay, and holiday pay, among other standards. The program application included a section on "optional arrangements costs," and the application guide gave examples of overnight help. It suggested that self-managers budget based on a flat rate for overnight help depending on how much "hands-on" work the attendant was expected to do, but it warned that if the attendant did not get at least six hours of continuous sleep, the ESA required one to pay hourly and equivalent to at least the Ontario minimum wage. Program materials also suggested that one could offer an attendant room and board "as a means of extending coverage over more hours in the day."[23] Given funding caps, more common than live-in work were the insecurities that came with intermittent need through short shifts filled by several workers. However, workers were only paid for time worked and not eligible for the minimum work period under the ESA. Self-managers could also recruit workers under a temporary contract labor program, in which case workers rights were even more restricted, although no one in my sample did so.[24] Limited funding and regulation that does not fully cover home-based work can exacerbate flexibility security tensions in the labor market.

Flexibility and Insecurity at the Labor Market Level

Self-managers valued a strong form of labor market flexibility through hiring and firing because they sought to hire someone who was compatible with them as a person, not with the job in the abstract. Their hiring criteria focused on interpersonal compatibility as well as reliability and availability. When asked about what she looked for in hiring people, Kerri said that "the main thing is their attitude." She elaborated on the importance of their attitude "towards this kind of work, the willingness to do it," as well as "towards somebody who has a disability . . . that they're taking into consideration how to treat the person." She also mentioned the importance of their "willingness to take direction." Similarly, Jennifer initially looked for people with an "outgoing attitude" who were "responsive to me as an individual." Self-managers felt that an attitude of openness to taking direction was "something you can't teach," in the words of Diane. Rather than considering education or formal training, Diane asked the following when interviewing workers: "Do you think you'll like the work? Do you think you can do the work? How do you think you and I are going to be able to get along?" Others considered training or experience as one factor alongside personality. Personality could trump training, but training could not trump a personality and openness to the independent living philosophy of self-determination. Doug said, "I look for somebody who is easygoing, who is understanding, I guess, and patient . . . and somebody . . . who doesn't really want to control." The emphasis on attitudes toward people with a disability and this type of work stemmed from a wariness of hiring attendants who might take control of the way things were done, as this was viewed as a threat to their autonomy. In line with independent living philosophy, formal training and experience in this field were not identified by one self-manager we interviewed as a deciding factor in whether to hire a given person. Yet several did hire some people with training. Jennifer hired people ranging from nursing students to those who were "borderline literate." This range also reflected who was available.

Insufficient hours of work largely drove labor market insecurity for workers. Monthly hours of service to the self-managers in this study ranged from 34 to 176, yet because their needs were intermittent, those needing significant hours of service hired multiple people on short shifts. Only one of the self-managers in this study hired only one worker, and some hired six or seven. They hired workers under arrangements ranging from thirty hours a week to a couple hours of backup a month. Similarly, hours of direct funding work among the personal attendants ranged from Mike's twenty-five hours a week for one self-manager and eight hours a week each for two others to the infrequent hours worked by Patti, who had another full-time job and worked through direct funding only as a backup. These figures may imply that weekly hours were stable, but they were generally not. For example, self-manager Kerri, who received approximately forty hours of service a week, employed four women. She tried to give them roughly equal hours but did not guarantee anyone a certain number of hours; if she needed someone, and one was working another job (which all of them had), she would give those hours to one of the personal attendants who was available. We interviewed one of these personal attendants, Mathilda, who said that she often worked two to three hours a night, five to seven times a week ("it depends"). She also worked forty hours a week during the standard workday through an agency. Sometimes people combined DF work with a full-time job, but others pieced together multiple temporary DF jobs to make a living.[25]

Funding increases in the late 2010s raised workers' hourly wage and provided more hours to self-managers, thus augmenting security. Self-managers had some discretion regarding what they paid workers, within the funding parameters. Most self-managers paid close to the maximum funded rate. Some paid workers for travel time, if they lived far away. All the personal attendants in this study earned more than the required minimum at the time of the interview, but only one received travel pay. However, even if the self-manager received the maximum amount of funding, one would likely hire at least two people as main attendants, plus a backup, given intermittent needs, resulting in poverty earnings for the workers.

Insufficient funding can exacerbate the flexibility-security tension, and most self-managers in this study felt they did not have sufficient funded hours. Robert explained how his accountant had to put him "on a diet" for six months or so, by cutting back his three workers by fifteen minutes a shift each, because he had overspent and risked going into the red. Similarly, Doug described increased funding for the personal attendants to get a pay raise and even some retroactive money but said he did not put the money toward a raise but rather toward more hours of service. He felt like he was in a kind of "legal limbo" and was nervous about whether he was "cooking the books." He speculated that others did this too. Paying workers less allowed him to have more hours than those for which he was officially budgeted. Doug had a lot of turnover and felt better pay would attract higher-quality workers, yet the heart of the problem was insufficient hours of service. If self-managers do not have sufficient hours to cover their needs, they might not pay the funded wage rate and might even treat workers as self-employed and thus not pay into statutory employer benefits, such as EI and CPP. Whereas most self-managers said they had to ensure that their workers were eligible to work in Canada, one person who hired three immigrant workers said he had not done so and did not think he was required to. Two workers in my small sample said they were classified as self-employed contractors, so income tax and employer statutory benefits were not taken out as required by the program. One self-manager spoke of these arrangements too. The more clients a worker takes, the more likely this legal interpretation is.[26] Charlotte was critical of DF Program assumptions that they hire people very casually to work split shifts. She said it was unrealistic, especially given the low pay. "Tell me honestly, who's gonna do that?" she asked rhetorically. She viewed assumptions that she would have an unpaid person on call or a live-in in exchange for room and board as "restricting on [her] freedom." Diana was able to "overpay" some of her personal attendants out of pocket (over the rate on which her funding is based). Yet generally she felt that funding needed to increase in order to pay a competitive wage—at parity with other services and with benefits.

Insufficient funding coupled with intermittent needs to shape self-managers' ability to recruit and retain workers. One way people with individual employment relationships found workers was through registries. The DF Program had an online registry, called the Consumer Attendant Roster (CAR), which could provide support. A key informant who helped create CAR explained how self-managers could put in the hours they needed someone, the location of work, and any special requirements, and workers could put in their availability, education or training, and preferred location. While self-managers chose whom to hire, they could receive assistance with CAR if they needed it. As the informant explained: "So I thought that CAR, the Consumer Attendant Roster, should be almost like a dating service. That, instead of matching up two people who want to date, matched up someone looking for an attendant with someone who wants to be an attendant." This key informant did not have a sense of how much self-managers used CAR or how well it was working, nor did this person have the resources to do a study of it. At the time of this interview, there were only approximately one hundred attendants on the roster in the entire province. One of the self-managers in this study had tried to use it but had trouble finding workers because the information was out of date. Susan, who had one personal attendant who worked four to six hours a day but was looking for another, characterized recruitment as a "major barrier" within the Direct Funding Program. She had not used CAR but rather word of mouth and ads. The CILT website response to the frequently asked question of whether it was difficult to find workers did not mention CAR and instead suggested general methods of recruitment, like Kijiji (eBay's online classified advertising service), newspaper ads, and postings at local store bulletin boards, although there is a link to CAR elsewhere on the site.[27] There was also a self-managers network—an email list—to share information on peer-recommended personal attendants.[28] This reflects the responsibility placed on the self-manager for finding personal attendants and the value placed on peer support. Most self-managers in this study found workers through people they already knew. Over half found workers through nonprofit, government-contracted agencies from which they had previously received services, especially when they first entered the DF Program. Several found personal attendants through the networks of a current worker of theirs; a handful found workers through personal networks, including other self-managers, people from church or the neighborhood, friends, or family. Only four self-managers found a worker through ads, and most of these people used personal networks as well. Two of the personal attendants interviewed found a job through CAR, others through people they had previously worked with in agencies, and others through personal networks. Despite the difficulty of recruitment, self-managers emphasized the importance of labor market flexibility because they saw hiring the right person as a way to gain flexibility at the intimate level.

Managing Flexibility and Security at the Intimate Level

Most self-managers we interviewed characterized themselves as friendly employers. Linda expressed this seemingly contradictory viewpoint when she said: "I'm the boss, but there certainly is not a hierarchy about it." Similarly, most workers spoke of themselves in ways similar to what Christine Kelly has called the "frien-tendant" or the personal attendant who was also a friend and sometimes a disability advocate.[29] Having hired based on a personality open to meeting the specific needs of them as a person, self-managers could usually eschew a feeling of hierarchy in the daily labor process, and so could workers. Yet also necessary to obtaining flexibility and security at the intimate level was significant relational work on both sides to navigate the line between friendship and employment around two possible tensions: time versus task and knowledge versus skill.

Embodied Knowledge and Relational Skills

Self-managers sought the flexibility to direct and change how their intimate bodily support was provided based on their knowledge of how their own bodies worked, reflecting the independent living philosophy that underpins direct funding. But enacting this embodied knowledge required self-managers to develop and use relational skills to negotiate the line between friendship and employment. Their effort to be *friendly* employers was key to how they obtained flexibility at this intimate level. For example, Charlotte made multiple references to hiring and firing "control," yet she also described the relationship with her main personal attendant as a caring one, noting that it was on "more of an intimate level" and that the worker was "a lot more of a loving person" compared to agency workers with whom she had worked in the past. Similarly, while Linda noted the "control" given to her by the program, she also took interest in the lives of the personal attendants, explaining, "I care about the person as much as they care about me." A friendship-like relationship was not always what the self-manager intended or desired. For example, Doug said: "You always think that when you're going to hire an attendant you're going to be able to direct them and not pay much attention to their personal issues or how they're feeling. . . . You're just going to be able to keep it kind of clean. But that doesn't happen." Doug generalized that his and others' "unpredictable needs" required workers to go "above and beyond," which in turn meant that self-managers were "obligated to listen to their troubles," and they got "drawn into their lives and social events." Given this reality of give and take, "it can't be a typical professional relationship at all," admitted Doug. In short, caring relationships developed over time.

At the same time, self-managers felt they continuously needed to regenerate a professional relationship so that workers did not take advantage of their friendliness. That is, they needed to be a friendly *employer*, not just a friend. For example, Kerri talked about DF workers as "friends" and "neighbors," but at the same time she characterized this as a "business relationship," in which she was "the employer." Louise characterized her relationship with personal attendants as friendly yet distinguished it from friendships outside the job. She said she did not like to act like a boss, but she did so when necessary. Several mentioned previous experiences: times when they got too close and put up with certain things that they did not like. Jeff also said that if workers thought you were friends, they might try to "take control." Interestingly, this was the only time Jeff mentioned control in the interview, so he did not use it in reference to himself having it or wanting it but rather as resistance to workers taking it. Jennifer said she would not consider all personal attendants friends, but with all of them she did "share in a friendly way" when they were at work. She contrasted her situation with "needy or lonely" people who might want a "best friend." Diane also characterized her relationship with personal attendants as "friendly but not needy." These self-managers are doing the skilled relational work of balancing the reality of caring relations against the marginalization that can come with dependency. Given the latter, they also expected personal attendants to likewise engage in skilled relational work to understand their needs.

Most personal attendants my assistants and I interviewed accepted self-managers' friendly direction and saw this acceptance as central to their job. For example, Adelia previously had worked with her self-manager through agency-run attendant services and thought he had left this program because he did not get along with people, saying that he was "angry at everybody." She felt that she was able to work with him in both types of services because her motto, which she repeated several times in the interview, was to "not take it personal," and she characterized herself as patient and having a "long temper." The skill of exercising patience was a key way personal attendants smoothed over the knowledge-versus-skill tension. During our interview with self-manager Charlotte, the personal attendant sat in on part of the interview and interjected when we talked about training, saying, "I had to learn too, from Charlotte." Joking was another relational skill that personal attendants frequently used. Personal attendant Mathilda said Kerri was "very picky" about how she wanted things done but suggested that this worked out given their good relationship. She relayed how she would tell Kerri that she was being too picky and jokingly threaten to quit, and Kerri would laugh and say she could *not* quit. Yet she also admitted that Kerri was "a boss first" and stressed this boss-worker relationship when she said: "I respect everything she says and listen to it and, you know, do my job the way I need to do it." Maintaining the continuously blurring boundary between friendship and employment also takes skill. Sandy said the self-manager she worked with, Louise, was "a very nice friend." As examples of the friendship, Sandy said they respected each other and listened to each other. Sandy said that when Louise was "snappy" she would wait and let her cool down and then ask her, "Are you okay? Do you want to talk?"—"like a friend." Sandy also recounted one time, when she was having personal problems, how Louise sensed it and asked if she wanted to talk, thus underscoring the importance of reciprocal relational work.

Self-managers valued in personal attendants not just a superficial emotional labor to act friendly but a deeper relational skill necessary to understand how to work with particular bodies in various situations. A key reason that self-managers wanted to direct how the worker did the job related to their knowledge of what was safe for their own bodies. For example, Diane, who had issues with bone density, said: "Usually the reason I'm asking for something to be done is in order to not hurt me. It's not like I'm just an idiosyncratic person." If doing things a certain way was not bodily necessary, Diane said she negotiated with workers. "I've had situations where, you know, attendants have said to me: 'Well, I can't do it like that, what about like this?' And if in my judgment it would be okay for me to do it, try it like that, I'll change my routine for them. But ultimately it's my decision." This quote was consistent with the attitudes of the other self-managers interviewed. One might consider this to be "control," but "flexibility" is a more fitting descriptor because Diane and others were open to changing how services were provided as long as they retained the ultimate decision about whether it was good for their body. Self-managers also made adjustments depending on with whom they were working. Jennifer allowed different workers to help her transfer into and out of her bed, tub, or wheelchair in different ways, noting that since one was good at transfers without a mechanical lift, that one did it that way, but others used the mechanical lift. Self-managers emphasized how much work it was to establish, in Susan's words, "the routine that an attendant and I get into." Similarly, Jeff required a worker who could do "certain tasks for a quad," so he looked for someone with experience working with other quadriplegics. Yet since, like Susan, he wanted someone who would come to know his routine, so he did not "have to keep telling them, 'oh, do this, do that,'" he also considered a good worker one who also had a personality that he could "get along with." In this way, the training that a self-manager valued, and provided on the job, was much more than just a physical order of tasks; it was also relational. Workers and recipients also used relational skills to smooth over tensions of time versus task.

Tasks of Daily Living at Various Times

Potential conflicts over what is done, when, and sometimes where take the form of a tension between time and task—that is, help with the range of changing activities in a given time period versus help with a defined set of tasks. Firstly, self-managers want scheduling flexibility because their needs change. For example, Linda had one full-time worker who worked a split shift and did not have another stable commitment in the day. This allowed her to extend the time between the shifts as Linda's needs changed. She described, "My attendant would normally take two to three hours in between the two shifts, but today, because I had somebody coming and it was important that I had some support and some assistance before, she only took one hour." Workers also spoke in relational terms when describing negotiations over scheduling. For example, Mathilda worked for Kerri in the evenings around her other job but said Kerri called her "for everything" and that if her (Mathilda's) phone was busy, Kerri would call her cell. She said she did not mind these calls because Kerri was "really, truly a good friend," and she described friendly activities outside of work, such as when Kerri took her on vacation, where Mathilda also provided personal support.

Self-managers also sought flexibility in the tasks done within any given shift, based on changing needs. As Linda said: "[The time] when someone comes in to work it would be depending upon the night I've had, and the morning I'm having, and the day that I am going to have. . . . So let's try and plan it out and see what we can do, but please be flexible, because, like, a day like today, I've had one thing right after another." Again, the relational work of being a friendly employer was key to Linda's ability to obtain task flexibility and scheduling flexibility. Rather than telling the worker "you have to do this now," she asked the worker and explained why her needs had changed, saying, "You get a lot more compliance and understanding and someone to agree with you if you tell them why." When we asked about whether compliance varied with different workers, Linda emphasized a deeper, relational work based on knowing workers as individuals who, like her, have changing moods. "If they have a low-energy day or a higher-energy day, or a better mood or not so good a mood, and me as well . . . we try to be very sensitive to each other's needs, to each other's moods." Linda spoke in relational terms—the "we" suggesting an interdependent philosophy, although she admitted that it did not always go perfectly.

An ethos of interdependence, rather than the independent-dependent dichotomy that underpins the traditional employment relationship, is also evident in the lack of a strict division of labor.[30] Most self-managers we interviewed had no strict division of labor between bodywork and housework or between the workers who did these tasks. For example, Louise had two main personal-attendants and no division of labor between them. She emphasized the importance of flexibility when she said, "They do for me what I need that day." This is more than just what labor scholars would call "functional flexibility" or the ability of employers to move workers from task to task.[31] For Louise and others it indicated the value they placed on support for their bodies and on housework. As Louise said, "They're not my maids . . . they're here to make life more productive." Jennifer argued that one of the key benefits of DF was that there was no imposed division of tasks, and she echoed Louise in valuing all aspects of intimate labor. "You don't have three different people coming in doing different functions. So doing my laundry is as important to me as dressing." She also underscored the importance that a single personal assistant could do things reserved for nurses in other programs—like bowel and bladder routines, catheters, enemas, digital simulation.[32] The lack of a division of labor also allowed for longer shifts more worth the personal assistant's time, Jennifer reasoned.

The labor valued by self-managers included support that allowed them to have guests and see family. As Kerri said:

> Let's say I'm going to have company over, and I'm going to prepare some things. They could do that because they're doing it for me, right? Basically, they're my body, right? So if I had to set the table or prepare some food, because that's part of their job description. . . . But not to serve guests or something like that [laughs].

Kerri echoed the independent living movement discourse of attendants as the arms and legs of the disabled person, when she characterized the worker as her body.[33] This philosophy could objectify workers and make their work invisible.[34] Yet here Kerri was also underscoring the value of personal support, conceptualized broadly as support with activities that people would do if their bodies were not impaired. Kerri distinguished this valued bodywork and housework from what she would consider akin to treating workers as servants—evident in her laughing at the suggestion that her able-bodied guests would not serve themselves. For Jeff, the line around what was acceptable to have personal attendants do regarding friends and family was drawn at not doing his visiting, able-bodied brother's laundry, since the brother could do it himself, but helping Jeff cook a meal for friends coming over was considered acceptable because it allowed Jeff to have a social life. Jeff said if a worker refused to help with these tasks he would fire them, because "if they are refusing, they shouldn't be here." At the same time, he said he did not like firing people and so tried to "give them a chance" and the "benefit of the doubt" and to "just try and keep communicating" since "it's like any relationship." Michael said he gave workers a job description when he hired them, but this description incorporated flexibility in tasks by defining them broadly. From the outside, there may appear to be a fine line separating personal support from work as a household servant, yet there was generally always a line, albeit one continuously negotiated between parties.

Most personal attendants did not experience as "maid" work the request for flexibility in what was done, when, and where, in large part because a broad and flexible definition of their work had been communicated to them upon hiring. For example, Sandy discussed a general, yet flexible, job description with self-manager Louise during her interview, which was in a written contract. Sandy helped Louise with housekeeping, shopping, and other errands as well as personal support, like bathroom help. The tasks did not change much, Sandy said, but she was "okay with that" when they did because she felt Louise was "a great boss." Similarly, Patti said she was willing to provide services to guests, like serving them tea, if that was something the person would ordinarily do but could not. During the interview with self-manager Charlotte, the personal attendant offered the interviewer a cup of tea but also made some for herself and sat down with Charlotte and the interviewer to drink it. "We get along so well . . . we are always laughing, aren't we?" the personal attendant said to Charlotte, who agreed. Jon said he was all right doing nominal services to family or friends, like making two cups of coffee instead of one. Noting that not all workers felt this way, he offered the following explanation for why he did: "I feel good in a way, because I have something to do while they talk." Adelia helped with meals, personal care, some cleaning, and sometimes shopping for the self-manager and said she would bring a drink to his able-bodied guest if he asked her to. It is clear from these interviews and others that what kinds of work were considered akin to servitude varied. This is why a key component of this job was the relational work to negotiate the line between servitude and support with daily living. For most workers it was as much about how they were asked to do the work as it was about what they were asked to do. They accepted a broad definition of the job if it was communicated upon hiring and requested of them in a friendly way. However, this friendly employment relationship was undermined by inequalities of gender and race in their complex intersection with disability.

Disability, Gender, and Racialization

Direct Funding Program self-managers, in this sample and beyond, were mostly non-elderly adults with physical disabilities who were relatively privileged in terms of class and race. They had more education and higher occupational status and income than the general disabled population. In my sample, nearly three-quarters had a university degree; only one had never been in the labor force; and most had worked in the disability sector or had been business owners. The majority were white and Canada-born, and men and women made up roughly equal proportions. The workers ranged from white, Canada-born students, art-ists, and contractors who sought flexible work arrangements, to Asian, African, and Latin American recently arrived immigrants who had little labor market choice. The majority of workers were women.[35]

Given that self-managers used subjective hiring criteria, hiring decisions had the potential to become racialized and gendered. Generally, self-managers wanted little division of tasks, but this could become gendered and racialized. Some people, especially women, wanted to hire people of their own sex for the most personal support. For example, Charlotte employed two women to do her personal support but got help from two men for transportation. Three of the women self-managers had all women personal attendants, while only one of the men self-managers had all women personal attendants. Several men hired women for intimate personal services. Yet some men preferred to hire other men for the personal bodywork and women for housework. This was particularly common if the personal help required was extensive. For example, Jeff, who had become a quadriplegic due to a neck injury and received the maximum hours, employed a white, Canada-born, forty-five-year-old man as his "stable guy" to help with his extensive morning routine twenty hours a week. Jeff split the other twenty-five hours a week between three other workers. A Caribbean-born man did his evening routine. Then Jeff switched between two Caribbean-born women for the one-hour dinner shift; one of these women also did shopping once a week. Yet not only did most self-managers reject a strict division of labor, there were also limits to the ability of self-managers to have a gendered division of labor, given a gendered labor market. Michael said that more women responded to his ads than men. Anil hired a man to do his routine in evenings but had a hard time securing other men; he only reluctantly hired women to do similar work in the mornings. Self-managers did not express an explicit preference for white work-ers in our interviews. Several white self-managers hired white Canada-born per-sonal attendants, while many white self-managers also hired personal attendants who were not white or whose first language was not English, although this also reflected who was available to do this work.

Self-managers said the ideal worker was one who understood people with disabilities, respected their unique needs, and thus wanted to do this work. There were certainly people in this sector who fit this notion of choosing this job, at least temporarily.[36] Take, for instance, Chris, a white, Canada-born man who was single with no children. He had a brother with a disability and had done volunteer work at a rehabilitation hospital as a teenager. He recounted a commitment to supporting people with disabilities as a form of "just kind of giving back" and also to "make a few bucks on the side." He did technical work in the film and music industries when he could get it. Chris described some control in the labor process, including turning down shifts with the self-manager when a work opportunity in the creative industries came up. When asked who decided what was done, whether he would do cleaning, and if he could refuse to do certain things, Chris's answer was telling. "Well, I guess it's him that decides what he wants to do, but it's usually a discussion. . . . I have free will, so, yes, I could refuse to do anything." Chris described how the self-manager had someone come in once a week to do "the real cleaning." In the meantime, if the self-manager had "made a mess or something," Chris said he would "certainly clean that up," but added, laughing, "I don't do windows. . . . I don't clean stoves." Chris was puzzled by our questions. "I can see where your question is maybe geared. . . . I can see it with other people. But, me, myself, you know . . . I'm like a friend." Chris's ability to negotiate the time-versus-task tension was connected to his choice in a gendered and racialized labor market, which stemmed from a college education and a trade, no dependents to support, and his location as a white, able-bodied, Canada-born man. Chris said he deliberately picked people who he would like to be around and who would like to be around him, someone he would be friends with, and this meant younger male adults, not a "crotchety old man." He described the job interview as an opportunity for both self-manager and himself to see if "there's a connection there." He said he wanted the person to look forward to "Chris coming," not just think "oh, my attendant is here." Chris's power in the intimate labor process also came from this location as able-bodied. When asked what he would do in the event of a problem, he said he would usually just communicate with the self-manager. Yet when probed on whether he would go to someone else for support, he said, laughing, "like if he didn't pay or something?" He suggested jokingly that he would use the threat of physical force to solve the problem: "Where's my paycheck? You still want to use your arms?" Although this is a hypothetical situation that to Chris is laughable, it reminds us of the reasons why the IL movement is so focused on control over hiring and firing in an effort to ensure that workers do not control disabled people and their bodies. Chris was the only person who spoke of such a threat, and he might have been performing masculinity for the woman interviewer, given his location in this generally feminized job. Yet Chris was not the only one with labor market choice.

White, Canada-born Patti also had labor market choice, at least by the time we interviewed her. She had worked "full time, steady" for two DF clients, for nearly three years, while in university. One was quadriplegic, and the personal bodily and emotional support was intense, so when she could, she quit that job but kept the second one. When she finished her degree and got a full-time supervisory job in a home care agency she "tried to quit" the second job, but the self-manager convinced her that he needed her help occasionally with some things he felt she could do better than his other personal attendants, like accounting in his small business or going to shows with him. Patti continued to provide backup help in these delimited areas not because she needed the money but because she considered this self-manager a friend. Similarly, Mathilda talked about two types of personal attendants; one did this work because they needed money, and another did it because they liked it. She put herself in the latter category. Mathilda was happy with the contours of the job, which did not include housekeeping, help with family or friends, or heavy lifting and was in the evenings, when she had time. Most of the experiences recounted by the personal attendants we interviewed, half of whom were white and Canada-born, indicated respectful, working relationships with the self-manager—otherwise they either quit or were fired.

Personal attendants did not face equal conditions with regard to the choice of whether to quit. Immigrant workers recounted racialized tensions, at least some of the time, at the intimate level. Not surprisingly, those with the least labor market choice described the most negative experiences. Unlike most we interviewed, Sarina did not characterize her relationship with the self-managers with whom she had worked as friendly. She recounted several cases of tension over knowledge versus skill. Sarina said the self-manager she worked for was an "irritable person" and was sometimes "rude." She described little negotiation over how the work was done, even if safety was at stake. For example, she felt he wanted her to lift him a certain way, without getting too close, which was hard on her back. Sarina found the self-manager's particularity—like insisting on the exact cup he wanted to drink out of—was "frustrating sometimes." She said that she had "snapped back" a few times because she was so tired. She lamented, "He always wants things exactly his way, even though it doesn't make a difference to change it," which made her feel like she knew "nothing." This suggests that she did not understand why it was important to him to have a say over his daily life. Instead, she felt it was only reflective of power. "He makes all the decisions. I have to just do what he wants me to do." She felt that sometimes self-managers "like to boss people around, so they just think they have the power to make you do anything." Sarina generalized that when people were in a "bad mood," they could "take their disability out on the caregiver." Sarina also described several cases of time-versus-task tension. She said that she worked for someone with another worker who would leave the dishes for her to wash. Given that the other worker had more hours than she did, she wondered aloud, "Why is it that that person was here all that time and didn't have time to do that?" Sarina's answer was racism. "And it happens a lot when you're dark, I guess. So, if you're a white person you wouldn't see it because it doesn't happen to you.... And the guy I was working with, he was really ... he was just looking for somebody to do cleaning." Given this and other conflicts, Sarina did not want to keep this job, yet she could not afford to quit. "If they're good clients, I don't want to lose them, and if I have a bad one, I'm sorry to say that, but I don't want to keep them. I just keep them because I need the job."

In stark contrast to Chris, Patti, and Mathilda, Sarina had a seventh-grade education and had been unable to work for many years due to her lack of permanent residency in Canada. She described difficulty finding jobs in the broader personal support sector without a PSW (personal support worker) certificate, impossible to get without high school equivalency, which made DF and privately paying clients who did not require a certificate one of the few options open to her. She tried to piece together a living from multiple DF or private-pay clients and personal support work contracted through private temporary agencies but said, "None of it is guaranteed." Sarina was an example of the second type of worker in DF—one who did this work for lack of other options. Although the contrasts between Sarina and Chris in social location and associated labor market choice were the most extreme, several personal attendants recounted difficult experiences that in only some cases had led them to quit. Others were in between these extremes, and so was their power in the labor process—like Caribbean-born Jon whom we met above, who resisted some cleaning tasks but did others.

Self-managers achieved flexibility at the intimate level through a combination of the skilled relational work of being friendly employers and the workers' location in racialized and gendered labor markets. This was evident in the case of Robert and Pilar, which opened this chapter. When we asked Robert how the worker's tasks were determined, he answered simply, "By me." When we asked whether workers could ever refuse to do something, Robert said, "Well, not officially, because I will fire them," but in addition to this formal labor market flexibility given to him by the program, Robert discussed two other key dynamics. The first was the relational work of being a friendly employer. He said: "But I work with all these women, and I am very accommodating and flexible and personable. You know? It's like I said, what you sow, you reap. If you are nasty to them, they will be nasty to you." Second, Robert explained the role of the broader racialized and gendered labor market in making workers available and willing to do this work when he said: "The lady who is the pediatrician does my housekeeping. It sounds so stupid . . . because they are so qualified." The unequal position of immigrant professionals in the Canadian labor market also meant that Robert could get support with paramedical services at the low rate provided by the program. Pilar, who was a nurse in her country, felt Robert asked her to do some things she considered "medical," which she refused to do because she felt that she could be liable if something went wrong. From Robert's perspective, this was not a medical procedure but an activity of daily living that he was directing and thus responsible for. Robert did not force Pilar to do this task to keep her job, but he asked the other worker, the one who had been a pediatrician in her country of origin, who complied. Indeed, all three of the women Robert had hired were immigrants who had been care professionals in their countries of origin but could not practice their professions in Canada. The broader problem of immigrant racialization through downward mobility, as credentials from the Global South are not recognized or valued, was not something Robert could do much about. But his experience, like the experience of all of us, was more caught up with racialized labor markets than was evident on the surface.

Yet there is also an opportunity for chipping away at racialized and gendered inequalities through relational encounters at the intimate level. White, Canada-born Doug spoke of the complexity of crisscrossing social locations.

> My attendants that I've hired have been mostly of African descent. . . . And it's a learning process for both you and the attendant. I mean, with my second attendant, when she first started working for me she would just assume, she would make remarks, like, um, my parents have all this money, and she didn't understand how I could ever have anything go wrong in my life. But I kind of let that go at the time, and I think by the end of a couple of years working together I think she understood that maybe, yeah, I have it a lot better in some areas of life than her and some of her ancestors did, but I have other areas where I would, you know, have some disadvantages.

Years of working together across distinct lines of oppression might allow people to develop deeper understanding of the location of the other. However, we could also see a pitting of marginalization through disability against racialized and gendered worker precarity.[37] For example, Linda said she sometimes had difficulties getting her words out, so she tried to be understanding with people whose first language was not English. At the same time, her son who also had a disability needed someone with a "very kind, calm voice," and this need became racialized as she ended up firing the Black immigrant worker to whom her son could presumably not relate. She offered, "It wasn't a racial thing at all . . . it's more about attitude and tone of voice and mannerisms." Several self-managers insisted that race was not an issue but that language or accent was, given the importance of communication in this work. As race scholarship has argued for decades, contemporary forms of racialization draw not only on explicit skin color or phenotypical distinctions but also on cultural aspects like attitude and accent that become associated with particular groups.[38] How might openings for change in the complexities of crisscrossing social locations contribute to greater understanding across divides of race and ability? The potential for a more transformative politics will require more collective backing than is evident in the Direct Funding Program.

Limited Collective Supports

Self-managers and personal attendants were navigating complex inequalities largely as individuals. There was no collective support for personal attendants and only limited support for self-managers. The Centre for Independent Living Toronto (CILT) provided information about one's responsibility as an employer but little education about how various labor legislation applied to the case of household-employers of individuals. Instead, in line with the independent living philosophy, CILT encouraged peer support. A study of self-managers in the pilot of the DF Program found that they were satisfied with the level of support, and several of the self-managers we interviewed who were also key informants (involved in CILT) echoed this sentiment.[39] Some self-managers we interviewed, however, expressed a desire for more support. For example, one felt there was a "culture of fear"—that if you sought help or advice from CILT your services might be cut off.

Despite advice from CILT to self-managers on employer responsibilities, informality could creep into the individual employer-worker relationship in two ways. The first way was through confusion over whether these workers were covered, or covered fully, by key labor protections. For example, CILT informed self-managers of what they could and could not ask about during interviews in accordance with the Ontario Human Rights Code. The code states that one cannot ask about race, ethnicity, color, creed, nationality, and citizenship but that one can ask about English- or French-language fluency if it is a genuine requirement for the position. However, if the self-manager is the direct employer of a personal attendant, then the personal attendant does not have the right to equal treatment in employment without discrimination under the code, since the code excludes people who directly employ a person to provide personal care.[40] Similarly, another self-manager and key informant said that CILT gave self-managers a "quiz" on labor legislation, like the Employment Standards Act (ESA) that regulates wages and hours. However, there was still potential confusion over the regulations regarding overnight help. In one case, a disabled householder-employer argued that the worker she hired to sleep over was a "residential-care worker," a category excluded from the right to overtime pay set forth in the ESA. The employment standards officer agreed, but the worker took the decision to the Ontario Labour Relations Board, which ruled that the worker was not a residential care worker because the employer could call her to work at any time. Thus even if she was sleeping she was still at work.[41]

The second way informality could creep into the individual employment relationship was through lack of enforcement of labor protections covering these workers. One self-manager and key informant emphasized that there was "lots of support" for self-managers from CILT, especially when first setting up direct funding, including workshops, the self-managers network, bookkeepers, and playing "a big role" in making sure self-managers knew about what they could ask in hiring, given the Ontario Human Rights Code and about ESA regulations on firing. At the same time, this self-manager admitted she had "let someone go" without going through the formal notice and firing process set out in the ESA. She emphasized that no one "policed" whether self-managers abided by the law. CILT only gave information, and it was the responsibility of the self-manager to follow regulations or not. This person felt that if a certain self-manager had several workers calling CILT complaining about him or her, a staff person would look into it, but DF Program policies distance CILT from playing a mediation role that might lead to an interpretation of them as an employer.[42]

There is also evidence that if conditions are not improved in DF, workers who have other options will leave it, if they have the choice. For example, personal attendant Adelia, who was cochair of the health and safety committee at her agency job, said a lot of consumers did not want to use a mechanical lift. Adelia felt that this was especially problematic in DF, where most workers had little formal health and safety training. Adelia had worked for three DF self-managers in the past but went down to working relief for one when she received more hours from her agency job. Personal attendant Jon, who was also a member of the health and safety committee at his agency job, quit working for an individual client who did not have "proper equipment" and who Jon felt had less strength than he had said he had during their interview. Recruitment and retention are also closely connected to workers' labor market insecurity, given few hours and low earnings in this sector.[43]

Collective organizing to augment personal attendants' security at the labor market and intimate levels is crucial, yet there is no organizing in this sector. Personal attendants cannot organize a trade union or bargain collectively because they are legally deemed "domestic workers," but domestic workers have organized outside the limitations of labor law and worked to change the law in Canada, the United States, and elsewhere.[44] There have been tensions between organized labor and disability activists in Ontario around the Direct Funding Program, reflecting the conflict between labor market flexibility and security. During the government consultation for DF, the Canadian Auto Workers, Canadian Union of Public Employees, Ontario Public Services Employees Union, and Services Employees International Union, all of which were engaged in organizing workers in the agency and institutional long-term care sectors, "banded together to oppose the implementation of Direct Funding," according to one observer.[45] In line with this view, one union official said, "Our union would have consistently held positions that are fundamentally opposed to individualized funding or vouchers ... It just runs counter to everything the [union] would represent, our principles."[46] The unions argued that DF represented privatization of public services and divestment of government responsibility and were doubtful that funding would be sufficient to allow people to pay workers good wages and to fulfill the labor-related responsibilities of an employer, such as paying into Employment Insurance or workers' compensation. In the words of another union official: "I'm not saying that's all this was, a cheap labor strategy, but that was definitely part of it."[47] Indeed, some early Direct Funding Program advocates focused on the benefit to the Ontario government afforded by reductions in administration and labor costs in DF compared to other personal support services.[48] Others pushed the government to dedicate sufficient resources to pay living wages, but they were up against a politics of funding restraints and a culture of individual responsibility. In this neoliberal context, collective representation and backing for both sides are necessary if the goal is flexibility and security.

Ontario's Direct Funding Program assumed that labor market flexibility through hiring and firing would result in the sought-after flexibility at a more intimate level regarding what was done, when, where, and how. Yet the translation of labor market flexibility into flexibility in the intimate labor process also depended on the degree of worker insecurity and on the willingness of both sides to engage in ongoing relational work.

Self-managers' effort to manage tensions in the labor process through a friendly employment relationship went some way to their realization of flexibility and to supporting workers' security through a respectful working relationship. Recruitment was time-consuming, and people's needs were intense and ongoing, so most self-managers hired workers who respected them as people and were willing to accept their ideas on how they should provide support, rather than hiring workers based on a credential or experience in personal support work. Although self-managers could fire workers, they tried to avoid doing so in large part because of the time it took to teach workers how their body worked and to develop a relationship that made bodywork a seamless routine.[49] Self-managers rejected disembodied, standardized skills such as those taught in personal support worker credentialing programs or learned in long-term residential care. Instead, they managed the knowledge-versus-skill tension by using their knowledge of their bodies to foster specific skills in workers on the job. Specifically they valued and nurtured embodied skills in workers in line with their own embodied knowledge; they also cultivated their own and workers' relational skills and recognized their importance in this intimate body labor.[50] In exchange, most workers we interviewed accepted direction and did not experience it as bossy, in large part because it was understood beforehand as central to facilitating the self-managers' ability to contribute to society. Self-managers managed the time-versus-task tension by viewing work such as preparing food for guests and cleaning toilets as equally important as help with bodily activities and by minimizing a division of labor across workers and shifts. As a result, most personal attendants did not experience housework as "maid" or menial work. In these ways, flexibility does not mean control over another person but rather autonomy through negotiated relationships.[51] At the intimate level, actual practices are more in line with feminist scholarship on interdependence than with independent living movement philosophy and DF policy documents that focus on independence as control.[52] My findings support this strand of feminist theory but suggest the following contradiction: the possibility for interdependent relational work to bring flexible security at the intimate level but also the danger that individualized relational work will prop up labor market insecurity.

My analysis showed that the evident willingness of self-managers and personal attendants to engage in relational work and the still unmet labor market security of workers were both necessary for self-managers to realize the Direct Funding Program's promise of flexibility. However, within a context of insufficient funding and little to no collective backing, this program produced labor market insecurity for workers, in the form of insufficient hours, earnings, and protection. Moreover, the position of workers in the broader racialized and gendered labor market shaped their labor market choices, or lack thereof, and shaped their experience at the intimate level. Some workers will simply quit if they have other labor market options. Yet if the contrast between Chris and Sarina is any indication, individualized relational work could reinforce the reality that workers with a stronger labor market position, like white, native-born, able-bodied men and women, will be more likely to get out of certain types of work, thus reinforcing racialization. Similarly, if Robert's management of Pilar and other workers provides a clue, this program could reinforce the de-skilling of immigrant women. Recognizing the broad needs of self-managers and how they get them met by constructing friendly employment relationships with personal attendants, relationships that acknowledge gendered, embodied skills, could help value intimate labor too often hidden in private homes. Yet when racialized and gendered insecurity are mapped onto relational encounters at the intimate level, there is also potential to reinforce workers' insecurity. Thus, failing to address broader racialized and gendered labor market insecurity not only has implications for workers who are less able to negotiate what they do and how. It also limits the progressive potential to value all forms of intimate labor and to rethink skill.

The design of the DF Program promised flexibility to self-managers through hiring and firing. But while some recipients and workers' approached flexibility and security at the intimate level through relational work, flexible security was undermined by racialized and gendered labor markets. Workers and recipients also engaged in a form of relational work in my second case covered in chapter 4, yet they were less isolated as members of an immigrant community, and they were unionized. Can labor and community collective backing foster flexibility and security?

NEGOTIATING FLEXIBILITY WITH SECURITY IN LOS ANGELES'S IN-HOME SUPPORTIVE SERVICES

Maria, an eighty-six-year old Pilipina widow and mother of four, migrated to the United States through the sponsorship of her son in the early 1990s. Her son and daughter-in-law also became her personal support providers under California's In-Home Supportive Services (IHSS). Like Direct Funding (DF) in Toronto, IHSS considers the recipient to be the hiring employer, but unlike DF one can hire immediate family members. This leads to a dynamic between recipients and workers in IHSS that is different from that in DF. As Maria said, "Even though [my son] is not receiving a lot, he still takes care of me." What was done and when was negotiated not only with Maria's son but also her daughter-in-law, who did the bulk of the work. As Maria relayed, "The three of us will talk." Maria rented an apartment in the same building as her son and daughter-in-law so, she said, "If I can't cook, I will go upstairs and eat at their house." At the same time, her son's and daughter-in-law's full-time employment in other jobs shaped the organization of Maria's care. "Every Friday we do the laundry because that's the wife's day off," Maria explained.

Maria described a family care economy that provided her with the flexible care she needed; her daughter-in-law, Angelica, recounted a system of paid work that dovetailed with her filial duties and previous experiences. Angelica explained how she came to be the main hands-on care provider. Two of Maria's four children were men, so they were "not used to it." The youngest daughter could have easily done it since they lived in the same apartment, but she was "the youngest, and you know how it is in the Philippines. She is not used to looking after the elderly." The eldest daughter was a nurse, but she was "quite busy at that time."

Angelica had grown up with an aunt who owned a small clinic in the Philippines, and she had later studied as a nurse's assistant. Thus, she reasoned, "I'm used to taking care of the patients." Angelica also underscored the importance of the state paying families to care for their elders in the U.S. context. "You're busy here in America. Everyone has a job. You need money to pay your bills. And then you have to take care of someone like this." Yet if you are paid to look after parents, "you're going to take it seriously because that's like work as well."[1]

I start with Maria and Angelica's stories because they demonstrate several features of the IHSS program in Los Angeles that differ from DF in Toronto. Whereas most recipients and many workers were white citizens in DF, people of color, including immigrants, were overrepresented as IHSS recipients, while African American, Latina, and Asian women were overrepresented as workers, compared to their proportion in the overall population.[2] Pilipinx made up only 1 percent of IHSS providers, yet they represent the growing phenomenon of co-ethnic care—that is, care provided by immigrants to immigrants.[3]

At the labor market level, both programs gave "consumers" the flexibility to hire their own "providers" (as recipients and workers are called here), yet in IHSS the state was more involved in the employment relationship because it paid the provider rather than giving funding directly to the consumer. Many elderly IHSS consumers hire family, but when family is not available, immigrant seniors hire others from their language and ethnic group, and this goes for Pilipinx.[4] Like in DF, labor market flexibility shaped negotiations in the labor process, but in IHSS it shaped it differently. While DF self-managers forged and embraced a friendly employment relationship, consumers in the IHSS context of paying family or co-ethnic fictive kin were more ambivalent about their employer role and used family ideals and family-like practices to negotiate possible tensions at the intimate level. The state's reliance on filial duty and ethnic community through IHSS may bolster flexibility and security at the intimate level in terms of mutually respectful negotiations of what is done, when, where, and how. Yet, as suggested in the preceding chapter, collective backing is also important if the goal is flexibility with security. Indeed, another difference between DF and IHSS is that IHSS providers have a union. Coalitions between the union and disability and senior groups have sought to protect IHSS from cutbacks and pushed for wage increases, but can such coalitions support security and flexibility at the intimate level?

Context: The Independent Provider Model

The independent living (IL) movement of non-elderly adults with physical disabilities shaped the development of California IHSS, as it did for DF in Toronto,

even though elderly people have always comprised the majority of IHSS consumers. In California, disability advocates argued for shutting down institutions and
abandoning the "agency model" in which a service organization contracted with
the government to hire the workers who provide in-home services. Instead, they
felt the disabled recipient should be the hiring employer. This politics was largely
successful. The independent provider model, in which no agency mediated the
employer roles of hiring, firing, and supervision, became dominant in the vast
majority of counties.[5] Unlike DF in Toronto, however, IHSS consumers did not
receive the funding directly, except in a small number of cases.[6] Instead, the state
paid the providers and thus shared employer responsibility.

Funding levels, and the political will that determined them, also shaped IHSS.
Unlike in DF in Ontario, however, IHSS was means-tested, so the recipients were
by definition poor, like the workers. A combination of federal, state, and county
government funded IHSS, and each county's Department of Public Social Services housed it. Most people eligible for fully funded IHSS services in Los Angeles County were on a form of monetary assistance for low-income, aged, and
disabled individuals called Supplemental Security Income (SSI). If one's income
was above the SSI cutoff, one would have to pay a share of the cost, but only a
small portion of IHSS consumers in L.A. County did so.[7] The scope of services
for those eligible included activities of daily living (ADL) (e.g., help with bathing); related tasks (e.g., laundry, housework, and shopping); and "paramedical
services" (e.g., checking blood sugar).[8] Paramedical services and help with ADL
were seen as the core services.

Social workers approved or denied services within state guidelines. They
determined some services on a "time per task" basis, estimating the minutes it
took for a given task, the number of occurrences per day and the number of days
per week.[9] Routine laundry and shopping for food were subject to what one IHSS
administrator called "soft" state guidelines.[10] Social workers said it was possible
to give more hours than the "soft" guidelines suggested, as long as social workers
justified why and it made sense. For instance, if the consumer had to use a laun-
dromat, they could allocate more time for laundry.[11] The time allotted to light
housekeeping (e.g., vacuuming, dusting, cleaning the bathroom) were strictly
set.[12] Importantly, IHSS would allocate domestic services even if the provider was
the child or grandchild of the consumer but not if the provider was the spouse
or parent of a dependent child consumer.[13] Social workers interviewed the consumer and family member(s) to ascertain the names and ages of others in the
household, their relationship to the consumer, their hours in school or employment, and the reason they could not provide IHSS services to the consumer.[14]
IHSS funded limited services outside the home, at school or work.[15] The state
did not pay for accompaniment on walks or social activities like going to church,

but some consumers tried to squeeze such help into the minimally funded "other shopping and errands."[16]

Many consumers, providers, disability advocates, and union representatives felt the authorized hours are were insufficient.[17] Consumers who needed protective supervision (like those with Alzheimer's) were most likely to receive the maximum number of hours, but this did not cover twenty-four-hour help.[18] Seventy-nine-year-old Saturino, who had recently asked for a reassessment and received more hours, said his seventy hours a month were not enough given that he had open heart surgery, making it impossible for him to lift heavy things and do his laundry, housework, and errands. Some people with high needs complained that they did not have enough hours for overnight help. Carmen, who was seventy years old and had eighty-seven IHSS hours a month, was fearful when her blood sugar dropped at night when her provider was not there. "So I go to the fridge, I drink orange juice or eat sugar, raw sugar, two tablespoons, and then I drink water right after. Then I pray. I cry too." Extensive discussion among both consumers and providers about social workers' power to determine their hours revealed how the state shared an employer role with the consumer.

Innovative legislation and organizing moved toward the recognition of IHSS providers as employees with the right to unionize and bargain collectively, rather than as "domestic servants," as was the case in DF, or as independent contractors, as was the case before the legislation. The legislation, passed in the late 1990s, allocated employer responsibilities to four different entities: the consumer, the state government, the county IHSS program and the "Public Authority" (called the Public Assistance Services Council—PASC—in Los Angeles).[19] The consumer remained responsible for hiring, firing, and supervision, while the state was responsible for paying the provider. Consumers signed time sheets every two weeks, and providers submitted them; then the state controller's office sent the paycheck to the provider. Finally, the newly created nonprofit organization, PASC, became the employer of record for the purposes of collective bargaining with the government over wages and benefits. The PASC board included some IHSS consumers; it also offered optional consumer training and a registry to help consumers find providers and providers find jobs. As one PASC informant said, the new model gave "voice" to both workers and recipients.[20]

Passing such legislation was possible through creative labor organizing, including coalition between the Service Employees International Union (SEIU) and groups representing disabled and elderly people in the late 1990s and early 2000s.[21] Members of the coalition understood the alliance largely along social justice lines but recognized different positions of power within care work. As one disability advocate said, "Something we had to keep straight [was] that we joined [in coalition with the union] in some of the things that will work for people with disabilities but our positions are not coming from the same place.[22] Similarly, another advocate characterized the worker and recipient as "absolutely symbiotic" but felt "we have to always look at how to do this balancing act," remembering that "service unions" are necessary yet continuously asking "what does that really mean [for disabled and elderly people]?"[23] Disability advocates also spoke of developing understanding of workers issues through coalition. One person who organized others in her community to support the union "really looked deep down" and said to herself, "I am fighting for social justice for myself. What's the moral philosophy here? . . . I cannot do this at the expense of another person." This advocate shared the idea of "consistent ethical social justice" with her community and described how others began to repeat it.[24] As another disability advocate said, "Really, independence is interdependence."[25]

Union officials also spoke of the coalition in the late 1990s and early 2000s as recognizing different degrees of power. One able-bodied SEIU official spoke of working with younger adults with disabilities, who were the "activist core" pushing for the new model in alliance with SEIU, and recalled, "One of the hugest things I took away from [the coalition] was to understand and appreciate their world." [26] The union's organizing of workers also had to contend with gendered power relations. As this official recalled, women workers would rationalize, "Well, taking care of my mom or disabled child. I'd do it anyway." The union's organizing frames countered: "This is important work! You should get paid! Didn't you quit your job?"[27] SEIU activists also argued that the invisible work done mostly by women of color IHSS providers was essential to the economy, since it "saved the state of California a ton of money" while "keeping people out of institutions."[28] After years of building bridges of understanding and alliance, skeptics on both sides became convinced that they had more to gain by limiting turnover through unionization than they had to lose.[29]

This alliance across different interests was crucial to winning the new legislation, which was a move toward flexibility with security in the labor market. As one disability advocate explained, some in county government saw the legislation as pandering to unions, "but when we came along with them it led some credence to their claim that it was essential for higher wages," which in turn was necessary to limit worker turnover. There was also a realization that "without the union we couldn't have done it," since the union had more human and financial resources. In contrast, the advocate said, "The only power we had was based on our relationship with the county government . . . and that's very weak."[30] The SEIU made key compromises to gain the trust and support of the disability and senior movements, including giving up the right to strike, not challenging the right of the consumer to hire, fire, and supervise, and agreeing not to bargain over how providers performed the work in the home workplaces.[31] One disability advocate described it as a "pretty powerful advocacy" that was able to resist a proposal to no longer pay family members to be IHSS providers, and the advocate suggested that this benefited people of color especially because they were more likely to use family providers.[32]

However, the need for ongoing coalition building was also evident. For example, L.A. County created PASC as a buffer between itself and the union, so the PASC board was by law prevented from bargaining for wage increases unless the county had already approved the funding.[33] In this context, on at least one occasion the union targeted the county directly for wage increases, essentially going around the new legal structure of bargaining with PASC. One disability advocate characterized this move as "institutional disrespect" that the advocate felt reinforced the disrespect that disabled people received every day. The advocate described SEIU organizer Rolf in the mid-1990s as a "genius," saying that he had "never ever moved one step ahead without consulting us . . . no matter how painfully long our meetings were." The advocate felt that the union leadership of the mid-2000s, with Tyrone Freeman as president, needed ongoing "disability sensitivity."[34] Things got worse in the late 2000s.

Throughout its history, the SEIU's home care organizing mobilized workers and made alliances with the disability and senior movements in a social movement unionism that used a combination of protest and electoral politics in pressing the state for legislative reform.[35] For example, in Los Angeles, SEIU organized "coffee captains" who hosted regular meetings with coffee and snacks in their homes with attendees organized by voting districts (precincts) to mobilize workers to participate in protests and lobbying.[36] Yet, after winning the flexibility-security model that allowed for unionization and collective bargaining and preserved consumers' hiring and firing power, the social movement aspect of alliance and worker mobilization suffered, leaving a thinner political unionism.[37] In the late 2000s and into the 2010s, the SEIU faced a series of internal and external problems at the local, state, and international levels. The critique of SEIU for a lack of internal democracy is not new, but it emerged in full force in home care, given top-down decisions by the union's international office and financial problems inside local unions in the late 2000s.[38] The internal democracy problems were not only the result of a few bad apples. They also marked a structural problem related to a top-down viewpoint at the international union level that saw union democracy as out of reach in a context of low union density, justifying instead deals with politicians and sometimes employers as the only way to improve conditions.[39]

Eileen Boris and Jennifer Klein insightfully warned of the "Achilles heel of political unionism," especially its reliance externally on electoral politics, which characterized the SEIU organizing model generally, given the attack on government programs like home care and the ascent of a "right to work" (union-free) movement that promised to gut public sector unions.[40] In 2014, after several battles in lower courts, the Supreme Court ruled in *Harris v. Quinn* that requiring workers to pay an agency fee to a union (i.e., union dues) violated the First Amendment protection of freedom of speech, even if the workers benefited from the collective agreement.[41] This case was brought by workers in the Home Services Program of the State of Illinois, who, like IHSS providers, were paid by the government but hired by consumers, and the ruling set a precedent not only for those seen as quasi-public workers, like IHSS providers, but other public sector workers too.[42] *Harris v. Quinn* meant that unions that had been formed through sectoral legislation would have to strive harder to connect with workers to sign them up as members in order to sustain themselves and their political work.

Toward Flexibility with Security at the Labor Market Level

The union had some success in augmenting providers' security while preserving consumers' flexibility in the labor market through its social movement unionism. Unionization brought wage increases for IHSS providers.[43] The union negotiated health benefits as early as the mid-2000s.[44] In 2016, the union won pay for overtime, travel time, and waiting at a doctor's office.[45] Since the state paid employer taxes, providers were eligible for statutory benefits (workers' compensation, unemployment, disability, and an old-age pension), thus providing more security than in most types of home-based employment where the individual hires and fires.

The union-disability-senior alliance also made some progress in addressing workers' labor market insecurity by supporting access to multiple jobs within a broad care sector. Like in DF, the program developed a registry to help people find workers and jobs, but the PASC registry within IHSS was partly accountable to the union. The registry had an advisory committee with joint consumer and union membership. The union's collective agreement also included a procedure for resolution of complaints about the PASC registry.[46] Still, there was evidence of discrimination by employers through the PASC registry. One union official described how consumer-employers often asked for English-speaking providers and said, "If they don't feel that they are being understood or there is a little bit of an accent when our members speak, their first reaction is: 'No, thank you. I want someone who can clearly articulate the English language.'"[47] In response, the union developed its own registry, the Home Care Exchange, which also listed private-pay domestic care jobs. However, not one of the Pilipina providers we interviewed had used the Home Care Exchange or the PASC registry.

The Pilipinx elderly IHSS consumers we interviewed expressed a strong preference for having family assist them, in line with the notion of children's filial duty to parents. Pilipinx consumers equated family with trust. For example, Rosario, an eighty-seven-year-old woman who had previously hired her cousin, said: "I don't want other people coming to my house. Sometimes I give my keys to the provider when I'm at the adult day care." Gendered understandings of filial duty—that sons are responsible for ensuring their parents are cared for in their old age but daughters-in-law and daughters do the hands-on care work—were evident, albeit in ways modified by the IHSS program.[48]

Social workers played an active role in suggesting family providers to consumers.[49] This was clear in our conversation with Manny and Jinkie, who explained that their son and daughter-in-law, with whom they lived, had been "spending a lot of hours on us," prompting them to apply for IHSS. Jinkie explained: "Most of the [Pilipinx] seniors have their children as their provider." Manny chipped in to suggest that the government approved children as providers to save money. "Because if it's someone else, IHSS will pay more. If the provider lives farther, I don't think they will agree with just thirty hours and be there the whole day." Interviews with providers further demonstrated the specific role of social workers. Like others, Jovelyn became an IHSS provider when the social worker from the day care center her mother attended told her mother that she could apply to have Jovelyn as her IHSS provider.

Consumers wanted to choose whom to hire, but they were ambivalent about their employer role. Those with family providers highlighted the government as the ultimate boss, not themselves, because the government paid the providers and determined the hours, despite the fact that the program allocated some employer responsibility to consumers. Consumers with nonfamily providers were more accepting of the employer role, but they still viewed the employment relationship as multilayered and attributed much power to the government.[50] All consumers were uncomfortable with firing, even though the government reinforced this employer role. What the consumers valued most was the ability to choose the worker. As Joel said: "You're the only one who can say if you're compatible or not."

This choice was gendered. There was a strong preference for women in the family to provide the hands-on care work and housework. The experience of Evelyn and her husband Rodel illustrated this well. Evelyn took care of her mother-in-law, an eighty-four-year-old, legally blind woman with high blood pressure and diabetes. Before Evelyn and her husband migrated to the United States, the mother-in-law had a Pilipina neighbor as her IHSS provider. Afterward Evelyn's husband chose to look after his parents as the IHSS provider rather than working in an elder care boardinghouse with Evelyn. "He didn't like it, because he's not used to that work," Evelyn offered. When the husband got a night job, Evelyn quit her full-time boarding care job to assume the majority of the mother-in-law's care. As Evelyn explained, "During the day he's sleeping . . . so I have to be there during the weekdays." On the weekend, Evelyn worked for an elderly white woman who needed twenty-four-hour care, sleeping at the woman's home, while her husband looked after his mother. Evelyn consented to her gendered obligation to the extended family, yet she did feel an entitlement to the payment, telling her husband, "Your pay is mine, because I do the work. But it is in your name." This subcontracting of IHSS work within the family economy took into consideration the reality that the family had more income due to the husband's night job and Evelyn's weekend domestic job, but it also reinforced the gender division of labor.[51]

When family was not available, ethnicity became the means to gain flexibility. Consumers spoke of other Pilipinx as fictive kin. When Rosario's cousin told her he could no longer do the job in addition to his other job at a hotel, "because it's so tiring," Rosario recruited a man from her church who was already the provider for his mother. Rosario described this man as "like a son to me." She had asked him, "Do you want to be my provider . . . do the laundry, clean, and drive me?" and he had responded, "Sure, Mommy, I am actually looking for a job now." The connection between family, ethnicity, and trust was evident across the interviews. Many consumers also said they hired Pilipinx because it was easier to communicate with them. For example, Patricia said: "You can tell them in Tagalog." Delia made the same point in the negative, stating, "There are Spanish [Spanish-speaking] ones, but even if you speak English with them, it's hard to communicate."

Some consumers said they hired Pilipinx because they felt they were better care workers, drawing on a broader discourse that circulates globally about the Pilipina as the ideal care worker, although in IHSS this preference can include men.[52] For example, Alma said, "You cannot just get somebody that's Mexican that says: 'I want to be a provider.'" When we asked Alma why she preferred Pilipinx, she said, "We're the same culture," but she also described asking prospective providers "first of all, the family, the place [they're from]. . . . They're Pilipina, but from what place from the Philippines?" This reference to the family was a reference to reputation and class.[53] "As much as possible, I'm looking for at least, um, you have educational qualification." Preferably, Alma would have someone with some "medical knowledge," and this was likely since "there are those who come here, that are nurses . . . still looking for job." Others also linked the notion of Pilipinx as ideal caregivers to their experience doing this type of work. As Amihan said, "Usually, [Pilipinx] are used to this kind of job."

Dense ethnic networks among seniors and between seniors and potential providers operated in churches, senior centers, and neighborhood spaces in the Pilipinx community like in others.[54] When we asked Leizel how her family started receiving IHSS to look after her mother, she said that friends from a Pilipinx seniors group had said: "You take care of your mom, and you should be compensated." Carmela's provider was "an acquaintance from church" but also recommended by Myrna, who was in a senior's organization with Carmela; Myrna and Carmela shared this provider. Pilipinx consumer and provider networks were dense around the Historic Filipinotown neighborhood, even though it was mostly Latinx. Roberto recounted how a Pilipino, who had owned a restaurant in the neighborhood that went out of business, became his IHSS provider. One day the man saw Roberto walking with his cane and followed him. Generalizing from this and other experiences, Roberto said: "If they see you're disabled, they will approach you." The man followed Roberto to the rooming house where Roberto lived and asked if they were treating him well. Roberto had his own room but had to wait in line for the restroom. He also did not like that the others were "always drinking . . . too loud . . . and had a lot of people over." The man, who owned three houses, offered to rent one to Roberto and to be his provider. Roberto felt this was a "blessing." Similarly, Gloria said: "Sometimes they approach you in the bus: '*Manang* [older sister], do you have a provider? If not, here's my telephone number. . . . I'm with IHSS, but I have no work.'"[55] Adelaida expressed a common sentiment among consumers when she said: "We don't look for them. They are the ones who present themselves." The economic context made providers available, while ethnic networks connected precarious consumers to precarious workers.

Providers also spoke of the comfort that came with working with someone they knew and of their entry into IHSS work as shaped by co-ethnic relations in specific neighborhoods.[56] For example, Josie said her IHSS client hired her "because she's my friend" and "because she likes me." She concluded: "Here [in L.A.] [Pilipinx] help each other. There are many referrals." Ethnic networks were also dense between neighboring seniors. Imelda's four Pilipinx clients lived in the same senior housing building as one another, which was only a few streets away from where Imelda lived. This arrangement was also convenient because Imelda only had to go up and down stairs to work with them all in a given day. When others in the building asked her for help, she referred them to her daughter Riza.

In a context where people hire those they know, do family and ethnic relations smooth out flexibility-security tensions at the intimate level?

Negotiating Flexibility-Security Tensions at the Intimate Level

Consumers and providers alike, whether family or nonfamily co-ethnics, used ideals and practices of family and fictive kin to negotiate flexibility and security at the intimate level. Both sides valued flexible time and task boundaries in body labor and housework akin to the labor process of unpaid work in families, and both underscored the skilled relational work involved in sustaining family and fictive kin care economies.

Cultural Knowledge and Gendered Skills

The Pilipinx IHSS community did not see credentials as a threat to their embodied knowledge, as was the case with non-elderly consumers like DF self-managers. Some Pilipinx IHSS consumers had a background in personal support work, reflecting the concentration of Pilipinx in the broader health care sector in L.A.[57] Several providers had some type of health care training in the United States, including certified nursing assistant credentials, even though a credential was not needed to do IHSS work. Most providers received only limited training from the IHSS program, consisting of an orientation that covered first aid and CPR. Training beyond the orientation was not mandatory. Women who were subcontracted within the family or other subcontracted "relievers" usually did not even go to the orientation. Pilipinx consumers did not reject credentials, but they understood IHSS work as linked to women's work in families.

Consumers with family providers did not need to explicitly invoke family ideals, but they implicitly did so by emphasizing that they worked out disagreements with family providers through frequent discussion or taken-for-granted assumptions. Manny suggested that our questions about who decided what the provider would do were not appropriate, since his son and daughter-in-law were the providers. "Ah . . . that's for outsiders, those who are not family. Our children are familiar with our routine. We don't have to talk about it, they know the usual." His wife Jinkie elaborated, saying, "We explain to each other." Adelaida said she never had a difficult relationship with her daughter-provider and emphasized her own role in making sure they got along when she said, "It's not just the provider but you too."

Providers drew on experience from both previous care employment and unpaid family work in an effort to gain security at the intimate level. Lilia linked the relational skills of joking and smiling in intimate situations, developed looking after her mother unpaid, to her ability to encourage her sister-in-law to accept her paid help through IHSS. When her sister-in-law rejected her support with the shower, she joked, "Why are you so shy? We are both girls" and suggested "Let me scrub your back instead" in order to coax her into a more private and safe way to get clean. Reflecting the hybrid nature of this paid family work, Leizel said to be a good care worker you needed two things, "the mind and the heart." Leizel admitted there were times when she had to control her emotions. "Let's say she says something . . . you just smile, and then you change the topic to something that's funny . . . because they forget. . . . That's why I said you should know their condition. You can be an adult with them, you could be a child with them, or, uh, you could be a mother to them." Leizel had developed the skill of relating to older people in part through unpaid work. Yet she also said she drew on her knowledge about various health conditions from doing administrative work in hospitals and pharmacies.

Consumers with nonfamily Pilipinx providers drew explicitly on family ideals. Patricia said the provider treated her "like family." In turn, Rosario felt consumers should not "treat them differently [from family] . . . that's why [the provider] calls me Mommy." Delia emphasized mutual respect. "You need to learn how to get along with them, so they can respect you. . . . It's give and take." Consumers also spoke concretely about this give and take. For example, some consumers taught their providers how to cook. Rosario said, "My provider is male, so he doesn't know how to make *sinigang* [stew with tamarind broth], so I had to teach him. We eat together." Patricia agreed that "it feels good when you eat with someone, especially since you live alone." Consumers with nonfamily providers, like those with providers who were kin, used family ideals and family-like practices to negotiate service flexibility.

Providers working with nonfamily Pilipinx consumers also used family ideals and family-like practices to negotiate the potential knowledge-versus-skill tension. Providers referenced culture as a source of common knowledge. For example, Nenita said her consumer was specific in her requests: "She even told me, 'Do you know how to cook Bicol Express?' You know, with the coconut milk." Yet, laughing about this request, she did not experience it as "demanding" since she was used to cooking with coconut milk. Mylene said: "We consider them as our relative . . . because that's our goal: to make them feel that we care for them. That they are still part of the . . . community or the world as a whole." Yet care was not the only understanding of the work circulating in this community.

The care orientation of providers coupled with economic necessity.[58] Nenita said she took the IHSS job "because I just came, I have to do it to live, to pay the rent," and by the time of our interview she had moved on to a better-paying, non-care job. Providers also sought economic security through family-like practices. For example, the son of Imelda's client of thirteen years put his mother in a "convalescent," but after two years Imelda "felt pity on her," so she brought her to live in her own home. "I really treat them like my own mother," she said by way of explanation. Riza, Imelda's daughter, also looked after this woman, whom she "treated like a mother." When we asked why it was important to treat the consumer like a mother, she said: "Because you always see them, and you have to treat them well, and they're the ones who pay you, so it's, it's good to be nice to them, and it's in my nature to take care of an elderly person." Providers thus connected their use of family ideals and family-like practices at the intimate level with economic security. Providers and consumers also used family ideals and practices to negotiate another tension.

Daily Activities and Unpaid Labor on Family Time

Consumers and providers also used family ideals and practices to negotiate the potential time-versus-task tension, meaning the tension between a job made up of a set of narrowly defined tasks versus one that entailed help with a range of changing activities in a given time period. Consumers with family providers described a seamless, almost natural flexibility in what providers helped them with, and when, within extended family economies. Consumers' routines were family routines, especially among those who lived with their family providers or very close. In terms of the schedule, there was often a need for a conversation, given providers' other commitments, but consumers viewed changing the time or place as easy to do. For example, Delano said that he and his wife had an agreement with their grandson on the schedule, but also, if they needed to make a "reasonable" change or if the grandson needed to change things for "personal reasons," it was okay, "as long as he is performing his duty." Emphasizing the need to compromise, Delano said, "We're just humans. We don't always get what we want." Delano's wife, Estela, agreed: "Understanding each other is the key. If he can't come right now, then tomorrow or the next day."

Family providers accepted the consumer's direction on tasks but had more say about the timing if the provider had another job. For example, Leizel also worked a full-time job outside the home, so she had "to prepare the meals in the morning or at night for her, and then I already put it on the table and then . . . there's time for us to bathe." Sometimes negotiations were three-way. For example, Evelyn said the timing was very flexible, "because we're there," but sometimes she would ask her husband to do a given task, telling him, for example, "I don't want to go to the store; you go to the store." Despite some negotiation, family providers accepted housework as part of the IHSS job.

Family providers valued housework for one's extended family as labor in this context where the state paid for it. In the Philippines, Leizel had helped her mother with her personal care, unpaid, but for the housework she had been assisted by a housekeeper.[59] In L.A. she was the one doing the heavy housework but for her sister-in-law and for pay. "Like last week, the garbage bin, I cleaned it. Her neighbors were laughing at me. . . . Then I washed five bins of clothes the next day." Leizel said that her sister-in-law often did not want help with bathing and did not want Leizel to cook, because the sister-in-law knew how to cook well. Those with family consumers who needed more hands-on help also viewed housework as part of the IHSS job. For example, Divina said that if her mother or father-in-law did not want help with personal hygiene one day but needed their floors washed instead, she would do this work not because it is her filial duty but "because it's part of the work of the IHSS . . . not only to take care of them." Yet not all extended family work was paid.

Family providers stressed the difference between hours paid by the IHSS and their actual hours of work and described a seamless array of paid and unpaid work in these family care economies. Leizel laughed at the IHSS assessment of time it would take to do various tasks, down to the decimal points—"like .2 hours . . . and then that will be in like 30 days, 60 minutes"—but said that "you just don't say, 'Okay, I'm not paid, I don't want to do it.'" Instead, she said: "When you take care of somebody, it's not only the money that you are after, right? . . . It's also love and commitment for the person that you take care of because that is precisely what caregiving is." For Leizel, care work was about love, but that did not mean it should not be partly paid. Evelyn said there was a list of the "covered work," which in her case included making the meals, doing the laundry, and doing errands. She had "glanced" at the list but not really read it, and the consumer could request other things. She linked this flexibility to the fact that she had already been doing "the laundry and everything" before she became the paid provider.

Co-ethnic fictive kin also used family ideals to grease the wheels of this intimate exchange. Consumers understood their right to fire workers, but few had ever done so, they explained, because of widespread adoption of family ideals and family-like practices on both sides. Carmela suggested that her provider understood her hiring and firing power and appealed to familial sentiment to gain some security when the provider told her, "Don't replace me. I love you." Myrna agreed that providers "compromise," so it did not usually come to firing. Carmela received hours for shopping and being driven to doctor's appointments, given her diabetes, as well as some assistance with showering. She said of her provider, "When I had surgery, she drove me to the hospital and stayed there all afternoon." Consumers' needs too often went beyond the funded hours.

Consumers with nonfamily providers viewed assistance with housework as an important paid job that helped them live a full life, like DF consumers. Rosario stressed the health-related importance of cleaning the refrigerator, saying that "sometimes there is food that is expired." She also spoke of her role in setting the conditions of work, noting that since the refrigerator did not have to be cleaned every day she would "let them know beforehand" and "in a nicely manner." Similarly, Carmela did not need help with personal care, only "house chores," help for which she tried to ask nicely: "I don't criticize her. I try to be patient with her. I don't oblige her to work longer hours for me, since my time is limited too." Saturino agreed that although he was the boss, he also needed to be "considerate." We see a similar value of consumers' need for flexibility among providers.

Providers with nonfamily Pilipinx consumers accepted the job as entailing a flexible boundary between housework and bodywork. For example, when the consumer told Nenita that she, Nenita, would cook simple meals, go to the market, and accompany her on the bus to medical appointments, Nenita inquired: "I do not, like, wash you?" When the consumer replied, "No, but you can go clean the restroom," Nenita did not reject the job. She insisted to us that this job was "not necessarily like a housemaid . . . not really like that." In describing the way they did their work, providers spoke of treating the consumer like family. Imelda said, "They want to be talked to because they have no one—to tell a story, while chopping, the vegetables . . . because I treat them like family." For those working with nonfamily, this job was ideally not like work of a servant or "housemaid" but rather like family work.

To providers it was important to treat people like family and to be treated like family—meaning not to be treated "like a maid in the Philippines," to quote Perla. This dynamic was evident in the way Jovelyn made sense of her work history. Jovelyn had long brought food to one of her Pilipina neighbors as volunteer work through a Pilipinx seniors' organization. Yet when the senior moved to a building that was "very strict" in terms of cleanliness, the building staff advised her to hire Jovelyn as an IHSS provider to help with cleaning and laundry since she was often there anyway. So Jovelyn became her provider for a time, and she gained another IHSS client who lived next door. Jovelyn was not happy that the first consumer started to treat her like an employee rather than fictive kin. First she started "keeping me [beyond the agreed-upon schedule]," Jovelyn explained. "She started making demands . . . like bossy." When she suggested that Jovelyn sign in and out each time she came, Jovelyn told her: "You know, my time for you is only five hours. But you see, in the morning, I will come and then do whatever you want me to do, and then after my time we still need to go out and then come home at night." The consumer got "really mad" and terminated her. The social worker tried to patch things up, but when, after a month, the consumer asked Jovelyn to return to be her provider, Jovelyn declined because she "saw her real attitude." Yet, laughing, she told us: "I'm still visiting her and giving her some food" as a volunteer. Jovelyn and others emphasized their desire for an intimate security, with the recipient respecting the importance of their work. Family ideals were how providers and consumers alike made sense of their work, and they negotiated flexibility and security through family-like practices, but this did not mean there were no tensions within the family or ethnic community.

Tensions within the Ethnic Care Economy

Family and ethnic fictive kin economies organized the provision of care, but tensions were not always kept under wrap. Some consumers with family providers mentioned tensions in extended families as authority shifted to adult children with migration. As part of a conversation about how the children have other paid employment, requiring the parent-consumer to organize her needs around it, Rosa said: "The children are the boss . . . not us." Others with whom we were talking laughed in agreement. Tess said her daughter-provider decided what to cook because she, Tess, did not "want to meddle." Rosa said she did not want to meddle either, even though she felt her daughter-provider's cooking was "so bland." There were also tensions within families over money, although few admitted to this within their own family. Normie said: "I heard it somewhere, but some consumers ask for their share from the provider. . . . Is that okay with IHSS?" Rosario informed Normie, who did not have services yet, that IHSS would not allow this. A community worker present confirmed that: "If they found out, they would lose their job, and the consumer would not be allowed to have the services."[60] Despite these comments, consumers were positive overall about their relationship with family providers. In comparison, family providers mentioned more tension.

Interviews with family providers suggested that, even within extended families, there was the danger of care work becoming like that of a personal servant. Although this tension largely was shaped by insufficient funding, too much unpaid work was not its only cause. For example, Lilia did not think the pay was too low and did not have an issue with working over paid time. "With *Ate* [Older Sister], even if I'm already working beyond my hours, it's okay." She did care, however, about how her sister-in-law treated her in the course of doing her intimate duties. "This is what maids do," she told her sister-in-law. "Please, not too much." When the sister-in-law asked Lilia to wash the large bath mats, Lilia said to her, "*Ate*, this is so heavy, eh? I washed this so many times. . . . Throw it out, just buy a new one. I'm too tired." Some providers did not want to work for family because of such tensions.

Consumers with nonfamily providers spoke of more tensions than those with family providers relayed, not surprisingly. Consumers often reported conflict with previous providers since tension in these nonfamily cases nearly always led to firing or quitting. Gloria relayed: "My provider made me feel like I owed it to her that I received this service." Gloria felt that this provider had tried to "cash out" all her hours by asking Gloria to sign the time sheet folded. Saturino said: "Just don't abuse me. Because sometimes, I observe, some providers don't want to do their duties, like they forget. You have to keep reminding them. It should not be like that." When a community worker relayed a scenario in which a provider insisted on doing things her way, Joel stated that providers "take advantage too, especially if you're old."

Nonfamily providers discussed the potential for IHSS work to morph into servitude. For example, Josie had left IHSS work in part because her food-service job in a long-term care hospital was "much more stable," but she also suggested how intimate relations shaped her decision. When we asked if IHSS work was rewarding, she said, "If the patient is . . . not so mean"—and here she laughed—"you really enjoy being with them," but she said there were "demanding ones" out there. Similarly, Flordeliza said: "You know, they look at providers as maids." She gave an example of another provider she had observed being "ordered around" in a condescending way: "Carry my bag, cover me with the umbrella." A former provider, Nenita, agreed, recounting how one consumer said she was "sitting pretty" because she had an IHSS provider. Nenita suggested, "Maybe that is really a little bit of verbal abuse." Nenita had felt she "had to endure it" since she "had another job but it wasn't enough." By the time of our interview, she had left IHSS work. Delia, a consumer who had been an IHSS provider, insisted that consumers needed to be respectful and "appreciate the things they do for you. . . . They should not treat you like a maid." Switching to her current perspective as a consumer, Delia told other consumers, "You should only ask of them the things you cannot do yourself. So, if you can still do these things, help them out." Consumer Adelaida, who had been her husband's IHSS provider in the past, agreed with Delia. "Others here tell people that they have a maid, eh, but it's not like that." Indeed, flexibility with security at the intimate level might rest not just on ethnicity but also on whether ethnicity helps challenge class inequalities through collective organizing.

Union and Community Organizing

Alliance between consumers and providers was a key part of the SEIU's social movement unionism aimed at augmenting provider security while preserving consumer flexibility in the labor market.[61] This case study reveals how family and ethnic ties have supported that alliance. It also suggests that ethnic organizations are another site for alliance politics, which is important given the union's internal problems with democracy and the limits of an external strategy based on a narrower political unionism since the late 2000s. Nearly one-third of the consumers we interviewed were members of Pilipinx organizations focused on seniors' issues, voting and citizenship, or Pilipinx culture through dance or art, while almost half of the providers participated in civic or social Pilipinx community groups.

Union and Community Organizing for Flexibility with Security at the Labor Market Level

Pilipinx providers' and consumers' engagement with Pilipinx community organizations, the union, or both have mostly focused on labor market security with flexibility. Most nonfamily providers were supportive of the union for its efforts to augment labor market security through better wages, more hours, and benefits. Community worker and former provider Flordeliza spoke positively about the union since its activists were "the ones who negotiated for the $11 [per hour]." Similarly, Perla said, "The union wants $15 per hour. . . . That's what the union is fighting for. . . . It really should be . . . since the job is difficult." Several family providers also had positive views of the union for augmenting labor market security. For example, Lilia said, "The increase of the pay, they fight for that, they help you." Consumers with family often supported the union when their family provider did. For example, Delano said, "My grandson is a member of the provider's union. It's good for him because they have [health care] benefits from them." Some consumers with nonfamily providers were also supportive of the union. For example, consumer Saturino even viewed himself as a member of the union alongside providers since they deducted union dues from the check that went to his provider. In contrast, Marian said, "They don't need it. The union calls my daughter, but she doesn't want to join." This quote illustrates the need for the union to put more effort into engaging family providers and their consumers.

Several consumers and providers participated in efforts by Pilipinx community groups to secure this flexible program. One community worker described various events with consumers and providers. "We rallied. We were holding placards. . . . Even those who are in wheelchair[s] joined."[62] Similarly, Imelda explained how the government was threatening to shut down the program, but they "succeeded" in stopping them, thanks in part to providers and consumers having "demonstrated in front of the Capitol." Nenita had not been involved in the union when she was an IHSS provider: "Back then, when I came here, I just wanted to have a job." Yet later, as a member of a Pilipinx community group, she became active in the union, even though she had a full-time job in another part of the care sector. "Yeah, I even participated in a rally, in front of the [Los Angeles County] Board of Supervisors office. I had a placard: 'Raise our salary!'" Similarly, Marian, who as we saw above was not supportive of the union, said: "If they're trying to get rid of it [the IHSS program], we as friends must unite.... We were thinking about it; we need to meet at least once a week." One way the union could mobilize Pilipinx providers to engage in the ongoing work of augmenting labor market security would be to work with organizations with which they are already involved. This is even more important in order to address flexibility and security at the intimate level.

Community Organizing for Flexibility with Security at the Intimate Level

Some consumers and providers felt that the IHSS program should address tensions in the labor process, but actual support at this intimate level from IHSS was limited, underscoring the need for collective solutions. For example, Alma said that if consumers had a problem with a provider, they could "channel it to the social worker . . . then they can advise you to dismiss her." Interviews with social workers confirmed that providers sometimes contacted them to complain about consumers who asked them to do tasks they did not feel they should do. Social workers would clarify what the state paid for, but they did not "become the referee."[63] The main recourse for consumers was to fire the provider, and the main recourse for providers was to quit. Could the union intervene to support providers and consumers at the intimate level?

Few providers thought the union was, or would be, effective at addressing tensions at the intimate level. If family providers admitted to any tensions in the labor process, they did not think the union was a tool to address them. Lilia mentioned difficulties with her mother-in-law but had not gone to anyone at the union for support. Instead, she explained, "Sometimes, I call Ate's son: 'Your mom is so stubborn.' She listens to her son." Lilia recognized the union's effort to increase labor market security, but she said: "For the clients, I'm not sure they help out." This viewpoint was shaped in part by a notion of unions as engaged only in confrontation and the difficulty of reconciling this with her relationship with her mother-in-law. "I don't have a reason to fight, since I'm taking care of a family member." In contrast to her lack of participation in the union, Lilia was involved in her hometown association, where she organized support for poor people in her community in the Philippines. Her lack of involvement in the union linked not to anti-collectivism or lack of time but to the lack of connection with the union. In her words: "I don't know them. All I receive is a paper, so I just read about them."

Nonfamily providers also felt that the union was unable to help with tensions at the intimate level. Rosario said this about the union: "How would they be able to resolve the problem if the problem is between you and her?" Perla was one of the few providers who was optimistic that the union could help resolve problems with consumers in the labor process and said, "That's why I want to be a member." Yet she did not return her signed membership card after the orientation. When we suggested she mail it, she said the dues were "so expensive" and elaborated that union meetings were a "waste of time" since she would get the wage increase whether active or not. A feeling of exclusion from the union, or at least a lack of inclusion in it, fueled Perla's free rider behavior. She said there was no Tagalog translation in the union, and she explained, "They keep sending me a membership [pamphlet], but . . . they sent it in Spanish. I don't understand Spanish, so I couldn't fill it up." My interview with a key informant in the union confirmed that they could not easily distinguish between Latinx and Pilipinx providers because both often have Spanish-sounding last names.[64]

One way to address tensions in the labor process could be through critical education. As one disability advocate said, "There's always going to be a conflict between both sides. . . . The most we can do is educate our communities as to what they should and should not do."[65] Similarly, a union official explained how the union focused on education and training in the mid-2000s in order to "put a shield around providers, knowing that this is what the provider understands his or her job to be when they go in there, so that they can say no."[66] Yet few Pilipinx providers felt connected enough with the union to benefit from critical education.

These experiences of the Pilipinx we interviewed make sense within the union's thinner political unionism focused on electoral politics since the late 2000s. One union official explained that the internal democracy problems prompted more checks and balances on finances but that they did not dwell on it, given an upcoming election.[67] One Pilipina worker leader and volunteer organizer in L.A. said that there were only a few Pilipina organizers throughout the statewide union and speculated that most Pilipina IHSS workers were family providers and hard to reach because they had other jobs and thus less time to participate in their union. This member organizer and family provider became an activist in the schools, pushing for better education for her disabled daughter. Later she got involved in SEIU through another Pilipina IHSS worker, a woman she met while campaigning for Hillary Clinton for president in 2016. At the time of our interview in 2019, she was a member of the union's statewide executive board, a delegate of the L.A. Federation of Labor, and on the local organizing committee focusing mostly on nursing home workers. Given all of this volunteer union work and her ongoing family provider duties, it is not surprising that she had only begun to consider new ways to reach out to Pilipinx IHSS workers, for example, through Facebook.[68] In

2019, one union official shared an updated member leadership plan, but again the focus was on mobilizing members for federal elections the following year rather than a deep engagement with workers about labor process issues.[69]

Pilipinx organizations may be better positioned to support Pilipinx workers in the labor process. Some consumers saw potential in community organizing to support one another as they navigated their relationship with Pilipinx providers. Speaking of a senior day care center in the neighborhood that catered to Pilipinx as well as Korean seniors on IHSS, and the role of one of the community workers there, Manny said, "Ah, you can talk about . . . problems at home, personal problems. Like at the center, she tells us what kind of attitudes we have to change." Some tensions could be difficult to tackle, especially within families. When we asked the community worker whether consumers with family providers confided in other seniors at the center about problems with providers, she said: "I think that only happens if the provider is not a family member. Because if they are family, they will cover up for them rather than telling it to others."[70] Critical education would have to address subtle, even unconscious, tensions that workers often gloss over, through references to family and ethnicity.

Some providers participated in Pilipinx civic or social groups and saw them as a space to talk with family and friends about the daily challenges of this work. For example, referring to a civic organization whose office we used to conduct the interview, Evelyn said: "Sometimes the elderly comes here . . . if they have problems, to ask questions. We're gonna help them." Jovelyn felt ethnic community groups could help providers to better address problems than the union because "it's more relaxed . . . if you're questioning . . . easier to be interactive with Tagalog and the environment." There may be potential within ethnic community organizations to address tensions at the intimate level left unaddressed by the union.

California's In-Home Supportive Services program supported the labor market flexibility of consumers to hire and fire and increased the workers' labor market security. Unlike with Toronto's DF, the legislation governing IHSS recognized the state's employment role through payroll and collective bargaining over wages and benefits, thus creating a mechanism for augmenting providers' labor market security. Many have written about the coalition between the Service Employees International Union and the disability and seniors' movements that spearheaded this novel legislation in the late 1990s.[71] However, the union faced both internal democracy problems and external anti-unionism in the late 2000s and through the 2010s that flattened this early social movement unionism to a more limited mobilization focused on electoral campaigns.[72] Furthermore, at its best, the SEIU's social movement unionism did not reach the intimate labor process, and, in a context of internal and external problems, even gains at the labor market level could be difficult to sustain. Yet this case study suggests that engagement with immigrant communities could be a way forward.

At the labor market level, Pilipinx preferred to hire family, and when family was not available, they preferred other Pilipinx, due to a combination of trust, ease of communication and dense networks, as in other immigrant groups.[73] By allowing people to hire family, the state helped women sustain their filial duties to the extended family in a context where women's need to engage in paid employment undermined their ability to meet these responsibilities. The program thus provided the potential for security within families who added IHSS employment to the mix of jobs. Yet it also reinforced gendered divisions of extended family labor. This gendered labor market security with flexibility was also evident in the immigrant community through a vibrant co-ethnic care economy. In DF, in contrast, the segmentation of the labor market along the lines of race and class reinscribed insecurity. Racialization in the broader labor market shaped the development of co-ethnic care economies in Los Angeles, but, compared to immigrant and racialized DF workers in Toronto, Filipinx had more options outside the ethnic economy due to a combination of their facility in English, high levels of education, and experience in the broader elder care and health care sectors. In this context, Filipinx seniors could find it difficult to hire and retain their preferred Filipinx workers if tensions in the labor process are not recognized and mediated. Furthermore, workers need more than security in the labor market to sustain caring relations.

At the intimate level, Filipinx consumers and providers referenced consensual relations linked to an ideal or typical family and engaged in concrete family-like practices to negotiate potential tensions between consumers' embodied knowledge and providers' formal skill. IHSS providers developed knowledge of particular consumers' routines, as was the case with DF personal attendants, but both IHSS providers and consumers also referenced gendered family relations as a source of common knowledge and skill. Consumers not only said they treated family and co-ethnic providers "like family" but also wanted to be treated "like family" in terms of being provided support "with love" or "with the heart." Family providers did not exert expertise. Instead, they skillfully drew on experience in unpaid work and care employment to ease knowledge-versus-skill tensions.

Pilipinx IHSS consumers and providers also mediated the possible time-versus-task tension, between defining the job as a set of standardized tasks and defining it based on a range of flexible tasks in a given time period, by using family ideals and family-like practices. Despite the state's estimation of funding based on a "time per task" basis, workers said they treated people "like family" by providing the help they needed when they needed it, within parameters of other employment. Importantly, the state explicitly allocated funding for housework, as well as daily living activities, at an equivalent amount to that in DF, and recipients and workers in both contexts valued housework as an essential part of this service and job. The potential to value housework was greater in IHSS, given that the state compensated even immediate family for doing it. At the same time, both providers and consumers used family ideals to justify working beyond paid time, and some providers mentioned tensions at the intimate level. Whether working for extended family or for nonfamily co-ethnics, providers sought and valued respect at the intimate level. They articulated intimate security as the recipient treating them "like family," meaning not treated them as "maids."[74]

It is important not to romanticize individuals' use of family ideas and strategies or to assume their ability to solve problems. My analysis reveals not an uncritical use of the trope of the Pilipina as the ideal care worker but rather specific community relations, based in particular places like neighborhoods and community centers, that encouraged Pilipinx to "still help" even if consumers were "mean" or did "not care," to quote community worker and former provider Lourdes. On the other hand, that providers use family ideals and practices strategically to negotiate security does not mean they do not authentically care about the people they work with, but rather that authentic care is not at odds with strategic action for economic survival.[75] Instead, authentic care develops out of specific economic relations. Furthermore, romanticizing family and ethnic relations could entrap immigrant consumers and providers in underfunded family and ethnic care economies and lead us to overlook the need to discuss unpopular tensions and gloss over the importance of collective supports to address them.

Alliances between consumers and providers, including family members, have long been a key strategy of the SEIU at the labor market level, and there is evidence of support for this strategy in this case study of families and co-ethnics with similar class backgrounds. Yet there is also evidence for the need to figure out how to address tensions at the intimate level. Although most providers and consumers were supportive of the union for its effort to augment labor market security, they did not see how it could help resolve tensions at the intimate level. Sustaining this alliance requires active participation of both providers and consumers, yet few Pilipinx connected deeply with their union. Some providers participated in Pilipinx civic organizations, senior mutual support societies, and cultural groups, which could be spaces to address tensions at the labor process level.

So far in our comparative journey, we have seen how recipient labor market flexibility, through hiring and firing power, can result in racialized insecurity in contexts like DF, where workers have no collective backing, but that creative coalitions can push for innovative legislation aimed at mitigating worker insecurity while still preserving recipient flexibility, as was the case in IHSS. However, we have also seen that this labor market flexibility for recipients in both DF and IHSS translated into very little intervention by the state or the union in cases of tensions at the intimate level. The focus on labor market security also lends itself to a top-down political unionism, fueling anti-union sentiment. As a result, the smooth running of this daily intimate service relies heavily on dyadic relational work, drawing on ideals and practices tied to family, ethnicity, or friendship. The likelihood of tensions being displaced to the labor market through firing and quitting, found in DF (and other forms of domestic work), was mitigated in the L.A. Pilipinx care economy by family and ethnic ties, yet there were still some tensions left unaddressed. What if an agency mediates the recipient-worker relationship? Would workers and recipients still rely on relational work articulating ideals and practices of family, ethnicity, or friendship to negotiate flexibility with security at the intimate level? Would more limited labor market flexibility for recipients ensue, and would this translate into more labor market security for workers? Would unions be better able to support flexibility with security? In the next chapter, I answer such questions with an analysis of an "agency model."

AGENCY-LED FLEXIBILITY AND INSECURITY IN TORONTO'S HOME CARE

Penny, an eighty-year-old white, Canada-born widow, hailed from a stable, working-class background. After high school, she had gotten married and worked as a clerical worker but left the labor force when she had children, while her husband supported the growing family with his unionized job. Penny lived on income from a variety of sources—the Canada Pension Plan based on combining her limited and her husband's larger contribution as workers, a small pension from her husband's employer, and a modest payment from Canada's Old Age Security. She lived in a semi-detached home with her son, who worked late and was gone most weekends. Penny had started receiving home care after she broke her hip and had received services from a for-profit agency for three years. Unlike both IHSS and DF, in which consumers or self-managers hired workers directly, home care services were delivered by mostly for-profit agencies that hired personal support workers and sent them to clients' homes. In three years, the agency had sent Penny three different workers, with little input from Penny, but she speculated that had they continued to send one "unusual" worker she might have been able to switch since, she thinks, the company wanted clients and workers to be compatible. Like in other programs, funding levels influenced the intimate relationship between recipients and workers. In home care, the government cut back funding to cover only limited, hands-on bodily support, so the agency rigidly defined funded tasks accordingly and offered additional services only for a fee. Penny was grateful when the worker saw what was needed around the house and just did it as a favor, but surely workers cannot give such favors endlessly.

Leah, a Jewish married woman in her early forties, with no children, had come to Canada in the 1990s as a refugee from Poland, where she was a nurse. Since Canadian employers did not recognize her Polish nursing credentials, she got a job as a personal support worker. Indeed, agencies contracted by the government to provide home care services in Toronto, like those providing Penny's services, employ predominantly immigrants who have arrived in Canada in the past few decades. They come from Asian, African, Latin American, Caribbean, and eastern European countries, and many are professionals whose foreign credentials are not recognized.[1] The agency often sent Leah to Polish clients who spoke limited English. While her bilingual skills opened up work, she provided a disturbingly vivid account of the anti-Semitism she experienced from some clients. Since the agency needed to service the older Polish immigrant community in Toronto, and since they took little responsibility even though they were the legal employers, Leah faced the problematic choice of either employment or racist treatment. In other words, she encountered a trade-off in security at the labor market and intimate levels.

How do clients and personal support workers (PSWs), as they are called in the Toronto home care program, negotiate flexibility and security in a context of rationed funding and marketized services in a racialized labor market? The consumers of Los Angeles's IHSS program and the DF self-managers in Toronto did the relational work of building and sustaining a good relationship with workers, although of different kinds, in an attempt to gain flexibility at the intimate level and retain workers. Yet, unlike in these two programs, in home care an agency operated as an intermediary between the workers and recipients. The key questions then concern whether these agencies facilitate flexibility for recipients and security for workers. Do home care agencies stifle their clients' ability to negotiate flexibility with workers at the intimate level? Or do they facilitate it by treating state recipients like customers who can choose a compatible service worker?[2] Do they assist workers in navigating the relational encounter in a way that limits the precariousness and indignities of personalized employment arrangements? Or do they exacerbate insecurity?[3] A first step in answering these pressing questions requires understanding how the agencies operated within a medical funding model.

Context: The Medical Model and Contract Agencies

In the 1960s and 1970s, the Ontario government developed home care through public and nonprofit services based on cost sharing between the federal and provincial governments. In the mid-1990s, however, the federal government cut payments to the provinces, and Ontario restructured its home care program. The Conservative Ontario government introduced "managed competition" allowing for-profit companies to compete with nonprofits for service provision contracts. The government justified this move by claiming it would provide "consumer choice and efficiency," but the effort to contain health care costs, by closing some hospitals and transferring more medical care to home care, drove restructuring.[4] In the late 1990s, the government introduced regulations to ration in-home long-term care by giving priority to acute patients. While this program also provides services to seniors and people with complex medical conditions, regardless of age, the focus of my study is on those with chronic, long-term disabilities through aging or through ill health.

The Ontario Ministry of Health and Long-Term Care funded these services within a medical model premised on cure of acute illnesses. Personal support was not means-tested, so the recipients we interviewed had a more diverse class location compared to IHSS consumers in L.A.[5] Yet they were more likely than DF self-managers to be poor. People applied for services through government entities, which employed case coordinators and managed contracts with service-providing agencies.[6] To be eligible, people had to fit the case coordinator's assessment of physical need and ability to stay in one's home with the hours allotted.[7] The case coordinator set up the initial care plan and provided any training to the client or the client's family regarding the care. Unlike in DF, in which recipients had to be able to direct their own service, in home care a family member could direct the services with guidance from the case manager. Services could be professional, such as nursing or physiotherapy, or they could be end-of-life care, homemaking, or personal care, but the majority of funding went to personal care, defined as help with narrowly delineated bodily needs.[8]

Most clients we interviewed felt they did not have sufficient hours of support. Although this was also the case with IHSS consumers and DF self-managers, who wanted to see more hours to cover overnight needs and for errands and social activities, complaints from home care clients were much more extensive and related to basic needs. This was perhaps not surprising given that the maximum hours under home care were much lower than the maximum in both IHSS and DF.[9] The hours among those we interviewed ranged from half an hour to fourteen hours a week; the majority received one to four hours, once or twice a week. One agency manager said, "The average client is getting two hours of service in a week, which is very, very limited . . . and a huge number of clients actually only get one hour of service." In reference to her single bath a week, Alice bitterly said: "It's disgusting."[10]

Many people had experienced a cutback in services. For example, Thomas, who was in his early sixties and had bone and muscle damage from a car accident, was cut back from two hours to one, three times a week. He said the case coordinator justified the cuts by telling him that other people were worse off. So he "gave in to that. . . . Went, 'it's no problem. Don't cut me off completely, because I can't do what I used to do.'" Other clients also said that case coordinators told them that others needed the hours more. Even people who said they had enough hours qualified their statements. For example, Mona, who was in her seventies and received three hours a week for help with mobility and bathing due to tissue damage and broken bones, wished she could get more help but did not ask, rationalizing, "I'm selfish but not *that* selfish."

In addition to lower overall funding, home care clients were distinct from IHSS consumers and DF self-managers in another key way: home care no longer covered help with housework, even though family could not fill in all the personal support and housework gaps, since women were employed or looking after their own children (or both). Unlike in L.A., family members could not be paid workers under this program. Only ten of the people in my sample, nearly all men, lived with family. For older men, wives managed and did much of the hands-on personal care, and a few clients lived with daughters who cooked and cleaned after paid employment. Most people had more intermittent help from family or from friends with shopping and errands, but people also stressed the strain this put on family and friends whom they felt were "busy" or had "other responsibilities," and they emphasized how insufficient paid help limited their independence. Elderly wives of male clients expressed the need for help too. As Betty, the wife of Arthur, said about their one hour a week for help with bathing: "We're still trying to get other hours. . . . We need more than that." In the meantime, they paid for Arthur to go to an adult day care for a couple of hours three times a week, and they paid for overnight respite once in a while, so that Betty—who was in her seventies, had a double mastectomy, and lived with arthritis—could get the housework and shopping done and also have some rest. A few of the upper-middle-class people supplemented home care with private personal support workers, two of whom had live-in domestic workers. A good number of people paid privately for cleaning, and some paid for help with shopping or errands. This included the middle class in the sample but also poor people who exchanged cleaning for small bits of compensation or for favors, intermittently and precariously—for example, by paying an even less-well-off neighbor's cell phone bill. A few poor people were receiving means-tested cleaning from the city, but several were on a waiting list for it.

The government funded Ontario home care, but it distanced itself from responsibilities to workers by contracting services to agencies, increasingly for-profit ones. As in other contract-agency models, the legal employer was the agency that hired workers and sent them to clients' homes, but the state funder also influenced employment conditions. In the late 2000s, the Liberal government put the competitive bidding system on hold and in 2013 abandoned it, partly due to critique by unions, nonprofit providers, and academics. However, the workers and clients' lives were shaped by this system still, in large part through its negative effect on their collective representation.

When the Conservative government of the mid-1990s restructured the service delivery model from a non-competitive to a competitive one, it limited the collective representation of clients and workers. This government disbanded the voluntary board of directors that managed the early home care funding and replaced it with government-appointed executive directors and boards of directors, thus severely reducing input from clients.[11] Contracting out services also made it difficult to unionize because labor legislation assumes a direct and continuous relationship with a single employer.[12] Several of the nonprofit agencies that lost the contracts with the government to deliver services were unionized. When the for-profits gained contracts, the workers lost their union because this government also got rid of the "successor rights" that protected workers' union representation when their direct employer changed. As a result, most of those unionized worked for nonprofit agencies, although a few large, for-profits were unionized in Toronto. The lack of significant union presence in this sector, coupled with next to no collective representation for clients, shaped worker insecurity and client inflexibility.

Contingent Flexibility and Insecurity at the Labor Market Level

Home care clients had less labor market flexibility than DF self-managers and IHSS consumers. Home care clients did not hire their own workers, and agencies did not accommodate clients' personal preferences in the initial assignment of workers.[13] However, in non-unionized agencies (the majority), clients were able to switch workers based on highly subjective criteria. For example, when asked whether there were any conflicts between clients and workers, one manager from a non-union, for-profit agency said: "From time to time, you're dealing with personalities—you're dealing with people . . . 'I don't like the dress she had on today.' 'She didn't butter my toast the right way.' It can be quite a variety of things. . . . So, absolutely, there are times when they don't get along, and then that's when we would change the caregiver."[14] Rather than addressing the source of the conflict directly, issues about how the work was done were understood as an inherent personality conflict that could not be bridged. This emphasis on personality was similar to the sentiments of DF self-managers and IHSS consumers where there was no agency. The solution here was to try to find a worker with a personality suitable to the client.[15] Half of the clients in my sample had asked the agency to change their worker at least once, while nine others had not requested a switch but said they would if they saw the need. Only a minority of people had requested a switch for an objective reason such as physical roughness or alleged theft. Most of their reasons were more subjective, related to personality and attitude. Nevertheless, the degree of clients' labor market flexibility was contingent on a combination of the social location of the client and agency policies. Non-elderly, white, Canada-born men and women were the ones who most commonly demanded a switch in worker, and for-profit, non-unionized companies were more likely to accommodate such a demand. For example, Gordon, a white, Canada-born man in his early sixties, told the manager about previous problems with workers and said this about the new one: "I hope he's got a personality." In response, the manager from the for-profit, non-union agency that provided Gordon's services told him that if he was not happy with the worker to call them within a month. In contrast, Agata, an elderly, Jewish immigrant woman, said the non-union, for-profit agency had never asked her about the workers, adding, "Money talks, and I have no money." Even for-profit, non-unionized companies did not offer flexibility to all clients, only to the squeaky wheels, or more accurately to the wheels when they squeaked.

Within a context of rationed state funding, agencies tried to preserve their own flexibility and meet the needs of select, demanding clients by defining workers as casual. For-profit, non-unionized agencies were the most explicit and extreme in this strategy. For-profit managers (except one who refused to answer the question) said that all their workers were "elect to work" (a category in which workers were akin to self-employed contractors), "casual," or "100 percent part-time." These managers argued that classifying workers in casual employment categories was necessary to provide scheduling flexibility for clients. They also claimed it provided choice to workers, but interviews with workers illuminated the negative implications of such "choice."

When we asked workers whether they were assigned another client if they lost one, they explained that this was far from guaranteed. As Vanessa said when we asked whether she worked full-time or part-time, "Well, it's called 'full-time part-time' because if there is no work then you know," and she explained how it "depends on the distribution" of hours through the agency's coordinator. Sometimes workers lost clients because of the nature of the client's illness or impairment. In these situations, the scheduling coordinator was likely to try to get them a new client, but this was not guaranteed and rarely based on seniority. Comments like "maybe," "they try," "it depends," and others conveying contingency were common among workers' description of the implications of losing a client. Wenna summed up this precarity well when she said that waiting to get a client with equivalent hours "could be a day, could be a year." Vanessa recounted an altercation with a male client who had yelled at her for not coming on time after he failed to answer the door when she knocked and who had later barred the door when she tried to leave. When asked whether she had gotten a new client in this instance, she said: "I took a while. . . . There was a time when there was no patients coming in because they were waiting for their contract." This is only one example showing how insecurity of employment could occur even if the client was at fault.

Coordinators in charge of scheduling had the power to give some workers the clients and not others, especially in a non-unionized environment. Not all of them always exercised this power, of course, but workers spoke of coordinators who showed preference for certain workers over others. Martina said that "nothing" would happen if she turned down a client but also said that if she did it frequently the coordinator would then think "something is wrong with you." Some workers said they could always "pick up" shifts, especially if one was willing to work on Saturdays, travel farther from home, or cover for people on vacation or out sick. At the same time, however, picking up hours by covering for other workers did not necessarily lead to long-term clients. Several workers recounted that sometimes the agency just sent them to hold a client until the regular worker returned. To the extent that a client preferred the initial worker and that the worker wanted to go back to that client, the agency would rejoin them; but if the client began to like the replacement worker better, it was more likely the original worker would lose the client if the replacement worker wanted to stay. As Penny said about her previous worker: "She was lovely. . . . Unfortunately she took two months' holiday and lost all her clients, but I gained Rachel, who's such a sweet person." In a non-unionized context, management could pander more to the clients who requested flexibility than to workers who requested security, when it suited them.

Employment insecurity combined with insecurity in wages and benefits, which in turn exacerbated contingent connections between workers and clients. Notably, home care PSWs earned much less than PSWs in nursing homes and hospitals.[16] Those classified as "elect to work" were not covered fully by the basic floor established by the Employment Standards Act (ESA), so they did not receive paid holidays, vacations or severance pay. The great majority of workers we interviewed said they had asked to leave at least one client. Given that agencies did not guarantee a new client with equivalent hours, and given that hourly wages and benefits were low, why would workers make this choice? The answer lies in the intimate labor process.

Insecurity and Inflexibility at the Intimate Level

Agency managers had rules related to tensions between workers and clients at the intimate level, but they did not enforce the rules or support workers and clients in negotiating tensions. This quote captures managers' hands-off approach well:

> Sometimes they don't feel comfortable advocating for themselves or to say no. . . . I mean, there's a lot of that, and it's so hard because it's community-based. We try to monitor them, but . . . how can we really monitor?[17]

Other managers likewise explained away their lack of supervision with reference to the self-sacrificial worker and the difficulty of supervising home-based services. Rather than proactively support workers or clients, they addressed problems ad hoc and after the fact. This limited supervision was evident in managers' approach regarding, and workers' and clients' responses to, the time-versus-task and knowledge-versus-skill tensions.

Body Risks and Invisible Relational Skills

Government policy shaped the way managers approached the knowledge-versus-skill tension and how workers and clients negotiated flexibility and security around this tension. The delivery of quality care was the responsibility of the agencies, but the government strongly encouraged agencies to hire people with a personal support worker (PSW) certificate.[18] The certificate could be from a community college, a private business school, or a public high school board. This meant that the training varied widely, but one common denominator was that care in long-term facilities, not in-home settings, drove the approach.[19] The agencies provided some training, but it was limited. Several managers mentioned mandatory yearly upgrading on things covered in the PSW course, often offered during paid work time. These included short refreshers on safe lifts and transfers, universal precautions like washing one's hands and other hygiene issues, stress management, incontinence management, infection control, and dealing with client abuse. Most agencies also offered some professional development courses on specific illnesses or impairments, like stroke, diabetes, or MS; the government often funded them, and thus they were usually free to the worker, but they were generally voluntary and on the workers' time.

In this contracted-out medical model, agencies did not recognize clients' embodied knowledge but instead viewed it as a risk to the workers and, by extension, to themselves. Any service that "invades the body," in the words of one manager, such as inserting an enema, was considered a "delegated act" for which a nurse took responsibility by authorizing and training a PSW to perform it.[20] As a result, agency supervisors were generally nurses. The government case coordinator set up the lifting or transferring routine in the care plan and provided client training, but it was then up to the contracted agency to ensure that the worker was providing the services safely. As one manager said: "If it's a safety issue, one of our registered [nurse] staff goes out to assess what is exactly happening. So you see, sometimes what the client wants is just risky to our employees."[21] For example, one manager recounted a situation in which a client's daughter had suggested the PSW transfer her mother in a way the mother preferred but the nurse-supervisor from the agency deemed unsafe for the PSW.[22] Another manager captured well the dynamic between agencies and clients also discussed by other managers when he said, "The client always has input. The agency always has the final say as to what is safe and what is not. Because we have an obligation to protect our employees under the Occupational Health and Safety Act."[23] Managers recognized the tension between workers' safety and client's knowledge, as these quotes reveal, but they largely left it up to workers to identify risk because the agency supervisor was rarely in the home workplace. Instead, the onus was on the PSW to call the supervisor if the client asked her to do something beyond her training, and the supervisor would come in, after the fact, to reinforce the training. This happened in cases where the worker identified a clear safety issue, but most of the time negotiating safety was more subjective and relied heavily on relational work.

Agency managers acknowledged the importance of workers building and sustaining a good relationship with clients, given the intimate nature and location of the work, but—characteristic of their hands-off approach more generally—they did little to recognize, support, or foster relational work, like listening and responding, as a skill.[24] This was evident in that they only required the worker to use her emotions minimally—to accept respectfully the direction of the client or the client's family, without becoming too involved.[25] Several of the managers of for-profit agencies spoke of training workers on "customer service." Others did not evoke this market logic but instead emphasized greater client influence in home care than in long-term residential care. For example, one manager said, "It's not like you're in a hospital setting," thus "the PSW is there to work with the client—so that they are not taking over or even setting agendas without the client's involvement."[26] Some managers said their agencies trained workers on managing boundaries around the relationship, but these trainings were usually not mandatory, and enforcement was again ad hoc. For example, one manager said that when workers "get into [doing] things that they shouldn't," management realized the need to reinforce the boundary between work and friendship. They did so simply by "reminding them about policies" and "re-orienting them," but there was little follow-up support.[27] This ad hoc approach shaped clients' relationship with workers.

Clients valued workers' training in the basics of body mechanics, safety, and health and were open to their ideas on how to do things as long as workers also exhibited relational skills. Home care clients valued very subtle relational skills, especially during bodywork. Penny described how she and her worker were talking about dry skin as Penny was having a shower. Penny mentioned that the best time to put lotion on was right after a shower, and when the shower was finished, the worker put lotion on her back. "So, you know, it's funny, you don't really have to ask her to do anything. She just sort of, you know . . . you just make a comment, and she does it." As this quote suggests, compared to DF self-managers, home care clients spoke less of directing their services actively. At the same time, more than the IHSS consumers, home care clients less readily chalked up workers' relational work to culture, as in a natural inclination based on gender or ethnicity. Home care clients spoke more of workers' relational effort, and this was evident in their critique of workers who did not give it. For example, Wayne, who was in his fifties, said, "Some workers are good, some of them are horrible. . . . If they come in and listen to the patient and don't dictate to them, then you have a better relationship." When asked to give an example of what a worker might dictate, Wayne gave an example of directing the worker not to put any salt in his food, but the worker made the decision to put the meat tenderizer, Accent, in his soup, which made it very salty. "I'm just, like, 'You're not here to be my servant, but you're here to listen to me and how I want certain things, and that's what your job is to do.'" Wayne elaborated that workers should "learn to respect what little privacy you do have," and if they did not he would "tell them to get out," although he admitted that he had never done so. In contrast, Anne said that she did not try to direct the worker because she did not "want to get on her bad side. I appreciate the way she treats me special." When asked to elaborate, she said: "Maybe she wouldn't come back again, and I'd have to go to a new worker and have them get used to me, and me get used to them again. That'd be hard." Similarly, Denise said, "You have to have patience. The known person is much better than an unknown person." In the context of the contingent home care labor market, where only the most entitled clients complain, some clients faced with the knowledge-versus-skill tension asked the agency to switch the worker or at least felt emboldened by their perceived ability to do so, while others suppressed critique of a worker, even if warranted.

Workers also underscored the connection of relational skills with more objective skills related to safety and how management overlooked this crucial link. For example, Anjali said she was filling in for a worker on maternity leave for a year.

The previous worker had left instructions on how she and the client had been doing the transfer from the bed to the wheelchair and back, but when Anjali tried it that way it did not feel right to her. She explained that although they were trained first in PSW school and then through various "in-service" courses offered by the agency on how to transfer people, "sometimes you don't always have to go by the book, because the book don't make it easy for you or the client. Depends on the client's weight or height or things like that. The book don't give you that." Anjali echoed others when she criticized the health and safety training for assuming a standard-sized worker and client, whereas different workers and clients could bear and handle different weight. Anjali respectfully asked the client: "If you don't mind, can I try my technique, and if you don't like it, I'll go back to hers?" The client agreed to try Anjali's way, and it turned out that the client felt more comfortable with Anjali's approach. He had been worried he might fall with the former worker's technique, but he had not alerted agency management to this fear or requested that the worker receive more training specific to his individual needs. When the original worker came back from maternity leave, the client requested that he keep Anjali instead. Anjali reasoned: "We don't try to steal hours from each other. . . . But sometimes what the company does is make the client happy." While it may be true that although most workers have PSW certificates they "all have different techniques," as Anjali said, this individualism, coupled with the agency policy of allowing the client to switch workers without much investigation, let the agency off the hook for training workers on the particular needs of specific clients. In other words, it allowed the agency to ignore the need for flexibility related to individual bodily needs and jeopardized workers' bodily security. It also rendered invisible the relational skills of navigating knowledge-versus-skill tensions.

Workers and clients were more willing and able to negotiate how the work or service was provided in a way that respected both recipients' embodied knowledge and workers' embodied skills if they had a long-term relationship, thus suggesting the intertwining of body-related skills and relational skills. For example, while Shanice never used the same washcloth "to clean the bum" as to clean "the front genital area," one client wanted her to use many separate washcloths for different areas of the body, like one for the back, another for the arms, another for the top of the leg, another for the bottom of the leg. Shanice did not feel that was necessary from a health and safety perspective and thought that the routine was "too complicated" and "very hard to deal with." Rather than asking the client why she felt she needed so many different washcloths or respectfully suggesting that three might suffice, Shanice said, "I just went there for one day. I'm not going to go back. I'm not going to let them drive me nuts. No headaches, no way." Yet Shanice was just filling in for this client. She said that if her regular client asked for something so complicated she would "really find some other way" lest she have a heart attack.

Similarly, clients valued the emotional skills with which some workers coaxed them into consenting to personal care, but they were only open to such coaxing from a worker with whom they had a long-term, close relationship. This was evident in our interview with Janet, a sixty-two-year-old with nerve damage and little use of her arms, who compared two of her workers. Janet relayed how some days: "I can't even get up, my head hurts so bad." So she would tell Virginia, her long-term worker, to wash the sheets next time, but Virginia insisted on washing the sheets because she did not think it was right for Janet to be in dirty sheets for two weeks. Janet explained: "She'll drag me out of bed, put me in the chair, all the lights off in the house, right? Because she knows how bad my headaches get sometimes." Janet was fine with being encouraged to get out of bed by Virginia, because she felt Virginia had a deep enough understanding of her situation that Virginia did her job with compassion. In contrast, she recounted how she did not accept the advice of a more short-term worker. With this worker, she had had a somewhat rocky relationship over a period of six months. Janet was upset that when she had asked the worker to make her chicken with Shake & Bake the worker had refused, saying it was unhealthy. Janet's reason for wanting the worker to follow her direction was linked to her own knowledge of the kinds of food she could eat. "She wanted to cook chicken in a curry way, which I can't eat—hot spices or any kind of curry, because, if I do, my throat closes up. Like, forget it—I choke to death." When the worker "wouldn't adhere to the [direct] complaints," Janet, upon the advice of others in her senior housing building, had called the agency supervisor to complain. The worker then came to Janet's apartment livid and yelled at her. Janet told her, "Get the F out of my house," and she refused to have her back. This was an extreme case of conflict, but generally such knowledge-versus-skill blowups occurred where no relationship had been established facilitating workers' skill at respectfully giving input and clients' willingness to accept their suggestions. A similar dynamic was evident regarding the time-versus-task tension.

Rescinding Tasks on Rationed Time

The government's rationed funding influenced the way that the agencies formally and informally approached the time-versus-task conflict, and this shaped how workers and recipients negotiated flexibility and security. Managers described their official rules as narrowly defined. For example, one manager explained that in the contract with the government they were "only allowed to provide certain services such as personal care, bathing, assist[ance] with mobility. We're not there as a homemaking service, for example."[28] PSWs could provide "light housekeep-ing," but the government defined this as the worker cleaning up the immediate area affected by the personal care tasks, such as mopping the bathroom floor after helping with a bath so the client did not slip when she stepped out. Manag-ers spoke of the care plan as an objective guide to what was to be done. As one manager said: "Our supervisors, when they go and do the visit, they go over the care plan with the client and then leave a copy. . . . So when the PSW goes in, they ask for that care plan, and they kind of see what needs to be done."[29] Managers also stressed that services were for the individual client. As another manager said: "They're only taking care of that room, that person, that person's laundry, that person's meal requirements, et cetera."[30] Despite such declarations, when time-versus-task tensions arose once again, supervision and support was ad hoc or, more commonly, left up to workers and clients to negotiate one on one. Workers and clients described how this minimal supervision worked with the contingent home care labor market to shape their response to the time-versus-task tension.

In contrast to the official definition of the services as a set of discrete tasks, home care clients—like IHSS consumers and DF self-managers—wanted flexible support to fit with their changing needs. Yet, unlike IHSS and DF, in home care the government cut funding for housework even though clients still needed it. For example, Eleanor, who was in her seventies and had osteoarthritis and had suffered multiple bone fractures, said the home care worker helped her mostly around the house because she wanted to "persevere" and "take a bit longer" to do her own bath and cooking. Thus, the worker changed the sheets on her bed and did the other laundry, cleaned her bathroom, and, "if she [had] any time left over, [might] dust or something." Justifying this division of labor based on need, Eleanor said: "I consider what she is doing for me to be personal care." She went on to detail how stripping the sheets and cleaning the bathroom required raising her arms and twisting her knee in ways that were painful, while cooking, doing her own bath, and sweeping her floors with a Swiffer, if done slowly, did not.

A few clients admitted that workers stayed over paid time to help with the housework and other tasks that the government defined out of the job. For instance, Claire, a fifty-one-year-old who had incontinence, mental health issues, and difficulties walking, said of her worker: "She will stay an extra half hour, forty-five minutes . . . and she doesn't get paid for it. But the difficulty I have in trying to get my laundry . . . I mean, there's just no way I can vacuum." Claire, like most clients, was grateful for the workers' unpaid help rather than expecting it or asking for it.

Several clients felt the government and the agencies knew that even though they no longer funded housework, clients still needed it and thus relied on favors from workers. Monica, who was in her early sixties and had mini-strokes that caused her to fall, articulated this viewpoint most explicitly. Having received services for some time, she showed us an early list of tasks that included light housekeeping and help with dressing but explained that she had begun to buy clothes with Velcro fasteners so she did not need help with buttons. While Monica knew that "they're not supposed to do the cleaning anymore," her worker not only helped her with "light housekeeping," such as wiping down the countertops and sweeping up the floor after meal prep, but also vacuumed, dusted, and washed the hardwood floors. Monica described how once the government case coordinator had visited, and Monica had mentioned that the worker helped her with cleaning, and the coordinator had responded that Monica should not tell her that. Laughing, Monica surmised, "It's sort of like this game that everybody plays, and it's because of the funding." In terms of the agency role in this game, Monica described how her ability to switch the worker gave her an advantage. She had only a couple workers who had said they would not help her with cleaning. "Of course, they don't come back either." She justified this strategy not only by her need but also by the notion that "they're in this profession because they want to help people." Yet she suggested that workers too knew the hidden rules of the game when she said, "They also don't want to lose their jobs." When we asked if she told the agency that she wanted to switch the worker because she did not clean, she said, "No. . . . I just say, 'Well, that one didn't work out. Perhaps it would be better if you sent someone else.'" With each new worker she asked whether one "would mind" doing some cleaning. Elaborating on her metaphor, she described finding a good worker who would meet her flexible needs, within this rigid system, as "like a game of checkers." Monica had been on a wait list for city-funded, means-tested cleaning services for a year. In the meantime she justified getting the worker to do this much housework because "those are the things I absolutely cannot do myself." Many clients spoke of unmet need and how some workers filled it through favors.

Client requests to switch a worker were risky because their success was contingent on a number of factors, and most clients would rather have a continuous worker than change workers frequently. As a result, a more subtle economy of favors was pervasive.[31] Most clients described not directly requesting flexible services from the agency but rather workers offering such services as favors. For example, following up on a comment from Jean about not liking to dust, we asked whether she would ever ask her worker to dust one day instead of doing the bath. Jean said: "No, I wouldn't do that." Instead, "the situation would be such that if she looked around and saw that there was something that needed to be done, because obviously I do not take an hour to bathe. . . . If they're conscientious about generally being a help to their clients, then they will on their own do other things." Jean would not ask the worker to do a particular cleaning task, since she knew it was no longer part of the job, but she still needed this help and so hoped the worker would provide it as a favor. Similarly, Wayne, who was in his fifties and spent most of his time in bed due to muscle degeneration, said his services included weekly shopping but that some workers would call to check in on him every day to ask if he needed them to pick anything up for him at the store. Like others, Wayne stressed that he did not request these tasks beyond the official job, but workers offered them. "If you do extra things because you want to, hey, much appreciated. . . . They don't have to, and I can't demand that of them, but some of them do that extra thing for you."[32] Yet this economy of favors could also disadvantage clients if it became the norm.

The most direct evidence of the negative impact on clients of reliance on favors for key service needs was in the experiences of those who had not cultivated close relationships with workers and, as a result, went without. For example, Dominic, who was in his forties and lived with HIV/AIDS, recounted "horror stories" of the poor quality of services he had received over the years, including workers who did not show up or showed up very late. Because transferring from his wheelchair to his bed was so painful, he would "void himself" but had to stay wet until the next scheduled visit. Sometimes the PSW would not show up but would say she had knocked on the door and that no one had answered. He had to videotape the building lobby to prove the PSW had not shown up. "It's brutal. It's just a horrible, horrible way to live." He recounted the problems with a reliance on favors in this context. He received two hours every morning for an extensive personal support routine of "showering, hair, teeth, rectum, legs . . . the diaper changing, cleaning of the dirty poo, the vomit, the diarrhea." Dominic said he was also to receive meal preparation and light housekeeping. "But there's always an excuse as to why they can't." He said he'd had an argument with a PSW because, instead of preparing a meal and tidying the house while he was in the shower, she had sat on the couch and watched TV. Dominic had requested other workers on many occasions, but he had had a series of workers with whom he had not been able to build a relationship. His experience vividly conveyed the downside of a reliance on favors for clients, but this was evident for several people we interviewed.

Nearly all the workers spoke of providing some services as a "favor" or of giving a little "extra" to some clients some of the time. Only three workers (out of fifty-two) never mentioned succumbing to the strong pull to provide favors to clients when presented with unmet need. The vast majority of workers gave examples of staying over their scheduled time, and two-thirds explicitly mentioned instances of doing so unpaid at one point or another. Workers explained how they often stayed over paid time to finish the basic bodywork because there was insufficient time to do it in a way that embedded the necessary relational work. For example, referring to the one-hour shifts, Leah said: "It's harder to do it when you have a, like, older person who cannot get up in the morning. And it's just no way. What you gonna do? Leave in the middle? And you can't rush them." A few people stayed over paid time to socialize with clients and framed it as a choice that they made outside of employment, on their leisure time. Some workers said they did favors because they felt clients valued their work. However, the most common reason workers gave for doing favors was that, knowing clients did not have other help, they felt obligated to stay.

Workers also did favors for clients because they perceived clients to have influence over their labor market security. Only a handful of workers explicitly linked doing favors to keeping a given client or gaining hours. This reflects the widely accepted viewpoint by workers, clients, employers, the state, and society that workers do this work because they are caring people.[33] Yet those brave enough to make this link in our interviews made strong statements. Several referenced how the ability of clients to complain and ask for a new worker pressured them to give favors. For example, Kela relayed a familiar "funny situation" in which clients would say they had already had their bath and would ask the worker instead to clean the house. Sometimes she called the office and told them the situation, but she got varied responses from the supervisor. "Sometimes the supervisor will say, 'Well, as she has had a bath, you know, help her.'" With little consistent direction from supervisors, other times Kela tried to negotiate directly with the client to say, "You know, you agreed for somebody to come and *assist* you with a bath. . . . And if you know you don't want [to] do that, tell her you don't need the bath. Tell her you need somebody to do housekeeping." However, this strategy was risky because the client might request another worker in hopes of getting one who would help more with housework. As Kela suggested, "Some of the workers, not only with my company but other companies, they *do* it because, say, okay, if I don't do it, I lost them—two hours." Vanessa recounted: "Many of us have reported [unpaid work], and maybe the supervisor is trying, but I don't think she listens. . . . I don't think [the government] knows. I mean, they know but they are not listening to you. It takes more than an hour." Only five home care workers felt the agency would pay them if they informed the agency that they needed to stay to finish the work, and one of these referenced a dire emergency.

Many workers spoke of rescinding favors once given. Workers generally did so by asking the agency to relieve them of a client with high needs. Carol described a client who would regularly ask her to go shopping with her, requiring getting on and off the bus, regardless of the weather, which would go beyond her scheduled time. When the client suggested she come for less time the next day, Carol "stuck it out" for a while longer, but then the client started to ask her to do more "extra things," and the extras got further removed from personal support, in Carol's view. For example, the client asked Carol to help clean a room she was renting out, which was clearly beyond the state-funded service, but Carol continued to feel obligated to help, as she described. "I did it because I care. You know, who else is going to do it for her?" Given ongoing requests, she explained, "One day I just said, 'I can't do it no more,' finished my shift with her, and that was it." For Carol the straw that broke the camel's back was the sense that the client was taking advantage of her kindness and being disrespectful. She felt the client was "quite difficult and quite miserable," but she tried to "lighten her day" even though she "put up with a lot of abuse." "[The client would] boss me around . . . be grumpy." Explaining her decision to tell the agency that she no longer wanted to go to this client, she said, "I treat people how they treat me, and I couldn't take it no more." Carol's experience was not unique. Half of the workers interviewed spoke of giving up a client for a reason related to the time-versus-task conflict.

In this context of a state-sanctioned and agency-condoned economy of favors, workers doled out gifts to some clients but not others. Nearly three-quarters of the workers reported both giving favors and resisting doing so. For example, when she first started this job, Tala stayed over her scheduled paid time in order to "pacify" upset clients because "you can't just leave them" and since "compassion sometimes has a tricky way." But by the time we interviewed her, Tala was adamant that workers should tell their supervisor if the client consistently did not want body care but asked instead for housework, "because otherwise if you did that, she's gonna ask for you to do that again." Tala said the agency would then report this to the government to revise the care plan to indicate that she only needed help with housework. Yet, since this service no longer included funding for housework, "sometimes [the client] will lose the hours or sometimes she'll get decreasing hours." This means that Tala would also lose hours. It is not surprising, then, that sometimes she did not tell her supervisor but threatened the client with doing so. A caring economy of favors is under strain not only due to rationed funding but also to racialization.

Racialization and the Trade-off between Employment and Respect

Racialization of the labor market also fueled tensions at the intimate labor process level. The majority of clients we interviewed were white and Canada-born, while most of the workers were immigrants from a range of countries in Asia, Africa, the Caribbean, Latin America and eastern Europe, demographics that fit with the Toronto population.[34]

Most managers said they would not tolerate overt discrimination. However, their willingness to allow complaining clients to switch based on subjective reasons allowed racialized preferences to come through the back door. Consider this quote:

> When a client calls and says I don't want someone of a color or nationality, we really go back and say, "We don't discriminate on those grounds. . . ." But what we find is we then get a call a week later, and they say, "I don't like her because she doesn't clean my bathtub properly." . . . Then we won't question it because it's a care or service issue.[35]

These agencies were bound by the Ontario Human Rights Code, which prohibited discrimination on the grounds of race, nationality, and citizenship. Yet this manager, like others in for-profit non-union agencies, followed the letter but not the spirit of this law.[36] Most of the white clients we interviewed did not express explicitly prejudicial views in the interview. Nevertheless, racialized tensions surfaced regardless of intentional harm.

Perhaps surprisingly, many workers seemingly accepted clients' labor market flexibility, through the ability to request that a specific worker not come back, even if the reason was racial. For example, Caribbean-born Tanice said: "I've been on two cases, I walk in, 'Oh, we didn't know they was gonna send me a girl like you.'" Tanice explained client racism in that "some of them are from the old country. They don't know better, and they weren't educated enough . . . Some people never have a Black person come into their home." Yet, she insisted, "we're only human." Tanice said that if a client did not want her in her home, the client called the office and said that she wanted another girl: "Not one like this girl." When asked if the employer honored the client's racist request, she said, "I'm pretty sure. I never follow up on it. . . . But I think they try to, because why would they want to send another Black girl to that place to irritate them?" Tanice insisted on the humanity of Black people in our interview but also consented to the customer service logic, even when explicitly racialized. Why?

Many workers consented to clients' racialized labor market flexibility in order to protect themselves from racist treatment at the intimate level. Vanessa, who was born in Guyana, said: "If it's necessary, they wouldn't send you back. I am not comfortable with this patient, they have been very rude and use profanities and, you know, racial, and things like that." In cases of significant, racial verbal abuse, Vanessa positively evaluated the agency's strategy to not send her back into an environment that made her feel unsafe. Similarly, Black, U.K.-born Clare felt that "if someone doesn't want me in their home, you shouldn't be there. There should be no coaxing, because anything can happen." Clare's comment that "anything can happen" suggests that a threat to her person could come from being forced into an isolated space with a racist client. If a client has hurled a racial slur or overtly said they did not like the color of a worker's skin, or even when a client's illness, age, or disability meant that one became aggressive, it made sense that workers would "choose" labor market insecurity.

Not all workers of color recounted explicit racial slurs, fears of violence, or overt rejection, but most discussed being treated like a servant. For these women, the expectation of cleaning when it was no longer part of the job was a racialized experience. Tanice recounted how some clients asked her to clean because they did not want her to "touch them personally ... or they might flinch when I go to touch them, they might pull away." Instead of bodywork, some clients "want you to vacuum ... want their roof fixed . . . bring out the dust cloths, the Windex, and the furniture polish . . . things that are not even close to personal care," to quote Caribbean-born Wenna. It was not only the tasks clients asked them to do but also the way clients asked workers to do them that was racializing. For example, when asked if she had ever experienced racism on the job, Liling, who was born in mainland China, said that sometimes clients would just say "'Hey, come here!' They don't call your name." In such situations, workers did not want to go back to that client. One client had asked Rosalyn to mop the floor, and when she said that was not in her job description, he told her to get out of his house. Rosalyn, who was a nurse in the Philippines and a live-in, contract domestic worker her first several years in Canada, complained to the agency. Rosalyn knew going in that other workers had had this same problem, but she took the client because she needed more hours. Only after several workers complained and Rosalyn went "personally to the office" did the agency act on the matter by phoning the client's government case coordinator, who relayed the complaint to the son, who spoke to the father and told the agency they would not ask Rosalyn to mop again and asked the agency to send her back. Yet Rosalyn declined to go back to the client "because there were these bad things that happened on the first time." As these examples suggest, workers of color spoke most extensively about tensions at the intimate level.

These examples and others too numerous to report underscore how the possibility that agencies would send a new worker rather than mediate tensions, albeit contingent on a number of factors, could push workers to "choose" between labor market security and a more intimate security of person. Can unions offer an alternative to this cruel trade-off?

The Challenge of Social Unionism

If unions are to improve workers' conditions in contract employment, they must reject a narrow business unionism focused only on workers' issues at the workplace in favor of a more social unionism that links economic and social justice issues also in the political realm.[37] Service Employees International Union Local 1/HealthCare began organizing home care workers in the late 1980s and represented the majority of unionized workers in Toronto. Social unionism was the "official discourse" of SEIU Canada, although practices of business unionism were still evident.[38] SEIU had some success in augmenting home care workers' security through social unionism at the labor market level.

Toward Labor Market Security through Social Unionism

The union tackled workers' labor market security by targeting both the state as funder and the agency employers to improve compensation, including hourly wages, pay for travel time, and benefits. Members' views were in line with this strategy. For example, union steward Vera explained how, when one employer said it did not have money to pay for travel time, "89 percent of workers were ready to go on strike just to improve our working condition. . . . And then they decided to go to our government for some financial help."[39] The union sought to address employment insecurity by targeting the state for reform of the service delivery model.[40] Union members identified the contract agency model as a source of their employment insecurity. Steward Danielle spoke positively of the union for its role in halting the competitive bidding system that so often put people out of work. Members also identified the agencies' hiring of them as casual workers as a source of their insecurity. The union also aimed to make temporary and part-time work more expensive to limit it, for example by bargaining with the agency employers for equality in benefits between full-time and part-time workers.[41]

The union framed its effort to improve labor market security as connecting quality care and quality work. It aimed to link an inside game of lobbying politicians to an outside game of engaging stakeholders.[42] Alliances with client groups have been very broad, short-lived, or recent.[43] For example, the SEIU local was a member of the Quality Care Alliance (QCA), a loose coalition of diverse stakeholders, including for-profit and nonprofit employers, senior's organizations, related charities, family support groups, government representatives, and individual seniors, family members, and workers, that was active between 2010 and 2012. The QCA sought security with flexibility at the labor market level through a PSW registry, a living wage for PSWs, and continuity of care for clients.[44] In 2017, the union also helped start the Ontario Caregiver Association, where they worked with service providers (like Red Cross), some client organizations (like the Multiple Sclerosis Society of Canada), and families to advocate for improved access to support unpaid caregivers.[45] Some workers we interviewed were open to coalitions with recipients to improve compensation. For example, Maribel felt clients could "speak on [workers'] behalf" to bring more value and recognition to the job. Yet others felt that while this might be a laudable goal, it would be difficult to put into practice due to the inability of the clients to "come out" and support workers, to quote steward Sarah. Workers' views on alliance with clients regarding employment security was also mixed. Leah suggested that an alliance between workers and clients could encourage clients to give positive evaluations of workers to the agency, thus supporting employment security. Yet others were critical of what they perceived as the union's acceptance of client flexibility, given its impact on their employment security. For example, Maribel said, "I think we don't have a union" and explained how she came to hold this view: after she complained to her supervisor that a client had cancelled service for the day and the supervisor had told her to contact the union, but the union had not advocated on her behalf. She explained: "They said there was nothing wrong. . . . They said that the client has the right to cancel the service." Maribel countered: "I *know* they have the right to cancel the service, but this is not right!" Indeed, addressing tensions with clients was difficult, given an enduring legalistic, bureaucratic unionism that was woefully inadequate in these decentralized contract services. This is starkly evident when we look at the intimate labor process.

The Negative Legacy of Business Unionism at the Intimate Level

Social unionism drove much of the union's effort to challenge labor market insecurity, but business unionism—legalistic, bureaucratic, staff-driven servicing of workplace problems—was also evident here.[46] Union officials recognized that client-worker relationships were strained, with tensions and problems that did not so clearly come from inadequate funding or the contract agency model, like verbal abuse, covert racialization, or sexual harassment, but they did not have a clear strategy to address them. The Quality Care Alliance pushed for standardized education and certification of PSWs, and the Ontario Caregiver Association sought support for family caregivers, but these coalitions did not address tensions in the labor process.[47] When asked if the union tried to regulate relationships between workers and clients, union officials described this as a legalistic procedure that was hard to maneuver given the individual home worksites where one might not even know her steward.[48]

The lack of strategy to address tensions with clients at the intimate level weakened workers' support for the union. For example, Aneta evaluated the union positively for its effort to improve labor market security. However, she also expressed the desire for a group separate from the union with which workers could discuss workplace issues: "We never discuss any of our problems because we don't have too many meetings. And we don't know each other." Aneta emphasized how they might address tensions with clients collectively, such as union meetings. Similarly, May felt that the union had improved compensation but did not help workers address problems with clients. She envisioned an alternative organization that would address worker-client differences: "One group to defend us, [to which] we can bring our issues, you know, our concerns about the job, what we will face every day. You know, dealing with the clients. Yeah, someone that sees us." Similarly, Chejtel felt that the local did not pay sufficient attention to home care workers within the larger union structure. She said: "We are a little part of some *big* union." Indeed, this is a big local that includes all personal support workers in the province, including those working in hospitals and long-term care facilities (as well as some nurses). Union steward Clare linked being treated like a maid to the widespread devaluation of care work:

> They refer to me as "the cleaning lady." . . . A lot of workers really feel that's why the way we are looked upon in society or in the health care organization is that *you* are really just at the bottom of the list. . . . And when you really think about it? Yeah, we are. We are. Because we don't truly have the support we should have. . . . We don't have the recognition that we should have.

Clare, despite her position as a steward, did not think the union helped workers with daily problems. "I believe I can stand up for some that are afraid to or [don't] know how to. Because of SEIU I do that? Absolutely not." Clare argued that workers were only assisted when individual union stewards, like her, who genuinely cared about coworkers' well-being, made the effort to help them resolve workplace problems. In this way, Clare had "become the union," which was a key goal of unions seeking to engage their members.[49] But she also criticized the union's capacity for improving the conditions of home care workers. "I really thought the union would be . . . an entity that looks after workers, so workers have a true sounding board." Clare's views echoed those of Aneta, May, and Chejtel: the union did not sufficiently support home care workers to address their unique tensions with clients in the labor process.

In this context, several union members felt workers and clients had different interests. For example, Tanice said: "We have different issues and different needs and different wants." Natalia linked this idea of different interests to conflicts in the labor process. "Clients are one side; we are on the other side. . . . We work for them, but it doesn't mean we work *with* them, because most of the time they look at us as like we are their maid. Very little number of people look at us as their equal." As these quotes suggest, the legacy of business unionism, focused on a legalistic approach to workers' issues at the workplace, undermined the potential of the union to organize for security with flexibility, especially at the intimate level.[50]

Home care was distinct from both IHSS and DF in that agencies were the direct employers. But these agencies did little to challenge the insecurity of individualized employment relationships and only contingently responded to the clients who requested flexibility. Clients' willingness to complain was shaped by their age, ability, and class. Agencies indulged clients' requests to switch a worker if clients couched them in relational terms and if the agency was able to produce a new worker when the client needed one; yet the latter was contingent on workers' availability, which was limited by casual employment contracts. Agencies did not assist clients or workers in navigating tensions at the intimate level. Instead, they chose to overlook a precarious economy of favors.

In home care, like in DF and IHSS, workers and recipients used relational skills that limited the discomfort of receiving and providing intimate bodily support. As in DF and IHSS, the state did not fully account for relational work in its funding, yet unlike in these settings, in home care the direct employers did not value this labor either. The agency employers only recognized workers' formal skills, narrowly defined around standard body tasks, through the personal support worker certificate. And they officially required only superficial emotion from workers, meaning the minimal amount necessary to respectfully accept the direction of the client or the client's family. Both the state and the agencies knew that deeper relationships developed but provided little support to workers or clients to navigate them. One might think home care clients would do less relational work than DF self-managers or IHSS consumers, since home care clients could get a new worker from the agency. Indeed, if the worker exerted expertise to the point where they were disrespectful, some home care clients asked for another worker, but others, especially poor, elderly, immigrant women, suppressed their emotions.

In home care, funding was even more out of sync with people's needs than in DF and IHSS, and this generated serious time-versus-task tensions. In this context, workers had little support negotiating the mismatch between a medical funding model and a client's long-term needs, and clients only had official influence within a narrow range of tasks directly related to their ailing bodies. Workers did extra tasks as a favor, sometimes on unpaid time, because they saw need and felt respected when they filled it, as was the case in IHSS and DF. Agencies rarely paid workers who stay over scheduled time because the government did not reimburse them for that time, as was the case in DF and IHSS, but here the government rationed hours to the bare bones, cutting funding for housework and even basic bodily support. This context undermined the willingness of workers to give extra care as a favor, which we saw in DF and IHSS and previous studies.[51] As still-needed housework tasks became major points of tension, the important relational work that made bodywork caring was undermined too. The economy of favors here was under strain.

Analyzing both sides of the care work relationship, and placing it within agency rules as well as government policies, underscored how tensions stemming from distinct facets of oppression emerge in the relationship. For instance, home care clients, like IHSS consumers, mentioned feeling uncomfortable receiving personal body care from a new worker, so they sometimes asked workers to do housework instead of helping with personal care. Yet in a context where housework was rationed out of the job, workers increasingly experienced this request as treating them like servants. The racialization of the labor market, largely along lines of white clients and workers of color, increased this tension. Not all workers of color recounted explicit racism, but most felt they had been treated "like a maid," which they linked to a history of racialized devaluation of women of color. Agency policies of sending new workers to problem clients until they got a squeaky wheel who insisted that something be done pushed workers into a trade-off between security in the labor market, through sufficient hours and income, and security at the intimate level, through respectful working relations. This churning affected clients negatively too by limiting their ability to get comfortable enough with workers to accept intimate bodily help. The negative impact of the economy of favors on both workers and clients underscored the need for new models of collective organizing.

SEIU's social unionism in Ontario attempted to link agency employers to the state in order to push for labor market security. Its success in augmenting compensation and reforming the delivery model rested even more on formal (parliamentary) politics than did the early social movement unionism through alliances with consumers in California. This reflected the fact that the hurdles were not as great in Ontario as they were in California, where coalitions with consumers were necessary to pass new legislation to make unionization possible. SEIU Ontario's success was also shaped by the reality that labor there had a seat at the table with the Liberal provincial government. For example, unions and workers centers were together able to push the Liberal government to reform the Ontario Labour Relations Act (OLRA) and Ontario's Employment Standards Act to protect precarious workers better. The resulting Fair Workplaces, Better Jobs Act of 2017, or Bill 148, reformed the OLRA to once again give home care workers "successor rights" that would protect their jobs if the employer that was contracted with the government changed.[52] Bill 148 reformed the Employment Standards Act to define travel pay between clients as work time subject to fair pay, and to secure their right to pay for public holidays, vacation, and severance.[53] However, in 2018, Ontarians narrowly elected a right-wing populist premier, Doug Ford, who quickly introduced legislation to repeal Bill 148, which his majority government passed as Bill 47, or the Making Ontario Open for Business Act.[54] Thus, like in the preceding chapter, the analysis here underscores the inability of a thin social unionism focused on formal politics to bring labor market security to precarious workers and emphasizes the importance of deep engagement with members and coalitions with recipient groups. Most of the home care workers we interviewed expressed solidarity between workers and clients and conflictual relations with the state and agencies. This suggests that more workers would support deeper alliances with recipients vis-à-vis the state as funder, engineer of the service-delivery model, and regulator of labor standards than was evident in union strategy.

The more profound and too oft misunderstood danger of a thin social unionism is that when workers feel their union does not help them address their particular issues in the labor process, they fail to support it. At the intimate level, SEIU in Ontario was no closer to figuring out how to augment workers' security than SEIU in California. The union implemented a new member development program in 2017.[55] More emphasis on member development could shift workers' negative experiences of a social unionism primarily focused on the political realm, but only time will tell. Part of the problem, which was also evident in L.A., is that organizing at the intimate level requires different strategies than does organizing for labor market security, and organizing at both of these levels is very labor-intensive. Furthermore, unlike in L.A., community-based immigrant groups were not filling the void in Toronto.

In home care, a medical model that rationed funding to narrow bodily tasks drove much of the contingency of flexibility and limits to security, and this in turn shaped union strategy. In the next chapter, we examine agencies of a different type: those within the independent living model whose funding is more in line with recipients' needs and where both workers and recipients have the backing of social movements. How do nonprofit, unionized agencies that also have consumer representation shape workers' and recipients' efforts to gain flexibility and security?

BARGAINING FOR SECURITY WITH FLEXIBILITY IN TORONTO'S ATTENDANT SERVICES

Gord—a white, Canada-born man in his twenties with cerebral palsy—directed several men to help him multiple times daily with the majority of his activities of daily living through Toronto's attendant services. Like in Toronto home care, agencies, not individuals like Gord, hired the workers. Yet, unlike home care, all the agencies were nonprofit. Jeff was among a cohort of Black Caribbean-born men who entered this sector in the mid-1970s and early 1980s through social networks with immigrant women. Since then more recently arrived immigrant women and men from African, Asian, and Latin American countries have entered the sector. Workers' social networks, together with the non-competitiveness of these relatively well-funded nonprofit services, facilitated unionization and upgrading of the job, in turn encouraging men to stay in this line of work along-side women.[1] On the surface, this context encouraged agencies to provide worker security but limit consumer flexibility, but the relationship between flexibility and security was more complex.

Gord and Jeff, and other consumers and attendants, as they were called here, recounted doing considerable relational work like others profiled in this book. Gord said that not all attendants followed his direction: "[They don't] take it as it comes." Yet as a consumer representative on his agency's board of directors, Gord also described how the board was working to clarify the job description around a flexible set of daily living tasks. Similarly, Jeff said the relationship with consumers was "not always smooth." Jeff had helped unionize his workplace, and he explained how the union was key to pressuring agency management so that today, "If they have a consumer that is not willing to compromise, then they [management] have to deal with it." In this context, relational work was done not by individuals in an attempt to keep the employment relationship intact but rather by collectivities with the aim to compromise on tensions at the intimate level.

In home care and IHSS, we saw that the union was able to win some flexibility with security but only at the labor market level. Could collective representation on both sides in Toronto's attendant services, through the board and the union, facilitate flexibility and security at the intimate level? Based on previous studies, I expected management to prescribe rules about how workers should feel in line with the agencies' altruistic motivation to support independent living.[2] What I found was that management actions were shaped not only by the independent living movement philosophy but also by the union, with key implications for flexibility and security. In attendant services, agency managers required relational work from both consumers and attendants to negotiate a mutually respectful employment relationship, and they stepped in to mediate when necessary because there was collective worker and recipient pressure on them to do so.

Context: Independent Living and Contract Agencies

Ontario attendant services were a variant of community-based independent living services for people with physical disabilities, services developed in the mid-1970s. Here I focus on the social support living units (SSLUs), which were accessible and affordable housing units linked to services available twenty-four hours a day, seven days a week. These supportive housing buildings generally housed twelve to sixteen people with disabilities plus able-bodied people. The services included both pre-booked periods, usually in the morning, at lunchtime if the consumer was at home, at dinnertime, and at bedtime, as well as help as needed in between bookings. Despite centralized services, SSLUs were not institutions, and services were individualized. Some people, such as those with spinal cord injuries, required several turnings or other help at night. In between booked services, consumers who were at home could call down to a staff office to ask for assistance with other things, such as putting on a coat so one could go out, picking up a stick that one used with a computer, or helping one go to the bathroom. In Ontario, all the agencies providing attendant services were nonprofit.

The Ontario Ministry of Health and Long-Term Care funded attendant services through the Toronto Central Local Health Integrated Network (LIHN).[3] These services were not means-tested, but the majority of recipients were poor, given the pervasive intersection of poverty and disability. Among the consumers we interviewed, there were roughly even splits between people with university degrees or some college and those with high school. The majority, however, had little to no labor force experience, while others were in temporary and part-time work. Roughly half of these non-elderly disabled consumers within Ontario attendant services were men. Like direct funding (DF) self-managers, most attendant services consumers were single and did not have children, although a few had some help from parents or siblings who lived close by.

Attendant services were defined broadly as help with activities of daily living (e.g., transferring and bowel routines) and related services (like food preparation, laundry, and shopping), as in the other programs that operated within the independent living model—DF and IHSS. Unlike in DF and IHSS, however, people did not hire or manage their own workers, but they did need to be able to direct their own services. Self-direction was defined as knowing, and being able to communicate to the attendant, what tasks one wanted the attendant to perform, when, and how.[4] People applied for attendant services through Centre for Independent Living Toronto (CILT), which assessed applications for basic eligibility and forwarded them to the service-providing agency picked by the person. Service-providing agencies reviewed applications and asked for updates or an assessment interview. Service providers made decisions to offer services based on eligibility criteria, individual needs, and available funding.

These services received better government funding than direct funding and home care. Among the SSLU consumers I interviewed, most received over twenty hours of pre-booked services a week, and several were close to the maximum, which was nearly double that.[5] In addition to booked services, people had shorter, on-call visits throughout the day or night (or both). Furthermore, funding was flexible in that it was based on a certain amount for a given consumer, but agency managers said they had the discretion to allocate more or less to an individual as needs changed in a day or over time. In this context, most consumers felt their own hours were sufficient. Yet both consumers and managers felt there was insufficient funding to raise attendants' wages and limit turnover. Indeed, most SSLUs had a wait list.

In attendant services, like in home care, the legal employer was a single agency. Yet, unlike in home care, here all the agencies were nonprofit. They ranged from large established organizations with multiple functions, such as the March of Dimes, to small ones that just provided attendant services, like Nucleus Independent Living. In the early 1980s, at least one agency in this sector tried to argue that the real employer was the individual receiving services, which would have rendered the workers "domestic servants" in labor legislation, with no right to unionize like in DF, but the Ontario Labour Relations Board ruled otherwise.[6]

The majority of agencies in this sector had collective representative for both consumers and attendants. Most of the agencies in this sector were unionized and only one in my sample was not. Local 40 represented the majority of workers in Toronto attendant services, so I focus on this union here.[7] All but one SSLU agency in my sample had consumer representation on its board of directors, while several also had additional committees or more informal groups or meetings in which consumers could give input. This reflected the broader population of attendant services agencies. The outlier was a large, long-standing organization developed through a charity model that predated the independent living movement and provided a range of services beyond personal support. Consumer representation in these agencies ranged from 60 percent of consumers on one board of directors, including the positions of president and vice president, to two general member positions on another board. The main role of the boards was managerial—liaising with the Ontario Ministry of Health and Long-Term Care over funding, setting policy, and overseeing an executive director—rather than involvement in day-to-day operations. However, the boards also intervened in serious conflicts at the intimate and labor market levels.

Security and Inflexibility at the Labor Market Level

In attendant services, managers worked hard to practice an independent living philosophy that supported consumer direction without labor market flexibility policies. Agencies did not schedule or assign attendants to consumers based on personality, compatibility or other subjective criteria used by DF self-managers, IHSS consumers, or private-sector domestic employers.[8] One exception to this lack of labor market flexibility was that they did accommodate a preference for women receiving services from women and men from men. Instead of labor market flexibility, managers developed rules around problem solving and conflict resolution, as described by one manager:

> I love doing this because it's all about problem solving. . . . The consumer has responsibilities under our contract. One of their responsibilities is to come to the table and try to resolve [issues]. It's their home. If they say, "I will not have Bill in my home," that's their business. . . . But that doesn't exclude our responsibilities to gainfully employ Bill. Let's say that Bill was a full-time staff person and a portion of his twelve-hour shift is there because of John the consumer and John refuses to have Bill in. Guess what? If John doesn't come to the table and find some

resolution, then John is effectively saying, "I'm canceling my services" whenever Bill is in.[9]

As this quote suggests, managers recognized conflict between consumer flexibility to decide who provided services and attendants' labor market security. In the SSLUs, full-time workers and part-time permanent workers, the latter of which were the majority, had guaranteed hours. Given this worker security, coupled with agency's commitment to consumer direction of services, managers in this model viewed conflict resolution as a key part of their job. One part of this comprised rules that required consumers to engage in relational work, to "come to the table," with the threat of canceling services as the alternative. Employers also required workers to engage in relational work. As one attendant, Albert, explained: "Our policy states that we are supposed to be capable of riding the wave. You know, like being able to work with different personality styles." Agency rules were not rigid but focused on process, requiring direct negotiations between consumers and attendants first. If this dyadic relational work did not suffice to resolve a conflict, however, workers or consumers could go to management for conflict resolution. And agency rules supported workers' security.

Workers' labor market security in attendant services was evident not only in job security but also in good wages and benefits, due in large part to unionization. The government set the minimum wage for all personal support, but unionization recognized seniority and allowed for consistent wage increases.[10] The union also negotiated prorated extended health benefits and better sick and vacation pay than in employment standards legislation for part-time workers.

Consumers did not make hiring and firing decisions, but in most agencies they had input into them. Sometimes they sat on hiring committees with management, and sometimes they were asked more informally and infrequently to attend an interview and give their views on whether they thought the candidate would be suitable for this type of work. During the workers' three-month probation period, consumers were generally surveyed about new attendants, and their views could inform whether a person was fired at this stage. For example, Gord recounted that "there was one person who didn't make the cut, and all of us agreed; it was during orientation." After the three-month probation period, however, firing had to show significant cause, given protections in Ontario's Employment Standards Act, which the union enforced through a collective agreement.

Interviews with consumers revealed the prevalence of conflict resolution over switching workers. White, Canada-born board member Ryan said requests for service with respect represented an issue investigated by supervisors.

> If you are not comfortable because you don't feel safe, you don't feel comfortable in terms of personality, the way they are following your

directions, you talk to the coordinator, and it's determined at that level whether you have a valid issue. And, you know, in many cases they try to do some conflict resolution.

In this context, workers had leverage to resist consumers' efforts to choose particular workers.

Union officials spoke of the de facto employer role played by the consumers in terms of preferences for certain workers and scheduling of shifts and the difficulties this could cause for workers in cases of discriminatory consumers. The union tried to limit the negative effects of consumer requests for flexibility in terms of reduction in hours or firing, through the collective agreement. A union official described their strategy to get language in the collective agreement ensuring that seniority determined hours. Still, such language in the collective agreement did not diminish the need for enforcement. The union official explained that when a worker lost working hours, they could file a grievance.[11] In short, managers did not usually value the seniority system as a principle of fair allocation of employment, but the union compelled them to accept it.

Lack of flexibility for consumers largely translated to workers' security at the labor market level. For instance, one Caribbean-born woman, Zoe, recounted that a consumer with "very complex care" refused to allow her to be trained to provide this care, even when the supervisor organized the training. This made the worker feel "inadequate at [her] job" and like she was not "pulling [her] weight," because the other workers had to do this consumer's "heavy" routine all the time. Yet the consumer's labor market flexibility was only temporary. Zoe explained that one day there was no other available worker so the consumer "had no choice" but to accept Zoe. Zoe felt: "From that day on, I think she saw me differently. Thinking that, 'okay, yeah, she knows what she's doing; she's capable; she can handle her job.'" The union's enforcement of policies limiting consumers' labor market flexibility not only supported workers' job security but could also cajole consumers into treating workers with respect. How did collective support help workers and recipients bargain for security with flexibility at the intimate level?

Bargaining for Security with Flexibility at the Intimate Level

Consumers and attendants bargained over the key tensions of time versus task and knowledge versus skill. These tensions emerged more frequently in attendant services than in the other programs since they could not be avoided through firing, as in DF and IHSS, or through a contingent labor market, as in home care.

Here agency policy encouraged compromises, and collective backing gave workers and consumers the ability to bargain.

Compromising over Knowledge and Skill

Agency managers supported the independent living philosophy, which called for recognition of people's embodied knowledge and emphasized the importance of attendants not making decisions for consumers. As one manager said, referencing the 1960s slogan of the IL movement: "In a way, you shouldn't say this, but we're just there as their hands or their feet but not their brains."[12] Yet agency managers qualified this seeming objectification of workers as the extension of consumers' bodies, as did this manager. They also recognized the importance of workers' and consumers' relational work as skill by requiring it and by providing support when dyadic relational work was insufficient.

Attendant services consumers rejected standardized skills learned in medical settings and recognized the importance of embodied skills, as did direct funding self-managers. Consumers felt attendants should not take over, speak for them, or make decisions on their behalf. Sometimes they echoed the IL movement slogan. For example, Audrey said, "[They are] your hands and feet, but they are not your mind." Through this emphasis on their minds, consumers asserted their need to define their unique needs. As Jane insisted, "I don't necessarily like something the same way as someone upstairs does, or downstairs or down the hallway. Each person is an individual and should be treated that way." Others emphasized more of a partnership that explicitly recognized the importance of workers' relational skills. For example, Pamela rejected an interpretation of IL philosophy as incompatible with committed, smart workers. "But you are not a robot; this is why I need a person with a brain, who does teamwork with me, who's proactive and takes pride in their job. [Otherwise] I could get a trained monkey." Pamela and others realized that flexible care required also recognizing that workers developed skills on the job. Indeed, attendants viewed "not taking control" as "the hardest part in the job," thus requiring the greatest amount of skill, to quote Danni. This sentiment from Danni and other attendants echoed the importance DF personal attendants placed on following consumer direction, but here workers had collective backing.

These unionized attendants felt empowered to resist seeming objectification and to assert their embodied and emotional skills. Referencing the Berkeley origins of the independent living movement, David said: "I'm not just, as I've heard said from the California thing, arms and feet or hands and feet. . . . When I read it, I went, 'That's really insulting.' I said, 'The interaction between myself and my consumer requires my mind, my heart, and for me a higher purpose.'" David said that if he were to take this slogan to its extreme he would make the consumer "micromanage" him by asking him excessively detailed questions throughout the shift: "Where do you want me to go? Where? Tell me, exactly where?" Here David described a resistance scenario mentioned by other workers and consumers. Instead, David explained, "I don't want to be micromanaged, but I also don't want to manage them either. . . . We have to dance together. We want to be comfortable and enjoy; then there's give and take and mutuality." For David and others, mutual respect was possible in this setting, but it required ongoing relational work, which was facilitated by union protection.

The knowledge-versus-skill tension was perhaps most evident in the realm of health and safety. Legislated health and safety protections for workers could conflict with legislation supporting consumers' self-direction. For example, one manager said that if the agency hired someone with a PSW certification, it "pretty much [has] to de-train them on certain things. Because—I'm quoting the Ministry of Health—in any kind of facility such as nursing homes, hospitals, et cetera, there's no such thing as self-direction. Here, that's what it's all about." The manager elaborated that the Long-Term [Care] Act gave a bill of rights to consumers that included their ability "to decide what, when, where." Yet managers also had to contend with the Occupational Health and Safety Act, which gave certain rights to employees, like "the right to refuse work that they believe will endanger their health."[13] Given that these agencies did not rely on standardized training from long-term residential care (LTRC), this was a key area where management required compromises on both sides.[14] Some managers had significant experience that helped them adjudicate this conflict. Others brought in occupational therapists (OTs), particularly when faced with different interpretations by consumers and attendants of whether a certain way of lifting was safe. Consulting an OT was not the same as valuing abstract professional expertise over a consumer's own bodily knowledge. Instead, OTs provided an assessment of the specific consumer and attendant transferring in a certain way in a particular home environment.

Attendants' experiences showed the importance of mediation by managers in the area of health and safety. For example, when asked if she could suggest doing things a certain way, Zoe said it depended on the consumer. "Some consumers are really headstrong. . . . You might do something that is unsafe, so . . . you try to tell them, and they take offense. And turn the other way." Health and safety issues included potential (and real) back injuries, consumers' smoke-filled home workplaces, and sexual harassment.[15] Again, there was the need for collective backing.

Disagreements over whether the consumer's apartment was a home or a workplace made the enforcement of health and safety by unions difficult. Whereas the union argued that it was a workplace when the worker was there, management argued that it was a home first—thus limiting access to health and safety representatives, shop stewards, and union representatives. As one union official said: "I can't necessarily waltz into someone's apartment and say, 'This is a workplace, and I think that we need to do an inspection.'" As a result, the worker generally had to tell the consumer when one felt uncomfortable. The official thought that this was a "proactive way of dealing with it" but underscored that it might not work for everyone, like in instances of sexual harassment.[16] Union efforts to get employers to require consumers to attend training have failed.

Consumer representation, alongside attendants', is essential if the goal is security with flexibility at this most intimate level of the body. At one agency that, tellingly, had no consumer representation, the union tried to mandate that all consumers have ceiling lifts installed in their apartments. This was a routine practice in LTRC but not necessary for many consumers living in supportive housing. In contrast, in organizations with consumer representation on the board, ceiling lifts were debated hotly. For example, agency board member and consumer Emily insisted that there were "issues of health and safety for us, not just staff." She explained that some of the attendants thought that her transfer into and out of the bathtub was a health and safety risk and wanted to use a lift, which she felt she did not need. She claimed: "If you knew anything about the way I transfer, I am not physically being lifted by them. I am doing most of the work. . . . They are lifting my legs possibly, but they are not lifting my entire body." This consumer contrasted her knowledge of how her body worked—specifically the amount of her body weight she could lift—with standardized protocol to use mechanical lifts. Similarly, another board member, Pamela, rejected the agency's "threat" to put a lift in her apartment. Asserting her rights as a tenant of an individual apartment unit, and asserting that she was not a resident of an institution, she asked the housing manager if she was required to do this; when the housing manager said no, the agency relented. Consumers like Emily and Pamela did not have the only truth about the delicate embodied work of transferring any more than workers who called for mechanical lifts to protect their backs did. Collective supports on both sides were necessary to allow consumers and attendants to resist the imposition of one group's rights over another and instead to force compromise.

Compromising over Tasks and Time

Managers described their rules regarding what was done, when, and where based on time. Rather than a predetermined set of tasks, they expected attendants to do the personal-support-related tasks the consumer wanted done in the time they had, with a few limits. One manager captured the time-versus-task policy well. He admitted that consumers sometimes said things like "that's my shower booking." Yet he described how the agency worked "very hard at trying to get [workers] not to think that way, because the consumer can do whatever they want."[17] This quote emphasizes how the time-versus-task rule allowed flexibility in what was done and when. The funded scope of services put limits on what could be done, but attendant services had a broad scope. Managers interpreted these independent living supports as services that allowed the consumers to do what they would do if they were able-bodied, which could extend to help with visiting family or friends. Most managers felt that helping to entertain able-bodied guests or helping with housework responsibilities toward adult, able-bodied family members could be part of the job. These managers, however, facilitated compromises between attendants and consumers on the parameters of help with friends or family. For example, when asked about help with family members who come to stay, one manager said, "All that has to be negotiated with me." He elaborated, "We would definitely pick up after family members and do housekeeping, but then they [family] would have to be doing something as well," especially if the stay was more than a day or two.[18] This manager and others underscored how the time-versus-task rule was a policy of flexibility, requiring workers and consumers to "give and take" and facilitating their ability to do so. Most agencies said attendants could only refuse to do a task that was unsafe.

Consumers felt the time-versus-task rule was key to getting the necessary support for them to live a full life. For example, when asked who decided what was done, Ethan said he did but that sometimes attendants resisted. He relayed, "Let's say I want to clean up. He might say, 'I'm not here to clean up' and ask when the weekly housekeeping comes." Yet Ethan asserted his right to flexible help with cleaning. "But wait: it's my booking. In my booking, I can do whatever I want. I tell them to read the job description again. [Or] I say I'd call [the supervisor], and then they'll change." This example suggests that the agencies' introduction of a division of labor between a housekeeper position and the general attendant—supported by the union—could conflict with the agency policy of flexible tasks in the job description. Ethan needed to be assertive in this situation, by referencing the task flexibility policy. Others emphasized that the agency rules encouraging direct negotiation of tensions with attendants first, before going to management, encouraged them to do the relational work of compromising. As Ella said, if you do not try to work it out with attendants first, they feel you are "blowing the whistle" on them with management. As a result, consumers also needed collective backing.

Consumers described the importance of collective representation in supporting their flexibility. Gord said that some attendants saw the description of the consumer's usual preference in a given booking and wanted it to be "followed to a T," so they would know what their tasks were. Yet through the board, consumers were "slowly working on maybe getting these descriptions taken out of the book-ings" so they could emphasize the importance of flexibility. Emily said that at her agency the board members discussed key tensions—such as regarding help with pets. Emily herself did not have pets but felt that telling consumers how many pets one could have was a violation of their rights as a tenant. "You go to the Landlord Tenant Act, [and] stuff like that isn't even in there, and if you say a person can't have this or can't have that, isn't that sort of breaking a different type of law?" She asserted that the board ought to make more time to train new attendants on the independent living philosophy. More broadly, Jane admitted that, in one-on-one negotiations, "the attendants could say that whatever hap-pened, and there is no way to prove it." Thus, she emphasized the importance of the board investigating whether tensions arose for multiple consumers.

Attendants felt they needed a union in order to navigate the fine line between independent living support and servitude in agencies with consumer representa-tion. One union official described struggles with consumers over what the job entailed as comprising an issue of "respect and dignity in the workplace" that was above monetary issues in having prompted workers to unionize in the first place. This official elaborated that "because they didn't have the ability to speak up and challenge their employer, what they were faced with was doing things that were not necessarily part of their job," giving examples of picking up after consum-ers' able-bodied partners or teenage children and cleaning the whole house. The official recounted workers saying that if they tried to talk to their managers about such problems, "they just weren't getting anywhere . . . and then always the fear of losing their jobs." Neither the union official nor the workers the official referred to were looking for a standardized set of tasks. They realized there was "a bit of a gray area [in] how much work we do for able-bodied family members." It was also about how they were being treated by the consumer and the family. "I guess the able-bodied family members at times would be very verbally abusive to the workers," the official recalled.[19] The union tried to regulate the boundaries of the job through the collective agreement, although this was difficult. One strategy was to frame pet care as a health and safety issue that workers could refuse, while another was to negotiate a pet care policy in the collective agreement. The policy varied by agency, but the union's goal was to argue that it was not part of inde-pendent living, thus not part of this job.

With this collective backing, most attendants consented to the general time-versus-task policy, although most placed some limits on their consent, particu-larly after obtaining the security of unionization. For example, Caribbean-born Tina said, "Yes, it's fine," when asked if the consumer could request laundry or other housekeeping instead of personal support and elaborated on the flexibil-ity of tasks in home-based work in contrast to a strict division of labor. "They do have housekeepers . . . but if there's a bit of sweeping to do or washing the floors . . . again, you've got your time, and as long as you're not over, you know, you get it done. It's fine." Tina's tone, her pause when first asked about the issue, and the content of the answer all suggested acceptance of the time-versus-task rule, but there were clear boundaries to her consent based on how much house-keeping was required and how much time it took. Like Tina, other workers of color drew boundaries between care work and personal servitude.

The Intersection of Race and Disability

The vast majority of attendant services consumers in Toronto were white and Canada-born, while the majority of workers were immigrants of color. Consumers' limited labor market flexibility in this model reduced their ability to act on any racial preference through refusing services from immigrant attendants or attendants of color. Yet sometimes racialized preferences, often articulated as language needs, came up. Several consumers felt it was difficult to receive services from recent immigrants with what they perceived as insufficient English fluency. Complaints about the level of English fluency could be phrased as quality-of-care issues but could also be exaggerated and contribute to racialization. In addition to complaints about the level of English fluency, consumers also recounted explicitly racist preferences that were not tied to English fluency, usually relaying stories about other consumers. Yet given the inability to switch workers based on race, and even the unlikelihood of subjective preferences slipping in the back door as in home care, attendant services consumers could not easily realize racial preferences. Workers thus rarely spoke of formal "discrimination," but they did recount racialized tensions.[20]

In this context of labor market security and inflexibility, immigrant workers resisted racialized tensions at the intimate level. For example, Mexico-born Mercedes said that when she first started the job, "[One consumer] didn't like me because she says my English was no good. And she said she didn't like Latino people." This consumer told the manager she did not want Mercedes to work there, "but the manager didn't listen to her," and a consumer board member supported Mercedes's application. Mercedes was hired but described tensions with this consumer.

> She was making everything difficult for me. And I was sick and tired, and I spoke to her, and I told her to give me a chance to work. And I told her to have the chance to know me better, and . . . I don't ask her to like me but at least to give me a chance to work, and she has to know me

> before she judge me, right? And she went, "Oh, I'm sorry; I'm sorry," and after that she is very good to me.

Agency policy not only ensured the hiring of Mercedes but also supported her ability to gain a more intimate security in the labor process, where she would not be judged by race. Still, workers needed collective backing to enforce agency policy.

Workers underscored the importance of union support in the face of racialized tensions. For example, Caribbean-born Selina spoke of a consumer who "abused" workers, so management had talked to the consumer. But the consumer denied the accusations, which required workers to more formally protest, as Selina described.

> Well, they did not really believe some of what you were saying, but they get to find out that's really true because people were going to go to Labour Board and Human Rights because it was abuse. They give her time to think about the situation and have workshop on how you're supposed to deal with people, like respect, and the fear and everything, but it didn't work.

This example shows how managers' rules were necessary but insufficient. In some cases, attendants needed to take legal action, like going to the Ontario Labour Relations Board or the Ontario Human Rights Commission that adjudicated discrimination cases in Canada, and the union provided legal support. In addition, Selina said, if there was documented abuse of a consumer by a worker, "you're gone"—the worker would be fired. The difference from home care, however, was that a consumer lost services or an attendant lost one's job only if problems could not be resolved through formal conflict resolution and after significant investigation, with the backing of each side's representatives.

Local 40 recognized that consumer preferences could be explicitly or implicitly racialized. Its efforts to protect job security through the collective agreements and through grievances addressed the effects of racialized preferences, such as reduction of hours or loss of job. The union tried to address the root causes through antiracist education. A good example was its Resisting Abuse course. A union official explained that this course was developed because attendants too often put up with racist treatment because they felt the perpetrator had had such a difficult life due to disability. This course emphasized that while a difficult life could be a factor in bad treatment, mistreatment was still not acceptable.[21] In their collective agreements, the union won mandatory human rights and anti-harassment training for all managers and workers. Yet they had less success in involving consumers. Another union official thought that consumers did not come "because they don't think they are part of the problem." The official explained that the union suggested the agency require consumers to take some anti-harassment training before getting these services, but the agencies said they could not force them to do it but only encourage it.[22] In short, union officials recognized that consumers played a role in working conditions as de facto employers along with the agency as the legal employer. However, since labor protections were based on a factory model that assumed a direct relationship with a single employer, unions found it difficult to target both the legal and de facto employer through collective bargaining. In this context, their strategy was to redirect conflict to the agency. More broadly, the union tried to ensure that this job did not slip into one of servitude, yet they also sidestepped the complexities of the relationship, given the constraints of labor law.[23]

Collective support for consumers was also important because racialization was often unintentional and because disability intersected with race and immigrant status to shape tensions in this intimate body service. For example, board member Jane touched on subtle racialization through language tied up with the marginalization of disability.

> There are a lot of language barriers, actually. . . . Sometimes that's good because it teaches you about different cultures, et cetera. Sometimes it is frustrating, and sometimes the frustration can be called prejudice or whatever, but I think what needs to be realized is that all that we can do is tell people with our voices or whatever means of communication that we have, what we need. . . . When you are in the situation and the heat of the moment, people tend to misunderstand what you are trying to get across.

Similarly, board member Emily emphasized that communication was vital and linked to health and safety for some people, such as ventilator users or those with impairments affecting their speech. While consumers like Jane and Emily felt that their frustration with communication was misinterpreted by attendants as prejudice, attendants of color often experienced consumer frustration as disrespectful and as another example of racialization. Collective supports on both sides go some way to eliciting compromises over tensions in the labor process, but racialized tensions indicate the need for allied movements across the locations of race and disability.

The Promise of Social Unionism

Local 40 and its parent union Unifor viewed themselves as a social union that engaged not just its members on narrow workplace matters but also supported citizens on broader social justice issues.[24] In assessing how well this social union-ism supported flexibility and security, it is important to address both the labor market and intimate levels.

Security through Social Unionism at the Labor Market Level

Much of Local 40's efforts to augment workers' security in the labor market used standard union tactics: pushing for increased wages and benefits and job secu-rity through collective bargaining and strikes directed at the legal employers—the agencies. Yet union officials also recognized that the consumer and the state were de facto employers with influence over conditions. They thus modified their strategies in important ways.

The union tried to engage the agencies, which were all nonprofit, to bring in the state. For example, one union official recalled asking an agency: "How can [the agency] and the union work together on tackling and lobbying the gov-ernment?" The official saw this as part of social unionism "because not only is it about workers in getting additional funding, but we're also talking about the rights of people with disabilities, because we do a lot of work advocating for human rights."[25] Workers' experiences also illustrated how the state—as funder—acted as a de facto employer along the dimension of wages and ben-efits, requiring claims toward a broader public. Like home care personal support workers, attendants compared their work to that of care professionals and argued for more funding for wage increases. Local 40 was even more successful in bring-ing labor market security than SEIU was in home care (given the less competitive environment), and this, in part, shaped attendant services workers' more positive evaluation of their union. For example, Owen said he could think of no negative aspects of unionizing this type of work, and he underscored the importance of a social unionism that targeted the state. "As far as wages go," he said, "it's a sort of fall down from the government." When we asked if his union could help target the government, Owen said: "Yeah, definitely. I mean, you have to have a voice . . . otherwise they'll give as minimal as possible." Most attendant services workers agreed that the union gave them a voice vis-à-vis the government funder.

The importance of organizing consumers to support workers' labor market security was evident during unionization drives and strikes. Key to getting con-sumer support was the argument that low pay led to high turnover, which jeop-ardized quality services. This framing of the issue was similar to the "quality care, quality work" framing in home care and elsewhere, but in attendant services the union also directly engaged consumers. One union official described how before a strike they sat down to explain the issues with consumers one on one, issues like the difficulty of supporting a family with a single job on existing wages, because management was claiming that the union had unreasonable demands. The official recounted how "throughout the course of our strike, consumers were starting to come out on our picket lines, and they were starting to support us."[26] Similarly, attendant and union activist Jon described how some consumers initially felt, "Oh, you're striking me, eh?" So the workers "tried to explain that it's not you we're striking, it's the company. But they came around and started to understand." Such one-on-one organizing was also required for many of the workers, who worried about the impact of the strike on consumers.

The Limits of Social Unionism at the Intimate Level

This union viewed itself as practicing grassroots social unionism. Union officials used the term "grassroots" to emphasize participatory and democratic processes of representation and empowerment of workers.[27] Grassroots social unionism tackled workplace problems not only through the formal mechanisms of collective agreement language and filing grievances but also through critical education and politicization. As we have seen, this effort helped protect workers against unhealthy work and personal servitude and helped workers of color shield themselves against racialized abuse. Indeed, the attendants we interviewed were largely supportive of their union as a protective force in relation to agency employers (and, when necessary, consumers) at the intimate labor process level.[28] Attendants spoke favorably about the union's strategy to pressure the employing agency to mediate conflicts between workers and recipients. In addition, workers felt emboldened by agency policy requiring consumers to do the relational work to engage with them respectfully, a policy that the union enforced.

Most consumers also spoke favorably about their collective representation. Sixteen out of the nineteen consumers we interviewed from agencies with formal consumer representation felt they had some input, either through a board of directors or through other committees, into how managers ran the agency. For example, Emily felt her presence on the board was important to ensure that the balance of power did not tip toward workers after unionization. Some consumers emphasized not only the representational democracy of consumer membership on committees or a board but also the solidarity among consumers that fostered collective enforcement of agency policies, or changing policies if necessary. For example, former board member Gord said about consumers then on his agency's board: "A lot of the guys, you know, are your friends at a small place, so you talk, and they can take your ideas back. . . . As with all democratic politics, some of the great ideas do get lost. . . . What I can say is that at least there is dialogue, and it is accessible." Gord and others did not romanticize the influence of collective representation but expressed that it contributed to respectful negotiations with attendants and their union.[29]

Attendants and consumers have allied at the labor process level when an issue clearly affected both security and flexibility negatively. For example, union steward David said that one summer there were over one hundred unfilled shifts at his agency because of people calling in sick or going on vacation, and management was asking existing workers to cover the work in the same amount of time. As a result, David described how the workers "were ready to rise, not just strike but riot." He also explained how this speedup affected consumers since "that two-hour luxurious getup . . . was now 'you've got ten minutes, and, I'm sorry, I've got five more people to see.'" In this context, "the consumers advocated on our behalf," David said, so that any unfilled shift would be worth fifteen dollars an hour (at a time when the starting wage averaged fourteen dollars an hour). The extra money was divided among all the people who did the extra work. David said management agreed, but when they later tried to take this away both attendants and consumers "kicked up quite a fuss," and the union argued that this had set a precedent and planned to bring it to the bargaining table. Attendants and consumers also allied to reject the use of temporary agency workers. In our interviews, recipients complained about the use of temporary agency workers because they did not know who was coming in to do a highly personal routine. Workers also lamented that temporary agency workers had not developed the skill to do this intimate work, so they ended up continuing to shoulder the bulk of it.

Some issues, however, like racism or ableism, pit workers and recipients against each other more directly. Tackling these complex intersecting inequalities when they emerged in the relationship was a more difficult task, as we have seen. Most workers supported working out tensions in the labor process collectively with consumers, but they also felt that workers and recipients had different interests and needed their own space to discuss their unique difficulties. For example, Africa-born Peter felt the union helped "in protecting the workers" but also suggested the value of "having representatives of each group meet once in a while to talk about issues." Caribbean-born Zoe said such a forum could flesh out "your ideas of what the consumer's expecting from attendants and what the attendant's expecting from consumers." These workers envisioned a medium in which workers and recipients could develop mutual understanding. There were two types of doubts about the necessity and usefulness of a worker-recipient forum to address labor process tensions, however. First, a few white workers felt it was not needed because workers and recipients solved problems on an individual basis with support from management where necessary. Second, some racialized workers also did not support a joint venue for discussing issues but for a different reason. Evan, Kay, Jon, and Wayne, all Caribbean-born, suggested that it would be "stressful" or "hard," while Caribbean-born Tina felt it might get "too personal." These differences suggest the difficulty of building alliances to take on tensions at the intimate level.

Some recipients also had doubts about the extent to which they could ally with workers to resolve labor process tensions. Some former attendant services consumers felt that unionization limited their influence significantly, and this was a key reason they left for direct funding, thus underscoring the difficulties of creating and sustaining alliances between worker and recipient groups. Michael viewed the union as a key reason why workers in his former agency "wouldn't do anything." He said he had filed many "incident reports" but that they "never got anywhere, because the union was there." Although attendant services agencies supported flexible tasks in scheduled times, the union also pushed for more of a division of labor between housekeeping and bodily tasks, through specific housekeeper positions. More broadly, David thought that after the agency unionized it "became less receptive to consumer interests and concerns." Direct funding was "union-free," he said, and he felt that was why many consumers went on it, because they had "more say and more control" over how attendant services were operated. Indeed, such experience with and views of the union meant there was little support for alliances with workers among DF self-managers, especially at the labor process level. Overall these views suggest that unions need to do more work to engage with consumers around tensions at the intimate level and that they need to figure out how to organize and support workers within direct funding.

In attendant services, workers had considerable labor market security through relatively high wages, benefits, and job protection. Managers did not willingly support workers' security but rather the union pushed them to do so. This security coincided with limited flexibility at the labor market level in that consumers had little influence over which attendant helped them on a given shift. Nevertheless, attendants and consumers alike gave many examples of bargaining for flexibility and security at the intimate level.

In attendant services, like in home care, IHSS, and DF, workers and recipients did relational work in an effort to negotiate tensions at the intimate level. Like in home care, an agency mediated the direct relationship, but unlike home care managers, attendant service managers had rules that required consumers and attendants to do a form of relational work that entailed mutual respect. Attendant services agencies developed "feeling rules" for both attendants and consumers based neither on commercial motivations nor on altruism.[30] Instead, their process-oriented rules recognized the importance of flexibility for quality services and the link between respect and security at the intimate level.

Agency rules that recognized the embodied and relational knowledge and skills of both consumers and attendants, and that required consumers and attendants to bargain over the meaning of independent living versus servitude, went some way to supporting security with flexibility. When consumer and attendant efforts to negotiate mutual respect were insufficient to achieve compromise, attendant services agencies facilitated conflict resolution. The flexible "feeling rules" of these attendant services agencies embedded the social justice principles of two distinct social movements, the independent living movement and the labor movement. Unionization and consumer representation allowed both attendants and consumers to give input into agency rules. More specifically, the union and consumer representation empowered attendants and consumers vis-à-vis the agency, as well as in everyday interactions with one another.

Interviews with consumers, attendants, union activists, disability activists, and employers support the claim that, overall, attendant services included a process of collective negotiation marked by representative and participatory democracy for both groups and an outcome of compromises. Moreover, these interviews suggest that in unionized environments that also have consumer representation there are openings for change in the complex terrain of inequality where race and disability intersect. Yet there are some lingering difficulties. Consumers who left attendant services for direct funding felt they had insufficient flexibility and saw the union as one reason why. For example, union strategies to bring in more of a division of labor between housework and bodywork could limit the potential for valuing the range of activities to support daily living embedded in the broad independent living funding model, of which we saw glimpses in both DF and IHSS. Clearly, collective backing for both workers and recipients is necessary for security with flexibility. In the concluding chapter, I take up the question of what type of social movement might be best able to bring flexibility with security.

TOWARD FLEXIBLE CARE AND SECURE WORK IN INTIMATE LABOR

This is not a workplace. This is a home environment. [Personal support service] should not be invasive into one's living. It should be complementary. If it's complementary, how can that be unionized? Complementary is flexible . . . not my idea of what a unionized job is about.

Self-manager in Ontario Direct Funding Program, 2007

Part of the reason for the partnership between the union and advocacy groups is actually we provided very skillful Chinese organizers to do outreach and say: "have you heard of this great program that you don't have to send your parents to a nursing home, and you can have a family member be the care provider? We also have union protection. . . ." You also have to try to understand the demographic. How do you think the Chinese or the Russian or the Hispanic believe the provider should communicate with the clients? It might be totally different.

Chinese immigrant union and community organizer in California, 2015

Now that I have painted a picture of the distinct social inequalities faced by workers and recipients, and the tensions in domestic personal support—this intimate help with daily activities provided by mostly immigrant workers to elderly and disabled people—here I chart the potential for flexibility with security. This is no easy intellectual or political task as it requires recognizing the potential, but also the difficulty, of coalitions across difference. Some recipients interviewed for this book, like the self-manager from Ontario's quintessential independent living program—Direct Funding—quoted above, saw quality services as impossible with unions, holding the widely accepted view that unions cannot accommodate flexibility. Like some disability advocates in Toronto today, California disability activists were also initially skeptical of alliance with a union, fearing it would limit their flexibility. Yet, after years of coalition building, many disability advocates in California, along with seniors' organizations, allied with a union to create a new model of flexibility with security because it had become so difficult to recruit and retain workers, given their very low pay and lack of collective voice. What this partnership deliberately did not tackle, however, were the more tricky issues of flexibility and security in the intimate labor process—the decisions about what is done, when, where, and how in the home workplaces alluded to by the self-manager. Yet the evidence in this book underscores, time and again across the four cases, the importance of collectively negotiating at this level not only for workers but also for recipients. Unions also need to work with organizations embedded in immigrant communities if they are to connect with the many immigrant workers in this sector. The union and community organizer quoted above explained that partnership between unions and community groups was crucial to informing immigrant communities about how the newly unionized program could support not just individual workers but also the extended family, given that the program allowed hiring one's family member as a paid provider. The organizer also suggested that community-based organizations could be sites of developing understanding of how different demographic groups of recipients might relate to the people who provide this most intimate service.

My analysis in this book shows that an understanding of how gendered and racialized class inequalities shape intimate relations in the labor process, regarding what domestic personal support entails and when, where, and how the work is performed, is as important to worker security as fair wages, benefits, adequate employment, and other aspects of labor market security. Furthermore, taking seriously how recipients' viewpoints stem from their location within inequalities of disability and age, I have analyzed the conditions under which domestic personal support could be considered "caring" in terms of flexibility—meaning that what is done, when, where, how, and sometimes by whom is open to change and negotiation, with significant recipient input or direction. Charting the potential for flexibility with security requires both a comparative analysis of the levers that exacerbate or alleviate tensions between flexibility and security and expanded ways of thinking about and challenging inequalities.

Disability and Age in an Extended Relational Matrix of Inequalities

My analysis attends to workers and recipients in relation to each other as shaped by intersecting axes of inequality that work together to locate them in a matrix of power and privilege.[1] Intersectional analysis emerged from activists' experiences in social movements, so it is an important tool for charting not just inequality but also the potentials for progressive social change.[2] Key to this mapping of inequality and change is the notion that intersectional identities are not fixed but rather that the axes of inequality activated depend on the context. As I demonstrated in chapter 1, despite different class, citizenship, and nationality backgrounds, workers all entered a labor market stratified by race and gender. This reality shaped their work history, including entry into the most precarious segments of personal support, and it contoured their long-standing search for security. Recipients of social services experience a different "face of oppression" through marginalization vis-à-vis the state.[3] Specifically, feminist disability and aging scholarship theorize how the state and society devalue dependence and value independence.[4] Drawing on this work, I showed in chapter 2 how this reality shaped people's experiences of service provision and their quest for flexibility. With this framework, one can analyze how, for example, when workers emphasize their skill they do so not only as workers but also as able-bodied people whose assertion of expertise has implications for recipients' claims to knowledge about their bodies. And one can analyze how when elderly and disabled people ask for help with housework they do so both as recipients who are marginalized by their need for state supported cleaning but also, often, as white people embedded in race relations that have long structured the meaning of work provided for white households by women of color. In other words, expanding the matrix of inequalities to include not only race, class, and gender relations, which are the focus of most studies of domestic work, but also disability and age, brings to the forefront a more complex relational analysis.

Starting from the social relations between workers and recipients, one can map several unique combinations of intersecting inequalities. A comparison of inequality in domestic personal support and classic domestic work (private pay from householder to worker to provide in-home child care or housework or both) is useful because intersectional analysis has developed significantly by theorizing from the latter case. Yet domestic personal support workers are a more diverse group than classic domestic workers. This comparison first reveals that, in contrast to classic domestic work, in each of the cases in this book inequality between workers and recipients along the axis of disability, meaning the social relations that turn bodily need or impairment into marginalization, is at the forefront. The analysis of domestic personal support also makes visible inequalities in age, although these are not always as stark. In California, both in the Pilipinx case presented in chapter 4 and in other immigrant communities providing domestic personal support, many workers are past retirement age.[5] Yet still, recipients are older than workers; their experiences diverge not only in relation to disability but also because they are from a different generation. Age and ability are not inequalities domestic worker scholarship has contended with substantially, in large part because the "recipient" in their analyses is rarely the direct receiver (e.g., a child) but rather the indirect one (e.g., the employer mother).

The second and related way the combinations of intersecting inequalities in my cases of domestic personal support are qualitatively distinct from classic domestic work is that recipients of state-supported services are poor or at least not well off more often than not, making them similarly located to workers along lines of class. This is most evident in contexts where services are means-tested, such as the United States, as we saw in the Los Angeles IHSS case. Yet marketization and rationing in Canada have occurred as well, as we observed through the rationing of funding in Toronto home care. Even in Toronto attendant services, where there was little rationing and no means-testing, recipients were most often poor due to the correlation of disability and poverty.

To make matters even more complex, multiple combinations of how race, class, and gender intertwine with disability and age are evident across my cases of domestic personal support. In Toronto Direct Funding and in Pilipinx and other communities within Los Angeles IHSS, workers and recipients were usually similar to one another in relation to race and class, but in DF they were often both white and more middle class, while in IHSS they were generally both racialized and poor. In both IHSS and DF there was a clear preference among recipients for a worker of the same gender, especially for the most intimate services, although men could not always find other men to do this work. In Toronto attendant services, in contrast, the agencies guaranteed this gender preference so the interlocking of race with disability was at the forefront. Including cases of disability and old age support thus not only expands the types of inequalities considered but also extends the analysis of race and class from one between women to include relations between men. In contrast, in Toronto home care, agencies met women's preference for women workers, but they did not do so for men. This reflected not simply older men's lack of gender preference but also the for-profit organization of the program. Indeed, an extended matrix of inequalities needs to go beyond relations between workers and recipients to include the varied organization of domestic personal support programs.

Comparative Analysis of Personal Support Programs

With an expanded matrix of power and privilege, one can engage in comparative analysis that considers intersecting inequalities at three key levels of analysis: labor process, labor market, and state. One can also assess how unions and other labor and community-based organizations seek to contest these inequalities and mediate tensions between flexibility and security.

Tensions at the Labor Process Level

In order to analyze the levers that exacerbate or alleviate flexibility-security tensions, I start by comparing tensions at the labor process level across the four programs. The first possible tension is between recipients' knowledge about their bodily and emotional needs that drives their quest for flexibility in how they receive support on the one hand and workers' skills in relating to both bodies and emotions on the other. The second tension is recipients' appeal for a range of varying tasks at the times they need them versus workers' desire for the security of knowing what one's job entails.

I found the most positive scenario in Toronto attendant services, where both flexibility for recipients and security for workers were evident. Specifically, agency employers in this program both recognized and supported consumers' assertion of knowledge of the way their body worked and thus their requests for support in unique ways, yet they balanced this against recognition and support for attendants' skills in bodywork by providing on-the-job training of workers with particular consumers. They also mandated mutual respect, as was evident in their policies on conflict resolution. This active intervention of agency managers was important, given the potential for racialization of the time-versus-task tension especially. This case shows that agency management can support flexibility with security and holds lessons for other contract agency models. Yet my second contract agency case points to the need to examine varying types of agency management.

I found the most negative situation in Toronto home care, where neither flexibility for clients nor security for personal support workers (PSWs) was evident. Here agency managers provided very little training, even in the basics of body mechanics, and relied instead on often short PSW courses based on long-term residential care (LTRC), which was a very different context in terms of both recipient social location and work organization. Lacking the centralized workplace of LTRC, agency managers relied on the workers to identify risks to their health and safety in the home workplaces and provided little supervision or support. Managers decreased the chance of worker injury by disregarding clients' knowledge of their bodies and suggesting less risky options, like mechanical lifts, even when not necessary for a given individual. Emotional skills were also largely invisible, even though they were crucial to quality care. The time-versus-task tension was even greater. Agency managers and workers alike considered help with housework as a favor. Like in Toronto attendant services, in Toronto home care most clients were white, while most workers were not, and this tension over how much housework was part of the job became linked to workers' long-standing struggle for respect in a context of racialization. The difference was that agency managers did not mediate this tension in home care.

In the two direct provision programs, flexibility and security were more contingent on social location in a matrix of inequality, although in different ways. In Los Angeles IHSS, Pilipinx family and co-ethnic consumers and providers approached a version of flexibility with security at the labor process level. Consumers asserted knowledge of how their bodies worked but also expected services to reflect their cultural traditions. Both consumers and providers recognized Pilipina providers' gendered skills in helping with bodily needs and relating to people emotionally in a culturally sensitive manner. Overall, these consumers received considerable flexibility in the types of tasks they received, although the schedule reflected the providers' other jobs. One tension was the subcontracting of elder care, usually from husbands to wives, within the family economy. This is one illustration of how consumer flexibility and provider security were contingent on consensual family and ethnic relations.

In Toronto Direct Funding, the self-manager had the ability to shape interactions with workers the most. This is related partly to program design and thus provides insight into other models of individualized and direct funding. Yet social location also mattered. Given strict eligibility criteria, most self-managers were highly educated, white, Canada-born, middle-class people who had lived with disability for a long time. They were confident in their ability to communicate to workers how their bodies worked and how they should receive support; they were also skilled at the emotional work of building respectful relationships with workers in order to retain them. Self-managers' direct communication of the broad scope of the job also limited daily tensions over the amount and kind of housework. Personal attendants' security in this context, however, hinged more squarely on matching their social locations of race, class, and gender with those of the recipients. Many personal attendants in Toronto were white educated women with another full-time job in the personal support sector.[6] These personal attendants were able to negotiate respectful relationships with self-managers that recognized their on-the job development of specific skills through bodily routines and emotional exchanges with particular individuals, and they consented to providing a range of tasks on short or split shifts. The same is likely not true for recently arrived immigrants with precarious immigration status, some of whom were also working this sector. Now that I have summarized the degree and form of tensions across the four cases at the labor process level, I identify their origins not only in managerial rules and practices but also in labor market realities and state-level policies.

The Limits of Close Social Networks and For-Profit Agencies as Labor Market Intermediaries

The configuration of flexibility and security at the labor market level also varied, shaping flexibility-security tensions in the labor process in distinct ways. At the labor market level, I focused on how people were able to find and retain reliable workers and how workers could find sufficient employment for a secure standard of living. Most people needed assistance for fewer hours than that required for workers' income security, or their support needs were too intermittent for one worker to cover. Thus, most workers had multiple jobs, and most people received support from more than one worker. In flexible labor markets—whether flexibility accrues to individuals or organizations—people use two mechanisms to recruit workers and find work: labor market intermediaries (like registries) and social networks.[7] In this intimate sector, when permitted by the program, people more often turned to family, friends, or at least a recommended acquaintance when available, rather than go through intermediaries, but comparative analysis revealed the drawbacks of relying only on close social networks for recipients and workers alike.

In Toronto Direct Funding, individual self-managers hired, fired, and supervised and were thus not only able to communicate the contours of the job and how they would like to be helped but also to choose workers they felt were more likely to agree. They mostly found workers through peer networks or through workers with whom they had developed a close relationship when they received attendant services. The Centre for Independent Living Toronto (CILT), which housed the Direct Funding Program, did have a consumer attendant roster, but few self-managers used it. CILT had few resources to keep the roster updated, thus making it less useful for both self-managers and personal assistants than it might have been. The reliance on networks and the absence of an effective intermediary meant personal attendants faced considerable labor market insecurity: their employment depended on learning and accepting the routines and moods of specific individuals. If they failed, tensions were displaced to the labor market through firing or quitting. Without the option of a labor market intermediary, those workers who could not afford to quit might stay in unhealthy work relationships, thus undermining the potential for security and flexibility in the labor process.

The In-Home Supportive Services program in California, in contrast, attempted to address workers' labor market security in a context of consumer flexibility to hire and fire by requiring the program to have a nonprofit registry. Like the consumer attendant roster in DF, neither consumers nor providers were required to use the registry, but it did have the financial and organizational support of the program. Its existence addressed a pressing problem for many who found it difficult to find reliable workers, and the use of the registry by some workers was significant.[8] This was not the case, however, in many immigrant communities, including the L.A. Pilipinx community featured in this book. Instead, in co-ethnic care economies, consumers used family and ethnic networks to find workers who spoke their language and who could provide culturally sensitive services.[9] The Pilipinx case suggested that family and close ethnic ties provided a source of flexibility with security in the labor process. Yet some consumers lamented that Pilipinx workers did not stay in this line of work. This reflected their labor market position, given English language skills, education, and employment history in the broader care sector.[10] At the same time, women family members within care economies might stay in unhealthy care-work relationships because of gendered, intergenerational duty.[11] In these ways, IHSS moved toward flexibility with security, but it remained contingent on one's location within a racialized and gendered labor market.

In Toronto home care, clients and personal support workers theoretically did not have to worry about finding workers or work, but in reality their flexibility and security at the labor market level was also contingent on their social location. This was because the labor market intermediaries here were mostly companies seeking to turn a profit by doing little more than matching workers to clients. They therefore did not encourage changes in the match, but they did pander to the clients who complained the loudest. Yet clients marginalized by age, ability, class, gender, and/or race often put up with low-quality services. Another way in which flexibility and security hinged on social location was that, once a client did complain, agencies tried to honor even the most subjective reasons for a switch in worker, and this meant that racial preferences or, more commonly, implicitly racialized tensions over housework could slip in the back door. Agencies also treated workers akin to contractors with choice of client but no guarantee of employment, setting up a cruel trade-off between labor market security and a more intimate security of person in the labor process. Workers facing client racism might pick respect and safety over employment security. But what kind of choice is that? Workers who have security through other income are those who do well in such a system, but this reality is less likely for the majority of immigrant women in this sector.

By contrast, attendant services organizations operated not as matching agencies but more like traditional employers that managed and also invested in workers. Here workers had job security after a short probation period. As a result, consumers had little flexibility to choose who provided their intimate services. In this context, recipients and workers negotiated tensions in the labor process largely because agency management required them to do so as a condition of service or employment. This worked for most recipients I interviewed, but it is important to note that some consumers who had left attendant services for DF felt certain workers limited their flexibility over tasks and how they received services. This suggests the importance of multiple service models catering to different recipient populations.

Wages and benefits are other features of labor market security—necessary, although not alone sufficient. Home-based workers have long been at the bottom of the wage hierarchy in the personal support and broader health care sector in both Canada and the United States.[12] Yet Toronto workers had higher hourly wages than those in Los Angeles, especially those in the nearly entirely unionized, nonprofit contract agency model example of attendant services. Furthermore, workers in Toronto (including foreign-born permanent residents) had socialized health care, although it did not cover dental, eye care, or prescriptions for adults. In Los Angeles, many workers qualified for means-tested health care because they earned so little, but this was at risk of clawback as workers gained income security. Indeed, state policy shaped security greatly.

The Problems with Medical and Family Funding Models

The funding model for a given personal support program also shaped flexibility and security. It is not a coincidence that Toronto home care had the most negative outcome, namely, insecurity for workers and inflexibility for recipients. Here agency managers provided little support and relied instead on medicalized training that treated client knowledge as risk, made workers' emotional skills invisible, and intentionally overlooked the fact that many clients counted on unpaid favors from workers. One key reason is that it was cheaper for them to do so. The government introduced this commercial logic in the late 1990s when it allowed for-profit companies to bid for government service contracts alongside long-standing nonprofits. Today the few nonprofits left essentially operate like for-profits in order to compete, as elsewhere.[13] Tensions also flowed more directly from a medical funding model that rationed care through means-tested cleaning and an offloading of unmet need onto unpaid family members. In this context, workers rescinded favors once given. This was a highly precarious situation for clients, especially those who needed assistance with housework. It is perhaps not surprising, then, that this context was rife with conflicts, often racialized.

What was relatively new and implicit in Ontario home care—means testing and a family model—had always been the norm in California. Many more people in need in California rely on unpaid family or favors from friends and neighbors or go without, because they are caught between being unable to pay for long-term support and not being poor enough to qualify for IHSS. Nevertheless, for those people who did qualify, the funding model supported flexibility with security in the labor process in two ways. First, the state made a family model explicit by allowing people to pay even their close family members to be their providers. Second, whereas Ontario coupled an implicit family model with a medical model, California combined its explicit family model with an independent living model. Taken together, this hybrid family-IL model compensated a broad range of personal support, including housework. At the same time, however, funding levels for housework, especially for those who hired family, were insufficient to cover need in many cases. The Pilipinx case showed how the state could rely on ethnicity to solve this problem. On the one hand, by paying family members to help their parents, the state supported the ability of daughters to fulfil their filial duty and the ability of parents to receive culturally sensitive support, both of which were undermined by the need for daughters to earn in the United States. On the other hand, it reinforced inequalities of gender and generation within families. Similar dynamics were at work in other immigrant communities in California.[14]

In comparison, Ontario attendant services and Direct Funding had more universal funding, although long-term care was not subject to the Canada Health Act, leaving it to the provinces to decide on whether, and to what extent, to subsume the cost of socializing these services. As importantly, both DF and attendant services operated under an independent living model that had a broad definition of these services as activities of daily living, thus removing a key source of time-versus-task tensions exacerbated by the medical model.

In sum, both state policy and labor market structures shaped flexibility-security tensions at the labor process level. Yet this was not a set of static correlations. Instead, flexibility and security also depended on the level and form of social movements.

The Promise and Limits of Social (Movement) Unionism

How and to what extent do worker and recipient social movements and alliances between them help navigate tensions between flexibility and security? My comparative analysis suggests that security with flexibility in domestic personal support requires creative strategies because the process of achieving it must take place at the labor process, labor market, and state levels. Yet most organizing in this sector does not address the intimate labor process.

Recall that the most negative situation among my four cases for both recipients and workers was in Toronto home care, where neither group could count on flexibility or security at the labor market or labor process levels. Notably, this case lacked any type of collective representation for clients and, although some workers were unionized, alliances with client organizations were short-lived or recent. Social unionism focused on labor market security largely through formal politics, like efforts to challenge the precarity of subcontracting by mobilizing members to lobby government for better program design or fair labor standards, sometimes with recipient stakeholder groups.[15] The push for such reforms represented one version of a strategy toward security with flexibility, in that the union sought a regulation of standards within flexible employment relationships. But the election of a right-wing populist premier in Ontario in 2018 threatened these gains, revealing the limits of a state-centered social unionism. Furthermore, the union engaged little with workers on daily injustices in the labor process. Instead, a legacy endured of business unionism focused on legalistic grievance and arbitration procedures executed by staff representatives.

The attendant services case suggests what unions can do when shielded from competitive pressures and when they engage with the grassroots membership. Here we saw a social unionism at multiple levels. At the state and labor market levels, the union suggested allying with the (all nonprofit) employers to push for more funding but also engaged in strikes against those employers, as in home care and other contexts with contract agencies.[16] In addition, during organizing drives and strikes, worker and union activists reached out to consumers to explain the issues and garner their support. Social unionism also operated at the labor process level, although alliance between attendants and consumers here was more complicated because their interests were more directly at odds. Nevertheless, through the union and consumer representation on a board of directors or committees, consumers and attendants negotiated key tensions, like the ambiguous boundary between independent living tasks and domestic servitude and the tension between respecting consumers' embodied knowledge and recognizing that workers bring embodied and emotional skill to the job. These collectively bargained compromises hint at the potential of new forms of alliance politics. However, the union was not able to force the employers to mandate consumers to attend antiracism training, so racialized tensions remained insufficiently unaddressed. This shortcoming stems partly from the limits of a labor relations regime based on the factory model.[17]

These same limits are evident, and amplified, in Toronto's Direct Funding Program. Alliances are particularly important in individualized funding cases like DF where there is no entity intervening in the relationship between recipients and workers. Yet no disability-labor coalitions existed in DF. My research assistants and I asked self-managers and personal attendants if they thought they could work together to increase the quality of both services and employment. All the personal attendants supported having a union that allied with self-managers to push the state for sufficient funding, adequate employment, and better earnings— that is, social movement unionism. Most self-managers thought that higher wages or better benefits (or both) would result in higher quality services. Yet their support for alliance was lukewarm, in part because they associated worker organizing with overly limiting their flexibility in the labor process.

In California IHSS, social movement unionism moved toward a version of security with flexibility at the labor market level through alliances between labor and disability and senior movements targeting the state for the ability to unionize and increased wages and benefits, although they had to continuously defend gains against state cutbacks.[18] Yet the alliance never attempted to negotiate collectively the complex tensions at the labor process level. Internal democracy problems in the late 2000s revealed the depth of this problem, while external attacks on U.S. unions into the 2010s underscored the urgency of the workers owning their union. In a context of a thin, top-down social movement unionism, labor process tensions were either hidden under the surface, smoothed over by gendered obligations and ethnicity, or displaced to the labor market like in Direct Funding. There were some gains in employment security with flexibility. For example, the program had an advisory committee with joint consumer and union membership, and the union's collective agreement included a procedure for resolution of complaints about the registry.[19] The union also responded to discrimination against some immigrant workers by maintaining its own registry, which linked workers to jobs in the broader long-term care sector. However, none of the Pilipinx IHSS workers we interviewed had used the union registry, a nonuse also evident in other communities.[20] This is perhaps not surprising given the slight involvement of the union in members' daily labor realities. At the same time, when workers were individually motivated, and when they had the time to organize others in their community, there was room to push themselves into formal union leadership structures and to participate in protest and electoral politics.[21]

My analysis suggests that building the alliances between worker and recipient movements necessary for flexibility and security raises particular challenges for a democratic organization of domestic personal support.[22] Forming truly democratic alliances requires that the workers and recipients themselves have input into strategy based on their experiences in the labor process. Yet these experiences are highly varied and complex, based on multiple changing individual relationships between workers and recipients and shaped by intimate connections that are sometimes solidaristic and sometimes ridden with tension. Clare Stacey argues that home-based personal support workers craft a "caring self," given the relationships they develop with recipients and the little to no managerial oversight of their work, but suggests this caring self could be a resource to help unions connect with their members.[23] My comparative analysis both broadens and specifies this claim. Some workers and recipients interviewed supported alliance at the labor market level, but there was more ambivalence about alliances between workers and recipients to address tensions in the labor process. Where there was little racialized tension in the labor process, like in the California Pilipinx community, something like a caring self was evident especially, but not exclusively, among family providers. Here engagement with members would benefit from not just recognizing the gendered obligations within the caring self but also empowering women to challenge them. In the context of racialization in the labor process, as in Toronto home care, where the rationing of funding for housework fueled the tension between care work and servitude, many workers were critical of their union for not intervening to address such tensions, and some imagined an alternative organization that could better address workers' tensions with clients. In contrast, in attendant services, the union's effort to address racialized tensions through antiracism education, even if not successful in incorporating recipients, contributed to workers' view of their union as a protective force. Workers' engagement with their union in settings that also have recipient representation could help develop sites where workers and recipients feel safe hashing out differences and coming to compromises.[24] More broadly, the alliance between workers and recipients needs to take root at the intimate labor process level.

Toward Flexibility with Security through an Intimate Community Unionism

How does this comparative analysis point us toward more flexible yet secure domestic personal support? This work is a hybrid form: in-home personal support workers are "neither nurses nor maids," and their work constantly straddles the realms of paid and unpaid labor.[25] Personal support also brings together the worlds of labor and social service, complexly interlocking inequalities of race, class, and gender with those of age and disability that are experienced differently by workers and recipients—and recipients themselves are differently located in relations of age and disability. In order to reflect the unique realities of this work, I argue that we need an intimate community unionism that can organize workers and recipients in coalition across lines of difference to address problems at the labor process, labor market, and state levels.[26] My comparative analysis suggests that if we are to realize flexibility with security, we must recognize and mediate tensions in the intimate labor process stemming from complex intersecting inequalities; support and fund recipient- and worker-run, culturally sensitive labor market intermediaries; and implement a universal social funding model. To accomplish these objectives will require ongoing, deeply democratic,

universal social funding model

worker-recipient run, culturally sensitive, funded

labor market intermediaries

democratic   democratic

union-community alliances   union-community alliances

labor process tensions

recognized and negotiated

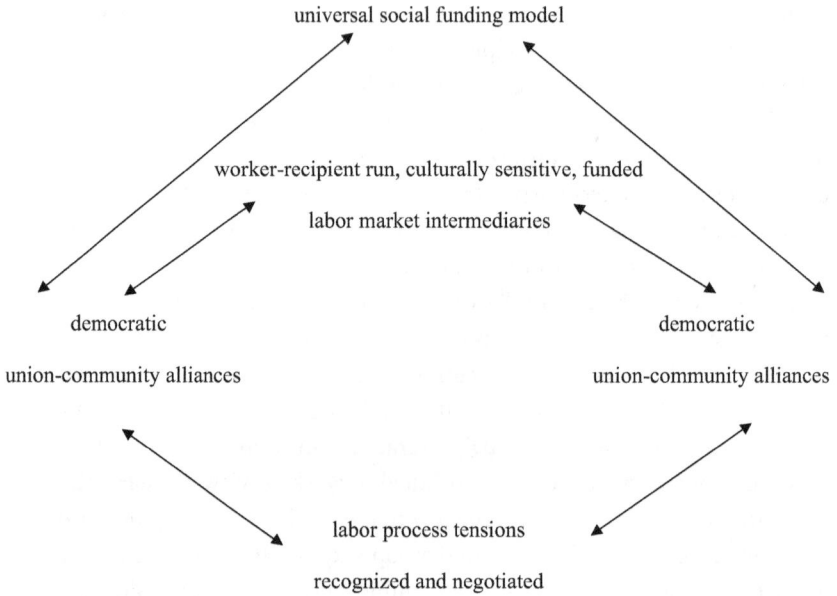

FIGURE 2.   An intimate community unionism

union-community alliances that cultivate grassroots leadership of workers and recipients (see figure 2). In what follows, I give examples of creative ideas and promising examples at each of these levels from my case studies and others to provide a glimpse of what an intimate community unionism could look like and accomplish.

A Universal Social Funding Model

My comparative analysis points to the need for a universal social funding model. This model would provide sufficient government funding to compensate people adequately to provide support with a broad array of daily activities, including assistance with bodily functions, emotional support, and housework. In order to truly value the people who receive personal support and those who provide it, we need to make it a public responsibility so that receiving personal support and some form of compensation for providing it is an entitlement of citizenship rather than charity, as others have argued.[27] This would require expanding greatly the compensation to family members who provide long-term care so that doing so is a real choice and not just a gendered obligation. Specifically, we need to make domestic personal support an entitlement under Medicare and the

Canada Health Act. Some scholars also call for universal rights not just to receive care but also to influence how one's support is provided, by extending programs like Toronto's Direct Funding that give people considerable flexibility.[28] More broadly, we must include the viewpoints of recipients and workers in program design and facilitate their ongoing ability to influence how their support is provided, in line with what Joan Tronto calls "democratic caring."[29]

How are we to accomplish this? A key step toward achieving such a transformative vision, as students of social movements know, is to frame it effectively. Care theorists argue that if we are to make care a public responsibility, we need to move beyond dichotomous thinking defined by the binary of dependence versus independence and instead recognize that everyone needs care (physical, emotional, or both), even able-bodied younger adults. Care is thus a relationship of interdependence.[30] At the same time, we need to recognize the ways in which care as an interdependent relationship is structured by, and infused with, power along lines of gender, race, class, age, and disability.[31] The difficulty comes in framing a politics that recognizes care—a concept that our society heavily imbues with gendered ideals of love, self-sacrifice, and devotion—in a way that acknowledges inequality and power. Some care scholars call for a joining of unpaid family caregivers, paid care workers, and care recipients in a "care movement" focused on the right to give and receive care with state support.[32] The need for alliance to increase the scale and authority of calls for transformative change cannot be understated, yet we should carefully consider how to frame it.

My analysis suggests that the hybridity of personal support labor and the complexity of inequalities in the sector mean that a social movement framed solely or primarily around care without sufficiently recognizing power inequalities could hinder alliances between workers and recipients rather than bolster them. Yet there is also tremendous potential in an alliance that recognizes power inequalities. For example, the coalition between SEIU and disability and senior movements around reforming the California IHSS program in the late 1990s and early 2000s recognized different interests stemming from inequalities of disability, class, race, and gender, as shown in chapter 4. Some disability activists used a frame of "ethical social justice" that was continuously aware of the dangers of fighting for social justice for oneself at the expense of another.[33] The union's frame was also not one of caring as in "taking responsibility for" but rather a more interdependent alliance in adversity or "the poor taking care of the poor," often within families.[34] It also had to contend with workers' gendered self-sacrifice linked to close relationships with recipients.[35] In these ways, the alliance in California in this period provides one way of thinking through a politics of interdependence that also recognizes power inequalities. Another way is evident in the new domestic workers' movement.

Starting from an intersectional approach that centers relations of race, immigrant status, class, and gender but goes beyond earlier domestic worker organizing by including age and disability, the U.S.-based National Domestic Workers Alliance (NDWA) frames its organizing as bringing recognition to "the work that makes all other work possible."[36] The NDWA organizing model is attentive to the unique combination of care and often racialized tensions in this type of work. This means recognizing that while some domestic workers have employers who value and respect them, "slavery by other names still exists in this sector."[37] The additional layers of complexity contributed by inequalities of disability and age, especially when the recipient is not the employer, are recognized in the Caring across the Generations campaign in partnership with NDWA and other organizations. This is a good example of a movement that encourages people to imagine and fight for policies that improve supports for elderly and disabled people and provide quality jobs and income support for the workers and family who assist them. Central to their proposed "care grid" is universal home care and the creation of high-quality home care jobs by increasing government funding for existing programs.[38] Yet the Caring across the Generations campaign has been criticized for overemphasizing love.[39]

If we are to win universal personal support, we also need a movement that engages the vast majority of people who do not qualify for means-tested programs. This requires recognizing how power inequalities pit marginalized groups against one another. As one California disability advocate said: "A lot of the times I think, *Well, why am I working?* you know, because a good portion of what I earn goes to pay my aide. . . . I can identify with some of these small business owners when they're talking about increasing the minimum wage . . . because I know that every time they raise the salary out there for attendants, that is more money out of my pocket."[40] This scramble for resources often takes place across social locations of disability, race, and immigrant status. While most vivid in the United States, Canada's erosion of provincial funding for home-based personal support could mean that more recipients will hire temporary migrant workers under conditions akin to indentured servitude, while others hire people with no citizenship status in Canada at all, under highly precarious conditions.[41]

In short, in order to push for a universal social funding model, we need a framing that accommodates complex overlapping and distinct communities of interest through a politics of interdependence that recognizes power inequalities. We also need to develop and fund labor market structures that operationalize complex intersectional interests.

Worker-Recipient-Run, Culturally Sensitive, State-Funded Labor Market Intermediaries

Study after study finds that labor market security—in the form of sufficient and predictable earnings and employment—is central to retaining workers in various types of intimate labor.[42] In addition, many studies emphasize the importance of fair labor standards across a broad sector, rather than directed at individual employers, in order to bring security to workers in flexible employment.[43] Finally, security with flexibility requires labor market intermediaries that provide opportunities for workers to find sufficient, fair employment through multiple jobs and for recipients to find high-quality yet intermittent support from several workers.[44] My analysis suggests that the development of sectoral standards and intermediaries need to have significant input of both workers and recipients and that they need to be state-funded.

One broad question we need to answer to move toward centering the diversity of workers and recipients' issues in domestic personal support is: what is the appropriate sector for setting standards and organizing employment? Some care scholars argue that we need to organize workers across a care sector encompassing elder care, health care, disability supports, and sometimes child care, provided by both professionals and the precariat.[45] Other scholars and some unions argue that long-term care and health care are unique sectors but still support organizing professionals with workers.[46] Both activists and academics base their call for sectoral organizing on the notion that more people united results in more power, especially if some of those people are relatively privileged. It is important, however, to understand the barriers to this strategy rooted in the class and racialized division of labor between professionals and workers, which organizing based on exclusive definitions of skill and credentials have reinforced.[47] Another way to go would be with an even broader grouping of intimate labor that includes tasks too often viewed by governments, society, and some professionals and their unions as ancillary to the core of care work, such as cleaning, laundry, and food preparation.[48] The notion of intimate labor encompassing housework, body-work, and emotion work is in line both with what most people need and with what most workers actually do in other people's homes—so a broad definition might be a first step toward recognizing the importance of all of these tasks. In addition, workers move across and combine various types of intimate labor, as illustrated in chapter 1, and thus need a range of labor market intermediaries.

In some subsectors of domestic personal support there are state-funded labor market intermediaries, but my analysis suggests that they too need to have the will and capacity to meet the need of diverse recipient groups and a multiracial workforce. For example, the registries in the California IHSS program were state-funded, but they did not provide sufficient language and cultural support to many immigrant seniors, making them less useful to workers in those communities. At the same time, organizations that are sensitive to recipients' language and cultural care needs often do not have the means to sustain effective registries. In California, registries operated by immigrant community-based social service organizations have thrived where state-funded and folded when funding was cut.[49]

Personal support workers need labor market intermediaries that both recognize their language and cultural skills and bolster their employment security. Worker cooperatives and hiring halls are two worker-oriented models that aim for security within flexible employment relations. In the private domestic work sector, worker cooperatives have been in operation for many years and continue to be a strategic choice of some domestic worker organizations.[50] Yet cooperatives vary in their emphasis on helping members get jobs for survival or fostering collective support to upgrade the job.[51] Unions operating in flexible industries, like construction, have long had hiring halls that provide their members jobs with unionized contractors. SEIU's Home Care Exchange in Los Angeles is a modified version of the hiring hall. But workers whose skills are under-recognized and devalued, like domestic personal support workers, have had trouble gaining enough control over the labor supply to advance employment security this way without government involvement.[52]

Labor market intermediaries need to have both significant input of workers and recipients and be publicly funded if the goal is security with flexibility. One tension here is the extent of power among various entities—like the government, worker representatives, recipient representatives, and employers who are not recipients—within the intermediary, since the balance of power shapes its goals and effects. In Ontario, the government funded a personal support worker registry with the aim of validating workers' education and training, ensuring recipients had high-quality care, and supporting employers to find workers and workers to find jobs. Yet unions were critical because the government initially put it under the leadership of an employer organization and because it established no fair way of reviewing complaints against workers, even while workers would be required to register in order to work for publicly funded employers.[53] Workers and recipients need to have input into the design of labor market intermediaries if they are to do more than support flexibility for agency employers and the state.

In recent years, unions, worker centers, and domestic workers' organizations have focused on broadening fair labor standards to cover flexible employment in domestic and care sectors with some success. Since home-based workers have long been excluded from labor standards legislation in North America or very minimally covered by it, their inclusion would symbolize a recognition of care work as labor worthy of state regulation. But there are still limits to the scope of their protection, underscoring the continued devaluation of labor through its association with unpaid women's work in families and with poor disabled and elderly people.[54] As one model, Australia sets minimum standards for wages and employment conditions in home care work through sectoral "awards" that, for example, require a pay premium for casual employment. However, these regulations have always been incomplete, and contracting out, amalgamation of many awards into one, and underfunding have resulted in a move toward informalization similar to what we see in North America.[55] Furthermore, it is difficult to enforce fair labor standards that do cover these workers if they must engage with legal bureaucracies as individuals. Some therefore call for legislation facilitating sectoral collective bargaining.[56] Writing in the UK context, Lydia Hayes argues that a sectoral collective agreement covering the adult social care sector would result in better enforcement because the workers, union, contracting government authorities, employer associations, and responsible employers would all have a stake in enforcement. She also suggests it would provide a framework for unions and disability and senior groups to ally to lobby the government for industry-wide funding to support good jobs and high-quality services, not unlike what we saw in California in the late 1990s.[57] My analysis suggests that workers and recipients' joint input into sectoral standards would be important for enforcement. Both sides also need to have a hand in designing culturally appropriate options to find work and services. For this to happen, alliances need to address tensions in the labor process.

Tensions Recognized and Negotiated in the Intimate Labor Process

Domestic personal support includes tensions, some of which stem from the funding model and the organization of the labor market but others that are not necessarily resolved through better and broader funding and labor market security with flexibility. We also need to recognize tensions that stem from different locations of workers and recipients within a matrix of inequalities, and balance the needs of both sides, but how? My analysis suggests that we need deeply democratic alliances between workers and recipients that negotiate tensions at the intimate level of the labor process.

It is clear that both workers and recipients need critical education, training, and support to negotiate tensions at the intimate level, but what kind and by whom? In California IHSS, one of the mandates of the Public Assistance Services Council (PASC) was to provide training to consumers in order to enhance the services. However, debates over training stemming from what I have termed the

knowledge-versus-skill tension ensured that consumer training was not mandatory. Disabled people have long had support from their own advocacy organizations, like independent living centers (ILCs), on ways to be a fair employer and
attain quality services.[58] Yet my analysis suggests that, despite such support, informality can creep in to individual relationships due to the complexity of labor
legislation in this sector and to the lack of enforcement. Alliances between recipient organizations and the labor movement could address these issues in creative
ways. For example, one ILC in Los Angeles that had a close working relationship
with the SEIU required any new consumers to go to the ILC's general orientation.
The orientation, offered in Spanish and English, gave tips on, for example, "the
attendants' role and the difference between them and a maid."[59] Hand in Hand,
a domestic employers' organization allied with the NDWA, also supports individuals so that they can be fair employers, including those employing elder care
workers. They provide similar advice as some ILCs on setting out expectations
in a written agreement. They also encourage individual employers to sign a "fair
employer" pledge, talk with other employers about it, and become a part of the
domestic workers' movement by, for example, contributing money to campaigns
for a domestic workers' bill of rights. One drawback of this approach is it relies
on employers' voluntary compliance.[60]

If the goal is security with flexibility, workers need critical education about
how the locations of disability and age shape people's quest for ongoing input
into their services, and they need training and support on how to negotiate this.
Questions of the amount and kind of training for workers, and who would provide it, have caused tension in labor and disability alliances. In Los Angeles, SEIU
and PASC, with input from some ILCs, jointly developed training modules for
workers in the early 2000s. However, when SEIU revised the training without
PASC input, disability advocates worried that the union was taking control and
that the training might become more medically oriented.[61] This example high-
lights the need for democratic alliances that negotiate compromises across different interests on an ongoing basis.[62] In Ontario, SEIU received government
funding to design a new PSW training project in the late 2010s, and the project
advisory committee included a home and community sector personal support
worker, a client receiving home care and her unpaid caregiver and partner, two
employers, and government observers.[63] Such efforts to consult representatives
of the various stakeholder groups are important, but they are not deep enough
to address many tensions.

What kinds of organizing models can engage deeply and continuously with
workers and recipients to address tensions in the labor process? Again, community-
based labor organizing provides inspiration. The National Domestic Workers
Alliance has a base in affiliate organizations across the United States whose goal

is not simply legislative reform but truly transformative organizing that builds leadership to push for broad and deep progressive change. Field director Lisa Moore explains how NDWA leadership development addresses the "trauma" of years of being told you have no worth, a message that comes from society, the state, employers, and parts of the labor and women's movements, and how healing from trauma "unlocks the true power of our base to lead," in no small part by building democratic organizations.[64] Asian Immigrant Women Advocates (AIWA) in Oakland is another illustration of workers' community-based organizing to advance the leadership of women workers. The main goal of AIWA, like of NDWA, is systemic social change. AIWA has designed a framework for leadership development among limited-English-speaking immigrant women in precarious employment, including domestic personal support workers. Based on AIWA's experience, it takes seven years to develop an effective leader.[65] The Workers Action Centre (WAC) in Toronto is another example of a grassroots organization engaging in long-term political empowerment of precarious workers to challenge the intersection of racism, sexism, and class inequalities.[66]

These are feminist models of community-labor organizing.[67] Sometimes they emphasize women's learned facility at relationship building and its importance in leadership. Always they recognize that leadership is something that is not inherently present or absent in people but that is in need of development. Feminist leadership development is found sometimes in unions, brought there by people with ties to other feminist organizing.[68] The feminist and antiracist politicization practiced by groups like AIWA, WAC, and the local affiliates of NDWA could build the leadership to ensure that immigrant women workers "have a seat at the coalition table," to quote one advocate.[69]

Worker centers or other community-based labor organizations could be sites to develop the leadership necessary to tackle the complex inequalities in this sector. For example, in the California IHSS model there were always limitations on how much the union could regulate the relationship between the individual worker and consumer.[70] From this viewpoint, just like worker centers in the past were able to boycott garment manufacturers while a union's hands were tied by National Labor Relations Act prohibitions on secondary boycotts, perhaps worker centers would have more leeway to address tensions at the intimate level because they are embedded in immigrant communities.[71] Indeed, AIWA started organizing Chinese and Korean immigrant women working in the garment and electronics industries and thus has a deep understanding of the complex relations between co-ethnic workers and employers who are intermediaries in a hierarchical system of employment inadequately coved by labor protections.[72] This kind of understanding, coupled with the trust from workers fostered by geographical, language, and ethnic connections, could make such worker centers places to address tensions in the labor process. However, one labor and disability advocate worried that a singularly focused labor politics could risk boycotting people in need and underscored that "any player who could bring power to the table" needed to recognize vulnerabilities on both sides.[73]

My analysis points to the need for a deep alliance between workers and recipients that recognizes the varying interests of each side in the labor process and hashes out mediated compromises. Democracy across difference takes ongoing commitment, perhaps especially when the state, economy, and society marginalize both groups. Relationships of trust arduously crafted by bridge builders organizing for labor market security with flexibility in California's IHSS in the late 1990s and early 2000s were not easy to sustain after the legislative win. Given the diversity of worker-recipient relationships in this sector, which are starkly evident in the various ways of structuring domestic personal support highlighted in this book, perhaps more attention needs to be given to decision-making and negotiating processes. Like feminist, community-based labor organizations, many ILCs have a notion of grassroots empowerment that works with people where they are to bring them to where they need to be to be able to push for rights and respect. In alliance with workers' associations with similar goals, they could at least recognize and negotiate tensions and hopefully come up with compromises in areas not resolved by more and broader funding or by well-funded, culturally sensitive labor market intermediaries.

Might community-based groups be sites of joint education and politicization of workers and elderly people? From the beginning, community-based immigrant organizations have been involved in forging connections between workers and elderly recipients in California, given the many immigrants wanting to hire their family. More broadly, community organizations in immigrant and perhaps other communities, including organizations serving seniors and civic and social organizations, could serve as places to build ties and mediate tensions between workers and recipients. A deep, feminist model of politicization through critical education and leadership development is key to unpacking the gendered underpinnings of tensions in families and communities of all kinds. Such organizing could couple the politics of framing this intimate work as indispensable with a deep and close-up analysis of interdependence at the micro-political level.

Imagine the power of such micro-level empowering practices if allied with the human and financial resources of large unions and with recipient social movements in a way that was democratic. We might conceive of a division of labor between local level worker centers, senior centers, and independent living centers on the one hand, and state-level alliances between unions and senior and disability organizations on the other.[74] The latter could focus on social movement action against the state for a universal, social funding model and for labor market security across a broad sector of intimate labor. At the local level, alliances could concentrate on the grassroots leadership development necessary to recognize and mediate gendered, racialized, disabling, and ageist tensions that manifest in the intimate relationships within specific subsectors, like agency-contracted elder care or directly funded and directly provided disability support.[75] Yet, from the evidence in this book, leadership development of workers on the ground would need to feed into broader mobilizations if they were to lead to progressive social change. Alliances between workers and recipients are bolstered by a frame of solidarity between them. Thus, addressing tensions between workers and recipients at the intimate level is not only difficult, time-consuming, and expensive but also might undermine the alliances necessary in targeting the state for adequate funding and essential to designing culturally sensitive labor market intermediaries and fair standards. Still, this does not mean we can sweep labor process tensions under the rug. The need to engage deeply and continuously with workers and recipients in domestic personal support is even more urgent given shifts toward right-wing populism in North America and Europe in the late 2010s that mobilizes anti-immigrant sentiment and villifies state welfare with real effects on the people who are the focus of this book. I hope the comparative analysis pursued here can help us to consider how to build deeply democratic alliances across multiple axes of inequality and at multiple levels—an intimate community unionism—to support both flexible care and secure work.

INTERVIEWS AND METHODS

For this book I interviewed 107 key informants who were knowledgeable about how personal support services were organized. These labor, disability, and senior advocates or activists, government representatives, and employers are listed in Table A1 along with the year I interviewed them.

TABLE A1 Key Informant Interviews

CODE	POSITION	YEAR INTERVIEWED
CALabor1	SEIU staff organizer in Los Angeles	2005
CALabor2	SEIU elected official in Los Angeles	2006
CALabor3	SEIU staff organizer in San Francisco Bay Area	2005
CALabor4	SEIU high-level staff in Los Angeles	2006
CALabor5	Community-based labor activist in San Francisco Bay Area	2015
CALabor6	Community-based labor activist in San Francisco Bay Area	2015
CALabor7	Elected member of a Labor Council in San Francisco Bay Area	2015
CALabor8	SEIU high-level staff in San Francisco Bay Area	2015
CALabor9	SEIU staff & community-based labor organizer in San Francisco Bay Area	2015
CALabor10	SEIU worker-organizer in San Francisco Bay Area	2015
CALabor11	Community-based labor activist in Los Angeles	2016 & 2019
CALabor12	SEIU high-level staff in Los Angeles	2016 & 2019
CALabor13	SEIU elected worker representative in Los Angeles	2019

(Continued)

TABLE A1 (Continued)

CODE	POSITION	YEAR INTERVIEWED
CASenior1	Senior advocate and community service worker in Oakland	2015
CASenior2	Senior advocate and community service worker in Los Angeles	2015
CASenior3	Senior advocate and community service worker in Los Angeles	2015
CASenior4	Senior advocate or community service worker in Los Angeles	2016
D1	Disability advocate in Los Angeles	2005
D2	Disability advocate from an independent living center in Los Angeles	2005
D3	Disability advocate from an independent living center in Los Angeles	2005
D4	Disability advocate from an independent living center in Los Angeles	2005
D5a	Disability advocate from an independent living center in Los Angeles	2005
D5b	Disability advocate from an independent living center in Los Angeles	2005
D6	Disability advocate from an independent living center in Los Angeles	2005
P1	PASC staff in Los Angeles	2005
P2	PASC staff in Los Angeles	2005
P3	PASC board member in Los Angeles	2005
P4	PASC staff in Los Angeles	2005
P5	PASC board member in Los Angeles	2005
P6	PASC board member in Los Angeles	2005
P7	PASC board member in Los Angeles	2005
P8	PASC board member in Los Angeles	2005
P9	Public authority staff in Oakland	2015
IHSSA1	Administrator from IHSS Program in Los Angeles	2006
IHSSA2	Administrator from IHSS Program in Los Angeles	2006
IHSSA3	Administrator from IHSS Program in Los Angeles	2006
IHSSS4	Social worker from IHSS Program in Los Angeles	2006
IHSSA5	Administrator from IHSS Program in Los Angeles	2006
IHSSS6	Social worker from IHSS Program in Los Angeles	2006
IHSSS7	Social worker from IHSS Program in Los Angeles	2006
IHSSA8	Administrator from IHSS in Los Angeles	2006
IHSSA9	Administrator from IHSS Program in Los Angeles	2006
IHSSS10	Social worker from IHSS in Los Angeles	2006
CCACS1	Social worker from a CCAC in Toronto	2005
CCACA2	Administrator from a CCAC in Toronto	2005
CCACA3	Administrator from a CCAC in Toronto	2005
CCACS4	Social worker from a CCAC in Toronto	2005
CCACA5	Administrator from a CCAC in Toronto	2005
CCACS6	Social worker from a CCAC in Toronto	2005
CCACA7	Administrator from a CCAC in Toronto	2005
CCACS8	Social worker from a CCAC in Toronto	2005
B1	Board member of an Attendant Services organization in Toronto	2006

CODE	POSITION	YEAR INTERVIEWED
B2	Board member of an Attendant Services organization in Toronto	2006
B3	Board member of an Attendant Services organization in Toronto	2006
B4	Board member of an Attendant Services organization in Toronto	2006
B5	Board member of an Attendant Services organization in Toronto	2007
B6	Board member of an Attendant Services organization in Toronto	2007
B7	Board member of an Attendant Services organization in Toronto	2007
B8	Board member of an Attendant Services organization in Toronto	2007
B9	Board member of an Attendant Services organization in Toronto	2007
E1	Attendant Services agency employer in Toronto	2006
E2	Attendant Services agency employer in Toronto	2006
E3	Attendant Services agency employer in Toronto	2006
E4	Home Care agency employer in Toronto	2006
E5	Home Care agency employer in Toronto	2006
E6	Attendant Services agency employer in Toronto	2006
E7	Attendant Services agency employer in Toronto	2006
E8	Home Care agency employer in Toronto	2006
E9	Home Care agency employer in Toronto	2006
E10	Attendant Services agency employer in Toronto	2006
E11	Attendant Services agency employer in Toronto	2006
E12	Home Care agency employer in Toronto	2006
E13	Attendant Services agency employer in Toronto	2006
E14	Attendant Services agency employer in Toronto	2006
E15	Attendant Services agency employer in Toronto	2006
E16	Attendant Services agency employer in Toronto	2006
E17	Attendant Services agency employer in Toronto	2006
E18	Home Care agency employer in Toronto	2006
E19	Home Care agency employer in Toronto	2006
E20	Home Care agency employer in Toronto	2006
E21	Home Care agency employer in Toronto	2006
E22	Attendant Services agency employer in Toronto	2006
E23	Attendant Services agency employer in Toronto	2006
E24a	Home Care agency employer in Toronto	2006
E24b	Home Care agency employer in Toronto	2006
E25	Home Care agency employer in Toronto	2006
E26	Attendant Services agency employer in Toronto	2006
E27	Home Care agency employer in Toronto	2006
E28	Attendant Services agency employer in Toronto	2006
E29	Attendant Services agency employer in Toronto	2006
E30	Home Care agency employer in Toronto	2006
TOUnion1	SEIU high-level staff in Toronto	2006
TOUnion2	CUPE elected worker representative in Toronto	2006

(Continued)

TABLE A1 (Continued)

CODE	POSITION	YEAR INTERVIEWED
TOUnion3	CUPE high-level staff in Toronto	2006
TOUnion4	SEIU high-level staff in Toronto	2006
TOUnion5	SEIU high-level staff in Toronto	2006
TOUnion6	Local 40, CAW high-level staff in Toronto	2007
TOUnion7	Local 40, CAW high-level staff in Toronto	2007
TOUnion8	Local 40, CAW elected worker representative in Toronto	2007
TOUnion9	SEIU high-level staff in Toronto	2015
TOUnion10	SEIU high-level staff in Toronto	2016
TOUnion11	SEIU high-level staff in Toronto	2017
TOUnion12	SEIU staff organizer in Toronto	2017
TOUnion13	SEIU staff organizer in Toronto	2017
TOUnion14	SEIU staff organizer in Toronto	2017
TOUnion15	SEIU high-level staff in Toronto	2018
TOUnion16	Local 40, CAW elected worker representative in Toronto	2001

CAW: Canadian Auto Workers (now Unifor)

CCAC: Community Care Access Centre

CUPE: Canadian Union of Public Employees

IHSS: In-Home Supportive Services

PASC: Public Assistance Services Council

SEIU: Service Employees International Union

Notes

INTRODUCTION

1. Glenn 2010; Martin-Matthews, Sims-Gould, and Tong 2012.
2. Lowell, Martin, and Stone 2010; Martin-Matthews, Sims-Gould, and Naslund 2010.
3. For exceptions, see Bourgeault et al. 2010; Martin-Matthews, Sims-Gould, and Tong 2012; Cangiano and Shutes 2010; Walsh and O'Shea 2010.
4. On "faces of oppression," see Young 1989; see also Bailey and Mobley 2019; Collins 2002.
5. Fine and Glendinning 2005; Fraser 1987; Garland-Thomson 2002; Morris 2001; Silvers 1995; Watson et al. 2004; Young 1989.
6. Labor scholars (e.g., Vosko 2000) critique the use of the term "flexibility," arguing that it is part of employer and neoliberal state discourse that disguises and justifies worker precarity. Yet they also analyze worker-led flexibility (e.g., Fudge and Vosko 2001b). See Cranford 2014a for a discussion of different types of flexibility. Here I develop an analysis of recipient-led flexibility.
7. Anderson and Shutes 2014; Bourgeault, Parpia, and Atanrackovic 2010; Cranford 2014a; Parreñas 2015; Williams and Brennan 2012.
8. See Michel and Peng 2012; Shutes and Chiatti 2012. Williams 2012 makes this point, but see Gottfried 2017 for an exception.
9. Cranford 2005a; Doty, Mahoney, and Simon-Rusinowitz 2007; Glendinning and Kemp 2006; MacDonald and Charlesworth 2016; Ungerson and Yeandle 2007; Trnka 2017.
10. Cranford 2014a; Doellgast 2012; Fudge and Strauss 2014; Vosko 2011.
11. Auer, Berg, and Cazes 2007; De Nanteuil-Miribel and Nachi 2004. Vosko 2011 (215–27) critically reviews proposals for a "flexible SER [standard employment relationship]" and begins to develop an alternative that could challenge global precarious employment by moving beyond the standard employment relationship as a policy norm while supporting gender equity and post-national citizenship. McCann and Murray 2014 begin to address the labor process level by proposing a model of flexible security in working time for domestic workers. See also Charlesworth and Malone 2017.
12. Cranford 2014b; Delp and Quan 2002.
13. I use the term "dignity" here as a synonym for "respect." Treating the terms as synonyms is common (see, e.g., Bolton 2007). Stacey 2011 argues that home care workers "find dignity in dirty work." Yet, although workers or recipients may seek to dignify, honor, or exalt both themselves and the other in the relationship in some situations, in other situations they might give less of themselves to the relationship, yet still act respectfully toward one another. To expect or give respect is thus a broader and more observable action than is dignifying or seeking dignity. The workers interviewed for this book used the term "respect," so I follow suit when referring to the workers and often when referring to the relationship—as in "mutual respect." I selectively use "dignity" when taking recipients' perspective, but many disabled recipients spoke of respect, as evident in other studies (e.g., Gibson et al. 2009).
14. Shakespeare 2000. See Kelly 2016 for a review.
15. Armstrong and Armstrong 2005; MacDonald and Charlesworth 2016; Shutes and Chiatti 2012; Ungerson 2004.

16. Cobble 2010; Fudge and Vosko 2001a; Kalleberg 2011; Milkman and Ott 2014; Rodgers and Rodgers 1989; Standing 2011.

17. Boris and Klein 2015; Ross 2013; Vosko 2000.

18. Boris and Klein 2015; Cranford 2014b; MacDonald and Charlesworth 2016; Ungerson and Yeandle 2007.

19. Cobble 2010; Fudge and Vosko 2001a; Smith and Neuwirth 2008.

20. Boris and Klein 2015; Cangiano and Shutes 2010; Cranford 2014a.

21. Cranford 2005a; Kelly 2016; Ungerson and Yeandle 2007; MacDonald and Charlesworth 2016; Trnka 2017.

22. Chun 2009; Cranford 2005a; Delp and Quan 2002.

23. Arat-Koc 1997; Constable 2014; Fudge and Strauss 2014; Stasiulis and Bakan 2005.

24. Goldring and Landolt 2011; Tungohan et al. 2015.

25. Glenn 2010; Parreñas 2015.

26. Aronson and Neysmith 1996; Cranford 2014b; Hondagneu-Sotelo 2007; Stasiulis and Bakan 2005.

27. Cranford 2005b. Glenn 2010 argues that there is continuity between domestic servitude—the dyadic relationship between mistress and servant—and paid health and elder care provided by organizations, in that workers' racialized social locations and precarious citizenship restrict their labor market choices. See also Aronson and Neysmith 1996.

28. Macdonald 2015 (153) uses "ethnic logics" to denote "strategies designed to match a certain set of desired services with the presumed characteristics of prospective employees" and examines ethnic logics in home-based child care work.

29. Diamond 1992; J. Rodriguez 2014; Kelly 2016.

30. Lord and Hutchinson 2003.

31. Camfield 2013; Clawson 2003; Cranford 2014a; Kumar and Schenk 2006. Union power has eroded in Canada, even in the public sector, and while there have been key gains in U.S. care work organizing, there is also regional variation in labor movement strength and differences in union strategies in the United States and Canada. Ross 2013; Milkman 2010 (1–2).

32. Armstrong and Lowndes 2018; Baines 2016; Burawoy 1978; Gottfried 1992; Leidner 1993; Romero 2002; Smith 1998.

33. Rivas 2003; Ungerson 2004.

34. Angus et al. 2005; Gibson et al. 2009; Meyer, Donelly, and Weerakoon 2007; Twigg 2000; Yamaki and Yamazaki 2004.

35. Zelizer (2010, 268–69) defines intimate labor as paid or unpaid work based on interactions that require one's particular knowledge about another and attention to that other from one or more people. This particular knowledge can range from secrets to bodily information, while attention ranges from taking out someone's trash to giving a bath. Intimate labor is thus a broader notion than emotional labor and goes beyond interactive service work. It is inherently relational, but this does not mean the intimate relation is practiced interactively.

36. Boris and Parreñas 2010 (8) use and extend the definition of intimate labor calling attention to the importance of the "daily praxis of intimacy."

37. The extension of the concept of "emotional labor" to different types of service work has been fueled through the use of a more general definition: labor requiring a worker to induce or suppress a feeling in order to generate a feeling or emotional state of another person (Hochschild 2012, 20). This definition has been applied to service sectors very different from the commercial services through which Hochschild developed the concept, including nursing homes (e.g., Foner 1995, 104–6). Hochschild later framed the contribution of *The Managed Heart* not as insight into the specific process of commercialization resulting in workers' alienation but as a more general understanding into the "pinch

between a real but disapproved feeling on one hand and an idealized one on the other" (Hochschild 2012, xiv). Yet this is closer to what she originally labeled "emotion work." Scholars have debated the form and effect of emotional labor in different sectors, arguing, among other things, that workers may derive some benefits from using emotions at work (Leidner 1993) and that Hochschild overstated the difference between unpaid emotion work and paid emotional labor and understated the amount of emotional autonomy workers have from employers (Bolton 2009; Lopez 2006). See Erickson and Stacey 2013 for a review.

38. Armstrong and Armstrong 2005; Bolton 2000; Cranford and Miller 2013; Erickson and Stacey 2013; Lopez 2006; Stacey 2011; Twigg 2000.

39. Baines 2016; Bolton 2009; J. Rodriguez 2014; Stacey 2011; Theodosius 2008.

40. Cranford and Miller 2013; Bolton 2009; Brook 2009.

41. Armstrong and Armstrong 2005; Stacey 2011.

42. Hochschild 2012. See also Erickson and Stacey 2013. This analysis of the meeting of emotions from the world of home and reason from the world of employment is in line with others' more explicit analysis of how care work bridges the "hostile worlds" (Zelizer 2011) of "work and care" (Ungerson 1999) or of love and money (Folbre 2012; Lan 2002; Stacey and Ayers 2012), and bridges love, labor, and welfare (Boris and Klein 2015).

43. Fuller and Smith 1991; Sherman 2007; Takeyama 2016. Cranford and Miller 2013 is an exception.

44. Aronson 2003; Gantert et al. 2008; Karner 1998; Piercy 2001.

45. Twigg 2000.

46. Meyer, Donelly, and Weerakoon 2007; Yamaki and Yamazaki 2004.

47. I use the term "relational work" to recognize that the emotional labor process in old age and disability support entails building a relationship. See also Zelizer 2011.

48. Duffy 2011 (12) pinpoints the commonality among different variants of what she labels the "nurturant care" approach as emphasizing care as a feminine "practice or ethic that encompasses interdependence, nurturance, and relationship," in contrast to masculine "values of competition, individualism and rationality." Duffy also includes under the "nurturant care" tent the work of economists like Folbre (2012) who seek to incorporate love into economic theory. This approach is more in line with my analysis at the labor market level in that it considers how to value paid relationships that include affection. Kelly 2016 usefully distinguishes between the early ethics of care scholarship and a political ethics of care developed by welfare state scholars (e.g., Mahon and Robinson, 2011; Tronto, 2013; Williams 2001).

49. Fischer and Tronto 1990 (cited in Tronto 2013, 148); Grant et al. 2004.

50. Tronto 2013, 148.

51. Duffy 2011; Garland-Thomson 2002; Kelly 2016; Morris 2001; Parreñas 2015; Silvers 1995.

52. In contrast to her broad definition of intimate labor, Zelizer 2010 (269) defines caring relationships more narrowly as "sustained and/or intense personal attention that enhances the welfare of its recipients." This allows us to see care along a continuum rather than assuming that all intimate labor involves care. See also Boris and Parreñas 2010; Cobble 2010.

53. Many scholars of domestic work begin with the concept of social reproductive labor—the labor of maintaining and reproducing people daily and generationally. This concept has more room than the concept of "care" for the analysis of racialized inequality (Duffy 2011; Glenn 2010; Parreñas 2015). Some of those developing a political ethics of care but writing less about domestic work (e.g., Tronto 2013; Williams 2012) use a broader definition of social reproduction that includes reproduction of people through the welfare state.

54. Hondagneu-Sotelo 2007, 216.

55. Parreñas 2015.

56. Rollins 1987; Roberts 1997.

57. Duffy 2011; Glenn 2010; Kang 2010.

58. Rollins 1987. See Hondagneu-Sotelo 2007, Macdonald 2015, and Stasiulis and Bakan 2005 for exceptions.

59. I conducted the earliest interview I draw on in 2001 and the latest in 2019, but the bulk of the interviews were done between 2005 and 2017. When I cite key informants in the endnotes I include the year each was interviewed. See the appendix and Table A1.

60. I also put an ad in senior magazines, but this method was not as successful in obtaining a sample of workers and recipients who were able to consent to an interview.

61. Jennifer Nazareno and I formed a partnership with Filipino American Services Group, Incorporated.

62. As is increasingly common in the community (for example, in the name of the Pilipino Workers Center), I use a P rather than an anglicized F in the terms "Pilipino" and "Pilipina," and I use "Pilipinx" to denote the plural for women and men, rather than lumping women in as "Pilipinos" or using the clumsy and unpronounceable "Pilipina/o." When I am writing specifically about women or men, I use "Pilipina" and "Pilipino," respectively.

63. See the acknowledgments.

64. Bailey and Mobley 2019; Collins 2002; Young 1989.

65. According to a 2017 press release from the Direct Funding Program, there were approximately nine hundred people on direct funding in Ontario, and the Liberal government budgeted for an increase to one thousand by 2018. See "Program Promoting Independence Grows Again," http://www.dfontario.ca/info/announcements.html.

66. Cranford 2005a; Doty, Mahoney, and Simon-Rusinowitz 2007; Glendinning and Kemp 2006; Kelly 2016; MacDonald and Charlesworth 2015; Ungerson and Yeandle 2007; Trnka 2017.

67. California Department of Social Services 2016, cited in Herrera et al. 2017.

68. Ong et al. 2002. In 1999, Doty et al., cited in Delp and Quan 2002 (3), estimated that 49 percent of IHSS workers were providing paid IHSS services to family members.

69. Delp and Quan 2002; Boris and Klein 2015.

70. Cranford 2014b; Cranford and Chun 2017; Chun and Cranford 2018a; Ibarra 2010; Stacey 2011.

71. My focus is on personal support workers (PSWs) in this provincial program, not nurses. As of May 19, 2019, there were an estimated one hundred thousand PSWs in the province, but this figure included PSWs working in hospitals and long-term residential care. See PSW Registry of Ontario, https://www.psw-on.ca/faq.html.

72. According to a 2008 report by the Attendant Services Advisory Committee of the Ontario Community Support Association, there were six thousand people receiving attendant services in Ontario, but this included nine hundred who were on direct funding. See *Unleashing Attendant Services* (Ontario Community Support Association, 2008), http://www.marchofdimes.ca/EN/advocacy/Documents/ocsa_report.pdf. This figure also includes outreach attendant services, which are more limited, scheduled services provided to people living in dispersed homes. Given space constraints, I exclude outreach from my analysis in chapter 6 because it is similar to the decentralized home care discussed in chapter 5.

1. GENDER, MIGRATION, AND THE PURSUIT OF SECURITY

1. Espiritu 1992; Dhingra and Rodriguez 2014.

2. Dhingra and Rodriguez 2014, 2.

3. Anderson 1993.

4. Armstrong and Armstrong 2005; England, Budig, and Folbre 2002.

5. Anderson and Shutes 2014; Cranford 2014a; Martin-Matthews, Sims-Gould, and Naslund 2010; Shutes and Chiatti 2012.

6. Arat-Koc 1997; Dhingra and Rodriguez 2014; Glenn 2010; Sharma 2012.

7. Dhingra and Rodriguez 2014; Foner 2013.

8. Dhingra and Rodriguez 2014; Goldring, Bernstein, and Bernhard 2009; Reitz, Curtis, and Elrick 2014.

9. There is no systematic method of counting immigrants without legal status in Canada, but estimates range from two hundred thousand to five hundred thousand, while in the United States the number is estimated to be twelve million, based on complex estimation techniques (Goldring, Bernstein, and Bernhard 2009). Even considering the larger U.S. population, it is clear that undocumented migration is more prevalent in the United States. In the Los Angeles IHSS program featured in chapter 4, undocumented workers had been able to be paid through this program in the past, but this ended with new legislation allowing for unionization in the late 1990s, according to several key informants.

10. In Canada, until 2014 there was a temporary domestic worker program specific to live-in domestic workers (Boyd 2017). People receiving direct funding from the Ontario government, featured in chapter 3, could recruit migrant workers through that program (Bourgeault, Parpia, and Atanrackovic 2010). However, the limits on the hours funded do not cover live-in work and thus makes this unlikely. It may become more likely, however, now that temporary domestic workers have been incorporated into the general temporary worker flow, which is growing (Goldring, Bernstein, and Bernhard 2009).

11. Foner 2013; Giles 2002; Iacovetta 1992.

12. Goldring, Bernstein, and Bernhard (2009) consider entry as a dependent on family as indicative of precarious citizenship status.

13. Anderson 1993.

14. Arat-Koc 1997.

15. Parreñas 2015; R. Rodriguez 2010; Stasiulis and Bakan 2005; Tungohan et al. 2015.

16. TOUnion10 2016; Tungohan et al. 2015.

17. Boyd 2017.

18. Parreñas 2015.

19. Romero 2011.

20. Glenn 2010; Ibarra 2010; Lan 2002; Parreñas 2015.

21. I was inspired to frame the issue in this way by a talk given by Sharmila Radruppa at the University of Toronto, February 14, 2018, about her research on how garment workers became surrogates in India. See also Smith 1998.

22. Vosko 2000. See also Boris and Klein 2015.

23. See Ameeriar 2017 for another way into the intimate level through the body, aesthetics, and the senses.

24. Classic studies of the labor process document how feudal serfs and later craft workers became subject to industrial management that broke down their work into multiple detailed tasks, increasing their alienation from the final product they were producing (Marx, *Capital*, vol. 1, 1976: 1, 283–306, 949–1060, cited in Burawoy 1978; Braverman 1974). Industrial workers largely accepted this managerial control over their tasks and resisted by seeking more control over their time—such as limiting the workday to eight hours or slowing down production while on the job (Burawoy 1979).

25. Hochschild 2012; Rollins 1987.

26. They also sought to control the time they gave to the job and payment by house rather than hour (Romero 2002).

27. Parreñas 2015, 10. See also Hondagenu-Sotelo 2007.

28. See also Stacey 2011.

29. Armstrong 2013; Hochschild 2012; Stacey 2011.

30. Boris and Klein 2015, 19.

31. Cranford 2005b.

32. Stacey 2011.

33. Hebson, Rubery, and Grimshaw 2015.

2. DISABILITY AND THE QUEST FOR FLEXIBILITY

1. Impairment is bodily injury, pain, or weakness. Disability is the translation of impairment into exclusion and marginalization. This decoupling of impairment and disability is central to what disability scholars call the social model of disability (Krogh 2004). The social model is a critique of the medical model that focuses on cure or the warehousing of people seen as incurable in institutions. Whereas the early social model focused almost exclusively on disability as external oppression, subsequent formulations have been put forth by scholars seeking to understand how the experience of impairment connects to disabling forces (Garland-Thomson 2002; Gibson et al. 2009; Hughes and Paterson 1997; Morris 2001; Shakespeare 2000).

2. My goal here is not to substantiate residents' lack of control in long-term residential care; there are studies documenting this (Diamond 1992; Kelly 2016). There are also studies of how facilities can be organized to support people's dignity and autonomy (Baines and Armstrong 2015; Lopez 2006). My goal is to understand how the meaning of nursing homes, rehabilitation hospitals, or other long-term residential care shapes people's desire for flexibility.

3. Wilder 2006.

4. I did not design this study to include mental health issues, but a few people in the study developed mental illness after a physical illness, such as a stroke or another debilitating disease that resulted in a break with employment or other meaningful aspects of their lives. Others had mental health difficulties that preceded physical impairment or illness and worsened afterward. Some people receiving in-home personal support have age-related cognitive difficulties, such as Alzheimer's, along with physical impairments. We did not recruit this population, but a few people with mild or developing cognitive difficulties did respond. Although they could consent to the interview, their family generally contributed significantly to it, and due to this, as well as the complexities of age-related cognitive difficulties, their experiences are not included in this book.

5. Angus et al. 2005.

6. Morris 2001; Garland-Thomson 2002.

7. D3 2005.

8. Grant et al. 2004.

9. Aronson 2004; Glenn 2010; Rodriguez 2014.

10. A 2002 government of Canada report titled "Advancing the Inclusion of Persons with Disabilities" reported the employment rate of disabled men (41 percent) and disabled women (32 percent), compared to 83 percent and 70 percent, respectively, for their non-disabled counterparts (Lord 2010, 29).

11. See also Heshusius 2013.

12. Wilton 2004.

13. Wilton 2004.

14. Parreñas 2015.

15. D2 2005.

16. D3 2005.

17. D5 2005.

18. CASenior4 2015.

19. Armstrong 2013; Bolton 2000; Hochschild 2012; Stacey 2011.

20. Kafer 2013, 27; Price 2010 cited in Kafer 2013, 27.

21. P8 2005.

22. Kafer 2013, 27; Price 2010 cited in Kafer 2013, 27.

23. D1 2005.

24. D2 2005.

25. B1 2006.

26. Bailey and Mobley 2019; Collins 2002; Young 1989.

3. MANAGING FLEXIBILITY WITHOUT SECURITY IN TORONTO'S DIRECT FUNDING

The Toronto Direct Funding Study began with a policy analysis that started in 2001, which was published in Cranford 2005a. Here I update the study and extend it to include interviews with people using and providing the services. As part of the first policy study, I sought an interview with the executive director of the Centre for Independent Living Toronto (CILT) at the time. The director did not want to grant me an interview but instead referred me to published materials by and for CILT in their library and on their website, on which I also draw. In 2007 and 2008, we interviewed fifteen self-managers and ten personal attendants. Many of the self-managers were also involved in starting the program or employed by it later. See the Appendix and Table A1.

1. Ameeriar 2017; Reitz, Curtis, and Elrick 2014.

2. Kelly 2016, 11.

3. Lord 2010, 35–36.

4. DeJong 1979; Lord 2010.

5. DeJong 1979; Lord 2010, 21.

6. Lord 2010, 49.

7. Lord 2010, 20–22; Valentine 1994.

8. For a history of the program, see Centre for Independent Living Toronto 2000 and Yoshida et al. 2000, and "History of Direct Funding" on the program website, http://www.dfontario.ca/info/history.html.

9. *Direct Funding General Information* (Toronto: Center for Independent Living in Toronto, 2012), https://www.dfontario.ca/df_public/general_information_oct2015_en.pdf.

10. "General FAQs," Direct Funding Program, http://www.dfontario.ca/info/general-faqs.html#Q7.

11. See Cranford 2005a for an analysis of this program within the context of neoliberalism.

12. "Application and Guide," Direct Funding Program, 2016, http://www.dfontario.ca/application/application-and-guide.html.

13. The maximum hours of funding one could receive was for most people 212 hours a month or an average of 7 hours a day, according to "General FAQs," Direct Funding Program, http://www.dfontario.ca/info/general-information.html#Q5. The government capped funding for housekeeping at four hours a week, according to "Application and Guide," Direct Funding Program, 2016, 6, http://www.dfontario.ca/application/applica tion-and-guide.html.

14. At the time of interviews with self-managers in 2006–7, the minimum and maximum rates were $11.39 and $13.33 per hour (Cranford 2005a, 125–26). The maximum funded hourly rate was $19 and the minimum was $16.50 an hour, according to

"Application and Guide," Direct Funding Program, 2016, 9, http://www.dfontario.ca/application/application-and-guide.html.

15. SM6 2007.

16. "Application and Guide," Direct Funding Program, 2016, http://www.dfontario.ca/application/application-and-guide.html.

17. "Application and Guide," Direct Funding Program, 2016, 8, http://www.dfontario.ca/application/application-and-guide.html.

18. The contingency fund was 5 percent of the overall budget according to "Application and Guide," Direct Funding Program, 2016, 8, http://www.dfontario.ca/application/application-and-guide.html, still current in 2019.

19. "General FAQs," Direct Funding Program, http://www.dfontario.ca/info/general-information.html#Q9.

20. Centre for Independent Living Toronto 2000, 128.

21. Centre for Independent Living Toronto 2000.

22. "General FAQs," Direct Funding Program, http://www.dfontario.ca/info/general-faqs.html#Q13.

23. *Direct Funding General Information* (Toronto: Centre for Independent Living in Toronto, 2012), https://www.dfontario.ca/df_public/general_information_oct2015_en.pdf; "Application and Guide," Direct Funding Program, 2016, 6, http://www.dfontario.ca/application/application-and-guide.html.

24. Boyd 2017; Bourgeault, Parpia, and Atanrackovic 2010.

25. See also Roeher 1997.

26. Cranford 2005a; Fudge, Tucker, and Vosko 2003.

27. "General FAQs," Direct Funding Program, http://www.dfontario.ca/info/general-faqs.html#Q2.

28. SM6 2007.

29. Kelly 2016, 27.

30. Fine and Glendinning 2005; Kelly 2016; Tronto 2013; Watson et al. 2004.

31. Atkinson 1987; Boyer 1987.

32. Independent living programs, including DF and attendant services (the latter discussed in chapter 6), have an exemption for these types of things in the Regulated Health Professions Act, based on the assumption that the recipients are capable of, and responsible for, directing their own services.

33. Meyer, Donelly, and Weerakoon 2007; Yamaki and Yamazaki 2004.

34. Rivas 2003.

35. See also Roeher 1997 and Centre for Independent Living Toronto 2000; Kelly 2016.

36. See also Kelly 2016.

37. This would be in line with white women's shifting of their gendered oppression through their greater responsibility for child care and housework onto more marginalized women of color identified in intersectional theorizing and studies of domestic work (Hondagneu-Sotelo 2007; Parreñas 2015; Romero 2002).

38. Omi and Winant 2015.

39. Roeher 1997.

40. Cranford 2005a.

41. Cranford 2005a. The determination of who is the employer is complex and varies depending on the purpose. For instance, a labor board might interpret the facts differently in determining who the employer was depending on whether it was

for the purposes of collective bargaining or for tax purposes (Fudge, Tucker, and Vosko 2003).

42. Cranford 2005a.

43. Cranford 2005a; Delp and Quan 2002; Howes 2005.

44. Boris and Nadasen 2008; Fish 2017; Fudge 1993; Hondagneu-Sotelo 2007; Stasiulis and Bakan 2005.

45. Goulet 1994, cited in Cranford 2005a.

46. TOUnion6 2007.

47. TOUnion7 2007.

48. Centre for Independent Living Toronto, 2, 43–44.

49. See Engman and Cranford 2016 for a theoretical elaboration of this dynamic.

50. The emphasis on relational skills is compatible with calls for feminist rethinking of skill (e.g., Armstrong 2013).

51. Stacey 2011.

52. Fine and Glendinning 2005; Kelly 2016; Tronto 2013; Watson et al. 2004.

4. NEGOTIATING FLEXIBILITY WITH SECURITY IN LOS ANGELES'S IN-HOME SUPPORTIVE SERVICES

The Los Angeles County IHSS case study is based on the following data. In 2006, I interviewed key informants: six administrators and four social workers across the five regional offices within the County of Los Angeles Department of Public Social Services that manages IHSS; three staff and five board members from the Personal Assistance Services Council (PASC), the public authority representing recipients within the L.A. program; seven disability activists outside PASC, including executive directors of independent living centers; four key informants from the Service Employees International Union local representing L.A. IHSS workers at the time (Local 434b), including appointed mid-level staff and the president. From 2015 to March 2019, I did key informant interviews with nine SEIU or community-based labor activists, four staff from community-based or social service organizations working with seniors who were IHSS recipients, and one representative from the public authority in the San Francisco Bay Area. See the Appendix and Table A1.

In 2016, Jennifer Nazareno and I partnered with Filipino American Services Group, Inc. (FASGI) to interview fifteen Pilipina IHSS providers with the help of a graduate student Valerie Damasco. Valerie also did focus group interviews with thirty-one Pilipinx IHSS consumers.

1. On shifting filial duty with migration, see Lan 2002; Cranford and Chun 2017.

2. Cranford 2014b.

3. CALabor12 2016; Cranford and Chun 2017; Chun and Cranford 2018b; Laher 2017; Lan 2002; Um and Lightman 2016.

4. Cranford and Chun 2017; Chun and Cranford 2018b.

5. Delp and Quan 2002.

6. Approximately 1 percent of IHSS consumers received advance payment to pay their providers directly, according to the State of California IHSS Management Statistics Summary Report given to me by IHSS in 2006. To be eligible to receive advance payment one had to be "severely impaired" and capable of managing one's financial and legal affairs or have a guardian or conservator. "Severely impaired" was defined as requiring more than twenty hours a week of personal care, preparation

of meals, and, when assistance with eating is required, meal cleanup, according to the IHSS Needs Assessment—Face and Documentation Worksheet given to me by IHSS in 2006.

7. Between 8 percent (IHSSA9) and 10 percent (IHSSA1) of the Los Angeles County IHSS participants paid a share of cost, according to interviews in 2006 and a 2006 IHSS program fact sheet given to me by IHSS.

8. IHSS Needs Assessment—Face and Documentation Worksheet, and State of California, Health and Welfare Agency, Request for Order and Consent—Paramedical Services form, given to me by IHSS in 2006; IHSSS7 and IHSSA3 2006.

9. The exception was paramedical service, where a doctor authorized and determined the time allotted to tasks.

10. IHSSA2 2006. In 2006, the soft guideline for laundry and food shopping was one hour a week, and for other shopping and errands it was half an hour a week.

11. IHSSS6 2006.

12. IHSSA3 2006; IHSS Needs Assessment—Face and Documentation Worksheet, given to me by IHSS in 2006. In 2006, time allocated to light housekeeping was set at six hours a month. Heavy cleaning, such as steaming carpets, washing windows, or washing walls, could be authorized once a year.

13. IHSSA2 2006.

14. IHSSS10 2006.

15. IHSS Needs Assessment—Face and Documentation Worksheet, given to me by IHSS in 2006; P4 and P8 2006.

16. IHSSS4 2006; IHSSS6 2006; IHSSS7 2006.

17. Cranford 2014b; Herrera et al. 2017, 22–24.

18. IHSSA3 2006. In 2006, the maximum funded hours were 283 per month for those deemed "severely impaired," while for others it was 195 a month.

19. P4 2005; chapter 3.45 of the Los Angeles County Code, Board Order No. 48 of October 7, 1997, Ordinance No. 97–0053, given to me by P1 in 2005.

20. P4 2005.

21. Boris and Klein 2015; Cranford 2014b; Delp and Quan 2002.

22. D5b 2005.

23. P4 2005.

24. P5 2005.

25. D2 2005.

26. CALabor8 2015.

27. CALabor8 2015.

28. CALabor4 2006.

29. D4 and D5 2005.

30. D3 2005.

31. CALabor1 2005; CALabor2 2006; P4 2005; P5 2005; P8 2005.

32. D5 2005.

33. P4 2005; P5 2005.

34. P5 2005.

35. Some scholars use the phrase "social movement unionism" to emphasize not only a social justice framing and repertoire beyond the workplace through alliances between labor and other social movements but also rank-and-file involvement (Johnston 1994; Lopez 2004), worker-led militancy, and union democracy (Camfield 2013; Kumar and Schenk 2006; Ness 1999). Others call this social unionism or community unionism. Given the proliferation of terms, I use "social movement unionism" sparingly when emphasizing a political unionism targeting the state through alliances between social movements.

36. CALabor2 2006; CALabor12 2016.

37. Boris and Klein 2015, 214–18.

38. Boris and Klein 2015; Early 2012; Yelson 2017. In August 2008, the *Los Angeles Times* reported that L.A. local president Tyrone Freeman had spent members' dues and monies from a related charity on himself and his family, sparking an investigation by the Department of Labor, the FBI and the IRS, although he was not convicted of felony until 2013 (Pringle and Branson-Potts, 2013). In 2009, the SEIU International Executive Board voted to put the Bay Area local United Healthcare West (UHW) in trusteeship and to remove home care and other long-term care workers from UHW and put them in the new statewide United Long Term Care Workers Union (ULTCWU). This prompted UHW officers and many staff to form a new union, the National Union of Healthcare Workers (NUHW), thus "setting the stage for years of decertification battles and contested elections between rival unions" (Boris and Klein 2015, 218). SEIU Local 521 in Santa Clara County was the second local to vote against the amalgamation of all home care and nursing home workers into ULTCWU, but their home care workers were amalgamated into ULTCWU, which became SEIU Local 2015 in 2015.

39. Boris and Klein 2015, 216.

40. Boris and Klein 2015, 218.

41. 134 S. Ct. 2618 (2014). See *Harvard Law Review* summary, November 10, 2014, https://harvardlawreview.org/2014/11/harris-v-quinn. See also *Knox v. SEIU, Local 1000*, 132 S. Ct. 2277, 2290 (2012), referenced in *Harvard Law Review* summary of *Harris v. Quinn*, November 10, 2014, https://harvardlawreview.org/2014/11/harris-v-quinn, and in the *Janus v. American Federation of State, County, and Municipal Employees, Council 31, et al.*, U.S. Supreme Court, October term, 2017, https://www.supremecourt.gov/opinions/17pdf/16-1466_2b3j.pdf.

42. In 2017, a California IHSS worker sued the United Domestic Workers of America, which represents workers in Orange County, and the state controller because there was only a limited period when people could opt out of coverage under the collective agreement and the payment of fees to service it (Roosevelt 2017). See also *Janus v. American Federation of State, County, and Municipal Employees Council 31, et al.*, https://www.supremecourt.gov/opinions/17pdf/16-1466_2b3j.pdf.

43. As of May 2019, Los Angeles County paid IHSS providers $12.60 per hour, according to the Los Angeles County Department of Public Social Services website, http://dpss.lacounty.gov/wps/portal/dpss/main/programs-and-services/. This compared to the state minimum wage of $11.00 per hour, according to State of California Department of Industrial Relations: "Minimum Wage," https://www.dir.ca.gov/dlse/faq_minimumwage.htm. In 2016, as part of the "Fight for $15" movement, unions and community-based labor groups helped secure yearly increases to the state's minimum wage, which is set to rise to $15 per hour and provide three days of annual paid sick leave by 2022 (2023 for those with twenty-five employees or less). For a description of this campaign, see United Domestic Workers of America, AFSCME Local 3930, http://www.udwa.org/2016/03/finally-15-an-hour-and-paid-sick-leave-for-ihss-providers/.

44. Those who worked eighty hours a month, for one or more employers, for two consecutive months had health insurance for the price of one dollar a month (Cranford 2014b, 222).

45. If IHSS providers worked over forty hours a week, even if for multiple recipient-employers, regulations stipulated that they should receive time and a half in their pay from the county government. If they worked for more than one recipient-employer on the same day, they were to receive pay for travel time between their

homes up to seven hours per week. The overtime legislation did include a cap of sixty-six hours per week, which affected a small number of IHSS providers. The state also required weekly changes to be authorized by the program, limiting the effectiveness of the overtime (Herrera et al. 2017, 31). For a description of the struggle leading up to this change, see "IHSS Homecare Workers to Begin Receiving Overtime Pay for the First Time in History," United Domestic Workers of America, AFSCME Local 3930, press release, November 4, 2015, http://www.udwa.org/2015/11/ihss-homecare-workers-begin-receiving-overtime-pay-first-time-history. On waiting at doctor's offices, see "IHSS Provider Wait and Travel Times," Disability Rights California, July 2, 2018, https://www.disabilityrightsca.org/publications/ihss-provider-wait-and-travel-times, accessed May 2019.

46. P1 2005.

47. CALabor12 2016.

48. Lan 2002.

49. See also Chun and Cranford 2018a.

50. See also Cranford and Chun 2017.

51. See also Lan 2002.

52. Guevarra 2014; R. M. Rodriguez 2010.

53. Thanks to Valerie Damasco for encouraging me to emphasize this point.

54. Chun and Cranford 2018a; Chun and Cranford 2018b.

55. "Manang" is also used as a term of endearment and sign of respect, not just as to literally mean "older sister."

56. See also Cranford and Chun 2017; Chun and Cranford 2018b.

57. Nazareno 2015; Parreñas 2015.

58. See also Kimura and Browne 2009.

59. "Katulong" was the Tagalog word used.

60. CASenior4 2016.

61. CALabor1 2005; CALabor2 2006; CALabor3 2005; CALabor8 2015; CALabor9 2015; Cranford 2014b.

62. CASenior4 2016.

63. IHSSA2 2006. See also IHSSS7 2006.

64. CALabor12 2016.

65. D4 2005.

66. CALabor2 2006.

67. CALabor12 2019.

68. CALabor13 2019.

69. CALabor12 2019.

70. CASenior4 2016.

71. Chun 2009; Cranford 2014a; Delp and Quan 2002; Mareschal 2006; Rhee and Zabin 2009; Walsh 2001.

72. Boris and Klein 2015.

73. Cranford 2014b; Cranford and Chun 2017; Chun and Cranford 2018a.

74. This finding contrasts with earlier work that emphasized references to treating workers "like family" as justification for exploitation, sometimes internalized by workers (Stasiulis and Bakan 2005; Romero 2002). Although family ideals can reinforce exploitation at the labor market level, at the intimate level these findings are in line with those of Parreñas (2015), who showed how being treated "like family" meant being treated like a human to Pilipinx domestic workers, and showed how they used family ideals to resist dehumanization and exploitation. The strategic use of family ideals to garner respect at the intimate level may be even more pervasive

in the paid extended family and co-ethnic economies discussed here, yet to under-stand exploitation and resistance to it we need to bring in the state as funder. Multi-level analyses are key to teasing out complex inequalities, given growing differences across care work in terms of who pays, who the various employer-like entities are, and in light of the aging of immigrants, especially poor ones, in North America. Thanks to Jennifer Nazareno for encouraging me to emphasize the difference of the co-ethnic case.

75. Scholars of emotion management debate the degree to which paid service and care workers have authentic feelings toward people they work with and whether their "emotional labor" is required by employers or other entities with power over them (Cranford and Miller 2013; Bolton 2009; Brook 2009; Hochschild 2012). In contrast, Zelizer (2010) argues for analyses that recognize the intermingling of love and money, as opposed to treating them as "hostile worlds." See also Boris and Parreñas 2010; Stacey and Ayers 2012.

5. AGENCY-LED FLEXIBILITY AND INSECURITY IN TORONTO'S HOME CARE

The Greater Toronto home care case study uses the following data. In 2005, I inter-viewed the following key informants: four administrators and four care coordina-tors from four of the five community care access centers (CCACs) that managed the home care program. In 2006, I interviewed three high-level Services Employees International Union, Ontario Local 1/Healthcare staff in organizing, research and bargaining, and public policy staff positions. Additionally, in 2006 research assis-tants and I interviewed fourteen managers of for-profit and nonprofit agencies that had CCAC contracts to provide services at the time. In 2007–8, research assistants interviewed forty-four clients and fifty-two personal support workers. In 2015–18, I interviewed seven additional key informants: four SEIU staff in high-level organizing, public policy, and leadership development positions and three staff organizers. I also consulted the SEIU website between 2015 and 2017 to update key changes. See the Appendix and Table A1.

1. Cranford 2014a; Martin-Matthews, Sims-Gould, and Tong, 2010.

2. The former is the argument in some disability studies that compare agency and individualized funding models (Doty, Mahoney, and Simon-Rusinowitz 2007; Lord and Hutchinson 2003). However, another body of scholarship suggests that an agency model that is also marketized, as in Toronto home care and in the UK, might instead treat clients like consumers, or at least profess to, resulting in considerable labor market insecurity for workers (Cranford 2014b; Shutes and Chiatti 2012; Schwiter, Strauss, and England 2017).

3. Although the former might seem the logical conclusion of strictly legal studies, where worker insecurity is tied in large part to the lack of regulation for employees of individuals in private homes, studies of temporary agencies and other labor market inter-mediaries suggest the later, especially when intertwined with workers' insecure citizenship status and gender inequalities (Fudge and Strauss 2014; Hondagneu-Sotelo 2007; Stasiulis and Bakan 2005; Vosko 2000, 2011).

4. Williams et al. 1999, cited in Aronson 2004, 169.

5. People are eligible for home care services if they are insured under the Ontario Health Insurance Plan (OHIP), which covers all Canadian citizens or permanent residents of Canada living in Ontario.

6. From the late 1990s to 2007, forty-three CCACs across the province determined recipient hours and distributed funding to (and managed contracts with) nonprofit agencies and increasingly for-profit companies that delivered services. In 2007, the government reduced the number of CCACs to fourteen, in line with fourteen new structures called local health integrated networks (LIHNs). In 2017, Kathleen O'Day Wynne's Liberal government of Ontario created a new provincial agency that would be a direct employer delivering home care—Personal Support Services Ontario—and planned to shut down the CCACs and expand the role of the LIHNs (Crawley 2017). But in June 2018, right-wing populist Doug Ford was elected premier, and the direct employer model was abandoned. The Ford government tabled reforms in the legislature dubbed the People's Health Care Act, 2019. Reforms included dissolving the fourteen LIHNs and merging their duties into one big agency called Ontario Health (Draaisma 2019).

7. Long Term Care Act 1994, Regulation 396/99.

8. The list of services included in "personal care" are washing and bathing, mouth care, hair care, "preventative skin care," routine hand or foot care, getting in and out of chairs or beds (or vehicles), dressing and undressing, eating, toileting, and taking a client to appointments. See "Home and Community Care," Government of Ontario, https://www.ontario.ca/page/homecare-seniors.

9. The maximum hours were eighty per month in the first thirty days, and sixty hours a month (or fourteen hours a week) thereafter, except under "extraordinary circumstances." If the CCAC determines that there are "extraordinary circumstances"—defined as palliative care needs, short-term stabilization needs, care for those awaiting emergency admission into a long-term care home, or a crisis where the unpaid caregiver is ill and the client cannot be left alone—they may provide additional hours for a thirty-day period (Long Term Care Act 1994, Regulation 386/99).

10. See also Aronson 2004.

11. Aronson 2004, 168, 171.

12. Cranford 2014a; Fudge and Vosko 2001a.

13. This contrasts with private pay agencies (Cranford 2014b; Hondagneu-Sotelo 2007; Stasiulis and Bakan 2005; Vosko 2000).

14. E24a 2006.

15. Unionized, nonprofit agencies were less likely to make a switch without first investigating the matter (Cranford 2014a).

16. The employers I interviewed in 2006 reported starting wages as low as $9 an hour for a non-unionized, for-profit agency, and as high as nearly $14 an hour for a longtime, unionized nonprofit agency. A union informant put home care wages between $10.50 and $13.50 an hour, depending on whether the agency was unionized (TOUnion4, 2006). Rates rose over time, but the gap between home care and long-term residential care remained (TOUnion15 2018).

17. E21 2006.

18. The managers I interviewed in 2006 said that 80–97 percent of the workers they hired had a PSW certificate. A couple of managers said they were able to retroactively exempt some workers with significant experience in the field who would not have passed the mandatory twelfth-grade written English test.

19. TOUnion15 2018.

20. E1 2006.

21. E21 2006.

22. E8 2006.

23. E25 2006.

24. See also Aronson and Neysmith 1996.

25. Cranford and Miller 2013.

26. E9 2006.

27. E21 2006.

28. E24 2006.

29. E21 2006.

30. E5 2006.

31. See also Zelizer 2011.

32. We might expect this passive waiting for workers to offer to help with housework to be more likely among women clients than among men. This would fit with Hochschild's (2012) theory of emotional labor. On the other hand, these are men marginalized by age and disability, which might temper their demands. While the number of men in my sample is too small for strong conclusions, it is important to note that a couple of the male clients were also passive in this way, while several women were direct. Comparing these findings with those of the previous chapters, where both women and men managed their own services within a program designed to facilitate their doing so, points to the need to examine how gender intersects with age and disability and also program design.

33. Baines 2016; Stacey 2011.

34. Cranford 2014a; Martin-Matthews, Sims-Gould, and Naslund 2010.

35. E24 2006.

36. There were more instances of nonprofit, unionized agencies challenging clients' racial preferences, and the challenges were more significant, yet few such agencies survived the 1990s restructuring (Cranford 2014a).

37. A social unionism that engages the state to improve conditions for workers as citizens, not just union members, is generally seen by scholars and activists as the dominant form of unionism in Canada, especially in the public sector. However, business unionism still exists, and different variants and degrees of social unionism are found among different unions (Cranford, Hick, and Birdsell Bauer 2018; Kumar and Schenk 2006; Ross 2013).

38. Baines 2013. As of 2017, SEIU represented 24 percent of home care personal support workers in Ontario, which came to 6,632 workers; 3,979 of these were in the Greater Toronto Area (TOUnion11 2017). The Canadian Union of Public Employees (CUPE) and the Ontario Public Service Employees Union (OPSEU) also represent similar types of workers but mostly outside of Toronto and in the community services sector, which services people with developmental disabilities and children with disabilities (TOUnion1 2006; TOUnion3 2006).

39. A union steward is a worker who serves as workers' representative at the workplace level. In 2013, SEIU held an Ontario-wide two-week strike of forty-five hundred home care PSWs working for one large nonprofit employer (TOUnion9 2015). Partly in response, the provincial government raised the personal support worker minimum wage by four dollars to $16.50 an hour, whether unionized or not, which took effect in 2017 (TOUnion15 2018).

40. TOUnion9 2015.

41. TOUnion4 2006.

42. TOUnion9 2015.

43. In the past it was involved in the broad Ontario Health Coalition, an alliance of unions and community advocacy associations that have long campaigned against privatization and funding cuts and on other issues affecting quality health care broadly defined (Cranford 2014a).

44. Connolly 2014, 1.

45. TOUnion15 2018. See also Ontario Caregiver Coalition, http://www.ontariocaregivercoalition.ca/.

46. See Cranford, Hick, and Birdsell Bauer 2018 for an in-depth analysis of social unionism from workers' perspectives.

47. Connolly 2014.

48. TOUnion1 2006; TOUnion5 2006; TOUnion15 2018.

49. Cranford 2007.

50. See Cranford, Hick, and Birdsell Bauer 2018 for an in-depth analysis of how these sentiments come out of workers' lived experience with social unionism.

51. Baines 2016; Bolton 2000; Ibarra 2010; Stacey 2011.

52. SEIU Healthcare, Submission to Changing Workplaces Review, September 19, 2015, and April 16, 2016, follow-up submission, given to me by TOLabor15. Bill 148 also included provisions to review bargaining units with a view to amalgamation, and requirements for employers to provide unions a list of employees, which would make it easier to organize contract employees.

53. TOLabor15 2018.

54. See "Bill 47, Making Ontario Open for Business Act, 2018," Legislative Assembly of Ontario, https://www.ola.org/en/legislative-business/bills/parliament-42/session-1/bill-47.

55. TOLabor10 2016.

6. BARGAINING FOR SECURITY WITH FLEXIBILITY IN TORONTO'S ATTENDANT SERVICES

The Greater Toronto attendant services case study was based on the following data. In 2001 and 2007, I interviewed four union paid staff and elected officials at the main union representing workers in this sector: Local 40 of Canadian Auto Workers (now UNIFOR). In 2006, research assistants and I interviewed sixteen managers of organizations that had government contracts to provide services. In 2006 and 2007, we interviewed nine disability advocates who sat on boards of directors of these service-providing agencies and were also recipients of attendant services. In 2008 and 2009, we interviewed twenty consumers living in social support living units (SSLUs) and nineteen attendants working in SSLUs. See the Appendix and Table A1.

1. Cranford 2005a.

2. Bolton and Boyd 2003; Cancian 2000; Cranford and Miller 2013; Lopez 2006.

3. People were eligible for attendant services if they were covered by the Ontario Health Insurance Plan (OHIP), if they were at least sixteen years old, if they had a permanent physical disability, if they required ongoing physical assistance with activities of daily living, if any medical or professional needs could be met by community health services on a visitation basis, and if one was able to direct one's own services. See Application Guide, Center for Independent Living in Toronto, http://www.cilt.ca/wp-content/uploads/2019/05/ASAC-Application-Guide-2019-05.pdf.

4. Application Guides, http://www.cilt.ca/wp-content/uploads/2019/05/ASAC-Application-Guide-2019-05.pdf.

5. The maximum hours of funding were approximately forty-two, or six hours a day of booked services, according to B5 2007.

6. Cranford 2005a.

7. Local 40 was initially an independent union but affiliated with the Canadian Auto Workers, which in turn amalgamated with other unions to form Unifor. Given its varied affiliations, I refer to this union simply as Local 40. Local 40 represented workers across six different employers, most of whom had multiple supportive housing buildings and some

of whom provided services in dispersed homes through Ontario's Outreach Program. The Ontario Public Service Employees Union represented two attendant services employers, the Canadian Union of Public Employees represented one, and the Service Employees International Union represented four. See Cranford (2005a) for a history of unionization in this sector.

8. Cranford 2014b; Hondagneu-Sotelo 2007; Stasiulis and Bakan 2005.

9. E26 2006.

10. For example, the starting wage for attendants in the mid-2000s was approximately $14/hour, according to interviews with employers. Yet long-term unionized workers earned up to $20/hour at this time, according to union informants. In 2017, the government set the minimum wage at $16.50/hour for all personal support workers in the province.

11. TOUnion8 2007.

12. E22 2006.

13. E26 2006.

14. At the time of research and writing, the government recommended but did not require a personal support worker certification in this sector.

15. See Birdsell, Bauer, and Cranford 2017 for more examples of this.

16. TOUnion16 2001.

17. E13 2006.

18. E14 2006.

19. TOUnion16 2001.

20. See Birdsell, Bauer, and Cranford 2017 for an analysis of how race shapes workers' consent as well as support for their union.

21. TOUnion8 2007.

22. TOUnion16 2001.

23. Chun 2009; Cranford 2014b; Fudge and Vosko 2001a; Hickey 2012; Milkman and Ott 2014.

24. A social unionism that engages the state to improve conditions for workers as citizens, not just union members, is generally seen by scholars and activists as the dominant form of unionism in Canada, especially in the public sector but different variants and degrees of social unionism are found among different unions (Kumar and Schenk 2006; Ross 2013).

25. TOUnion16 2001.

26. TOUnion16 2001.

27. TOUnion6 and TOUnion7 2007.

28. See Birdsell, Bauer, and Cranford 2017 for more examples of this.

29. One person I interviewed, however, provided a strong critique of the board at her agency, arguing that she and other consumers on the board were "token cripples" and that the views of "business people" who did not sufficiently understand the issues dominated board decision-making.

30. See Hochschild 2012 on "feeling rules" based on commercial motivations. See Bolton 2000, Cancian 2000, Lopez 2006, and Baines 2016 on altruistic motivations more common in nonprofit and social services and among care professionals.

7. TOWARD FLEXIBLE CARE AND SECURE WORK IN INTIMATE LABOR

1. Bailey and Mobley 2019; Collins 2002; Garland-Thomson 2002; Glenn 2010; Young 1989.

2. Chun, Lipsitz, and Shin 2013; Garland-Thomson 2002; Romero 2018, 1.

3. Young 1989. See also Fraser 1987.

4. Aronson 2003; Fine and Glendinning 2005; Garland-Thomson 2002; Morris 2001; Watson et al. 2004.

5. Cranford and Chun 2017; Chun and Cranford 2018b; Nazareno, Parreñas, and Fan 2014.

6. See also Kelly 2016.

7. Cranford 2005b; Hondagneu-Sotelo 2007; Smith and Neuwirth 2008; Vosko 2000.

8. D2 2005; D4 2005; Cranford 2014b.

9. P2 2005; Chun and Cranford 2018a; Chun and Cranford 2018b.

10. Nazareno 2015; Parreñas 2015.

11. Cranford and Chun 2017; Chun and Cranford 2018a; Chun and Cranford 2018b; Glenn 2010.

12. Duffy 2011; Grant et al. 2004.

13. Aronson, Denton, and Zeytinoglu 2004; J. Rodriguez 2014.

14. Cranford and Chun 2017; Chun and Cranford 2018b.

15. In Canada the term "social unionism" is generally used to describe a unionism that engages the state to improve conditions for workers as citizens, not just union members, and sometimes used to emphasize union democracy (Cranford, Hick, and Birdsell Bauer 2018; Kumar and Schenk 2006; Ross 2013). In the United States the term "social movement unionism" is more common. Yet since the latter term is used in numerous ways, I use it sparingly to emphasize a political unionism targeting the state through alliances between social movements. See chapters 4, 5, and 6 for an analysis of social (movement) unionism.

16. Ness 1999.

17. Cobble 2010; Fudge and Vosko 2001a.

18. In May 2019 the U.S. federal government released the Centers for Medicare and Medicaid Services final rule limiting home care workers' ability to use paycheck deductions for union dues even if they are union members, although the SEIU plans to challenge this in court in California and elsewhere. See the union's press release, "Trump Administration to Home Care Workers: Here's Your Poverty-Level Wage. Now Let Us Tell You How to Spend It," May 2, 2019, http://www.seiu.org/2019/05/trump-administration-to-home-care-workers-heres-your-poverty-level-wage-now-let-us-tell-you-how-to-spend-it.

19. P1 2005.

20. Chun and Cranford 2018b.

21. See also Chun and Cranford 2018b.

22. This is in addition to issues with top-down decision-making noted by others (e.g., Early 2012; Boris and Klein 2015; Yelson 2017).

23. Stacey 2011, 155. See Little 2015 for a similar claim based on a case study of the Quality Care Alliance, a coalition of consumers, workers, and employers. See Duffy 2010 for a review of the common argument for union-community coalitions connecting quality care and quality work.

24. Critics might argue that union engagement with workers and recipients at this level is only possible in more centralized workplaces, like the supportive housing buildings in attendant services. However, my comparison of centralized and decentralized services revealed that what mattered for worker security was not centralization but unionization, which was more likely among nonprofits whether representing centralized or decentralized workplaces (Cranford 2013).

25. Boris and Klein 2015, 19; see also Armstrong and Armstrong 2005; Grant et al. 2004; Stacey and Ayers 2012; Ungerson 1999; Zelizer 2011.

26. This concept of intimate community unionism develops ideas in Cranford et al. 2006 on community unionism by coupling it with insight from Cobble 2010 (281). Cobble wrote about the need for a "more caring unionism," by which she means a

unionism that would take the experiences of the mostly women and immigrant workers in a range of types of intimate labor "as prototypic rather than exceptional." Scholars and activists have used the term "community unionism" to refer to at least three distinct elements of union work, each of which is important here. First, sometimes they use "community unionism" to discuss coalitions between unions and community organizations representing other marginalized groups, especially in the service sector (e.g., Tatterstall 2010). Second, they use the term to emphasize organizing beyond a single, centralized workplace, given the predominance of small, disaggregated, service-sector workplaces. They thus emphasize community as spatial or social location and call for organizing within broader communities defined by labor market, geography, racial or gender social location, or combinations of these (e.g., O'Conner 1964a, 1964b). This community unionism seeks to improve labor market conditions by targeting the state rather than individual workplace or employers to improve standards (e.g., Fine 2006). Finally, sometimes scholars emphasize unions' use of community organizing tactics and strategies instead of, or along with, industrial union ones like strikes and collective bargaining. Community tactics include direct action, but crucial for this intervention are the longer-term strategies of critical education and grassroots leadership development (Chun, Lipsitz, and Shin 2013; Cranford and Ladd 2003; Cranford et al. 2006; Moore 2018). "Community unionism" encompasses all three of these elements more so than other terms used in the United States ("social movement unionism") or Canada ("social unionism"), especially the emphasis on grassroots leadership development. With these conceptual tools and my comparative analysis, I extend the concept of community unionism to the intimate.

27. Glenn 2010; Grant et al. 2004; Krogh 2004; Tronto 2013.

28. Doty, Mahoney, and Simon-Rusinowitz 2007; Kelly 2016.

29. Tronto 2013.

30. Fine and Glendinning 2005; Glenn 2010; Tronto 2013; Watson et al. 2004. Williams 2018 usefully conceives of care as made up of both autonomy and interdependence.

31. Duffy, Armenia, and Stacey 2012; Garland-Thomson 2002; Glenn 2010; Kelly 2016; Krogh 2004; Little 2015; Morris 2001; Silvers 1995; Williams 2001.

32. Duffy 2010; Folbre 2006; Stone 2000.

33. P5 2005.

34. CALabor1 2005.

35. CALabor8 2015.

36. Moore 2018, 4.

37. Moore 2018, 1. See also Boris and Nadasen 2008.

38. Poo 2015, 5–6. SEIU formed an agreement with NDWA to work together on the Caring Across the Generations campaign in California, Washington State, and Oregon (CALabor12 2016).

39. Thanks to Mary Romero for suggesting the importance of continuing to emphasize the problems with a simplistic "love" framing for domestic workers and their own families. As Eileen Boris (2018) put it succinctly: "Love is not enough. We need to build power."

40. D2 2005. San Francisco's Support at Home Program services middle-income people who are not poor enough to qualify for IHSS but cannot afford to pay for personal care (Herrera et al. 2017).

41. Arat-Koc 1997; Bakan and Stasiulis 2005; Bougeault, Parpia, and Atanrackovic 2010.

42. Aronson, Denton, and Zeytinoglu 2004; Howes 2005.

43. Charlesworth and Malone 2017; Cobble 2010; DuRivage, Carré, and Tilly 1998; Fudge 1993; Fine 2006; Hayes 2017.

44. Brenner, Leete, and Pastor 2007; Cranford 2014b; Vosko 2000.

45. Folbre 2006.

46. Hayes 2017. SEIU Local 1 in Ontario rebranded itself SEIU Healthcare and now organizes both personal support workers and some nurses in health care and long-term care (TOUnion15 2018). In California the international formed SEIU 2015 as one big "local" across the long-term care sector, and another "local" focused on the multiple occupations in the health care sector. Others have become general unions, like Unifor in Canada, which has had jurisdictional battles with SEIU.

47. Armstrong 1993; Duffy 2010, 132–35.

48. Baines and Armstrong 2015; Cobble 2010; Duffy 2011.

49. CASenior1 2015; CASenior2 2015; Cranford and Chun 2017.

50. Cranford and Ladd 2003, 29; Guevarra and Lledo 2013.

51. Salzinger 1991.

52. Fudge 1993.

53. Cranford 2014b, 186. It was SEIU's position that the Ontario Ministry of Health and Long Term Care should support a council of all stakeholder groups, including clients, families, workers, and employers, to develop the registry further (TOUnion15 2018). The registry opened in 2012 but closed in 2016 after a report that the employer association running it, the Ontario Community Support Association, did not fully do background checks or confirm education and employment history, although arguably they did not have the funds or clear mandate to do so (Zlomislic 2016). The government relaunched the registry in 2018 under the direction of the Michener Institute, a post-secondary institution with expertise in health-sector certification. However, the plan is to transition it to a permanent host in December 2019. See "Frequently Asked Questions," Personal Support Worker Registry of Ontario, https://www.psw-on.ca/faq.html.

54. Boris and Klein 2015; Charlesworth and Malone 2017; Gottfried 2017. For example, home-based personal support workers were finally included in the U.S. Fair Labor Standards Act in 2015 (as pushed for by unions and allies for years), but the scope is limited. See also chapter 4.

55. Charlesworth and Malone 2017; Fudge 2012. The sectoral awards in Australia set job classifications, minimum rates of pay, and conditions of employment by use of independent, quasi-judicial tribunals, like the Fair Work Commission, usually in response to applications from unions or employers. Initially they were a way to extend the benefits of a collective agreement to nonunionized workers in the sector. However, since the reform of the labor regime in Australia in the 1990s they have been seen as more like a safety net, as is the case with minimum or fair labor standards in the United States and Canada. The federal Social, Community, Home Care and Disabilities Services Industry Award sets minimum wages and working time conditions for most home care workers in Australia (Charlesworth 2017).

56. Fudge 1993; Vosko 2000.

57. Hayes 2017, 15.

58. Independent living centers in Los Angeles County provide support for disabled employers on how to communicate what they need and the parameters of the job in an effort to avoid a break in the working relationship, not unlike the Centre for Independent Living Toronto discussed in chapter 3 (D2, D3, D4, D5, and D6 2005).

59. "Personal Assistance Services Procedures" given to the author by D4 in 2005.

60. See the Hand in Hand Domestic Employers Network website, http://domesticemployers.org/. As of 2019, nine states and the city of Seattle passed domestic workers' bills of rights (Campbell 2019). However, the standards in the bills are difficult to enforce, so they are more an indicator of organizing strategies than an example of successful outcomes at this point. Domestic workers' associations have long contemplated the pros and cons of allying with employers to improve conditions (Boris and Nadasen 2008).

61. P5, D3, and D6 2005.

62. See also Rivas 2007.

63. TOUnion15 2018.

64. Moore 2018.

65. CALabor5 2015.

66. Cranford and Ladd 2003; Cranford et al. 2006.

67. Cranford and Ladd 2003; Chun, Lipsitz, and Shin 2013. Many worker centers focus on leadership development of various degrees, but not all engage in the long-term, feminist leadership development with links to critical education, politicization, and consciousness-raising described here. See Fine 2006 and Milkman 2010 for overviews.

68. Briskin 2011; Cranford 2007.

69. CaLabor5 2015.

70. CALabor9 2015.

71. CALabor5 2015.

72. Chun, Lipsitz, and Shin 2013.

73. P9 2015.

74. This idea is influenced by Milkman's (2010) analysis of worker centers in Los Angeles, but I place more emphasis on long-term politicization and bring in service recipients.

75. One drawback of community-based organizations, however, is that often their funding source constrains them from doing political work either directly and indirectly through the work of documenting tangible results (CALabor5 2015; Cranford et al. 2006).

References

Ameeriar, Lalaie. 2017. *Downwardly Global: Women, Work, and Citizenship in the Pakistani Diaspora*. Durham, N.C.: Duke University Press.

Anderson, Bridget, and Isabel Shutes, eds. 2014. *Migration and Care Labour: Theory, Policy and Politics*. New York: Palgrave Macmillan.

Anderson, Wolseley W. 1993. *Caribbean Immigrants: A Socio-Demographic Profile*. Toronto: Canadian Scholars Press.

Angus, Jan, Pia Kontos, Isabel Dyck, Patricia McKeever, and Blake Poland. 2005. "The Personal Significance of Home: Habitus and the Experience of Receiving Long-Term Home Care." *Sociology of Health and Illness* 27 (2): 161–87.

Arat-Koc, Sedef. 1997. "From Mothers of the Nation to Migrant Workers." In *Not One of the Family: Foreign Domestic Workers in Canada*, edited by Abigail Bakan and Daiva Stasiulis, 53–74. Toronto: University of Toronto Press.

Armstrong, Pat. 1993. "Professions, Unions, or What? Learning from Nurses." In *Women Challenging Unions: Feminism, Democracy and Militancy*, edited by Linda Briskin and Patricia McDermott, 304–20. Toronto: University of Toronto Press.

Armstrong, Pat. 2013. "Puzzling Skills: Feminist Political Economy Approaches." *Canadian Review of Sociology* 50 (3): 256–83.

Armstrong, Pat, and Hugh Armstrong. 2005. "Public and Private: Implications for Care Work." *Sociological Review* 53 (2): 169–87.

Armstrong, Pat, and Ruth Lowndes, eds. 2018. *Negotiating Tensions in Long-Term Residential Care: Ideas Worth Sharing*. Ottawa: Canadian Centre for Policy Alternatives.

Aronson, Jane. 2003. "'You Need Them to Know Your Ways': Service Users' Views about Valued Dimensions of Home Care." *Home Health Care Services Quarterly* 22 (4): 85–98.

Aronson, Jane. 2004. "'Just Fed and Watered': Women's Experiences of the Gutting of Home Care." In *Caring For/Caring About: Women, Home Care and Unpaid Caregiving*, edited by Karen R. Grant, Carol Amaratunga, Pat Armstrong, Madeline Boscoe, Ann Pederson, and Kay Wilson, 167–84. Aurora, Ont.: Garamond Press.

Aronson, Jane, Margaret Denton, and Isik Zeytinoglu. 2004. "Market-Modelled Home Care in Ontario: Deteriorating Working Conditions and Dwindling Community Capacity." *Canadian Public Policy* 30 (1): 111–25.

Aronson, Jane, and Sheila M. Neysmith. 1996. "'You're Not Just in There to Do the Work': Depersonalizing Policies and the Exploitation of Home Care Workers' Labor." *Gender and Society* 10 (1): 59–77.

Atkinson, John. 1987. "Flexibility or Fragmentation? The United Kingdom Labour Market in the Eighties." *Labour and Society* 12 (1): 87–105.

Auer, Peter, Janine Berg, and Sandrine Cazes. 2007. "Balancing Flexibility and Security: The Role of Labour Market Politics and Institutions." *Tilburg Law Review: Journal of International and European Law* 14 (1): 49–56.

Bailey, Moya, and Izetta Autumn Mobley. 2019. "Work in the Intersections: A Black Feminist Disability Framework." *Gender and Society* 33 (1): 19–40.

Baines, Donna. 2013. "Unionization in the Non-Profit Social Services Sector: Gendered Resistance." In *Public Sector Unions in the Age of Austerity*, edited by Stephanie Ross and Larry Savage, 80–90. Halifax: Fernwood.

Baines, Donna. 2016. "Moral Projects and Compromise Resistance: Resisting Uncaring in Nonprofit Care Work." *Studies in Political Economy* 97 (2): 124–42.

Baines, Donna, and Pat Armstrong, eds. 2015. *Promising Practices in Long Term Care: Ideas Worth Sharing*. Ottawa: Centre for Policy Alternatives.

Birdsell Bauer, Louise, and Cynthia Cranford. 2017. "The Community Dimensions of Union Renewal: Racialised and Caring Relations in Social Services." *Work, Employment and Society* 31 (2): 1–17.

Bolton, Sharon. 2000. "Who Cares? Offering Emotion Work as a 'Gift' in the Nursing Labour Process." *Journal of Advanced Nursing* 32 (3): 580–86.

Bolton, Sharon, ed. 2007. *Dimensions of Dignity at Work*. Oxford: Butterworth-Heinemann.

Bolton, Sharon. 2009. "Getting to the Heart of the Emotional Labour Process: A Reply to Brook." *Work, Employment and Society* 23 (3): 549–60.

Bolton, Sharon, and Carol Boyd. 2003. "Trolley Dolly or Skilled Emotion Manager? Moving on from Hochschild's Managed Heart." *Work Employment and Society* 17 (2): 289–308.

Boris, Eileen. 2018, October. "Expert Panel on Care and Carework in an Uncaring World." Presented at the Gender, Migration and Work of Care Project Conference, University of Toronto.

Boris, Eileen, and Jennifer Klein. 2015. *Caring for America: Home Health Workers in the Shadow of the Welfare State*. Oxford: Oxford University Press.

Boris, Eileen, and Premilla Nadasen. 2008. "Domestic Workers Organize!" *Working USA* 11 (4): 413–37.

Boris, Eileen, and Rhacel Salazar Parreñas. 2010. Introduction to *Intimate Labors: Cultures, Technologies, and the Politics of Care*, edited by Eileen Boris and Rhacel Salazar Parreñas, 1–12. Stanford, Calif.: Stanford University Press.

Bourgeault, Ivy, Jelena Atanrackovic, Ahmed Rashid and Rishma Parpia. 2010. "Relations between Immigrant Care Workers and Older Persons in Home and Long-Term Care." *Canadian Journal on Aging* 29 (1): 109–18.

Bourgeault, Ivy, Rishma Parpia, and Jelena Atanrackovic. 2010. "Canada's Live-in Caregiver Program: Is It an Answer to the Growing Demand for Elderly Care?" *Population Ageing* 3: 83–102.

Boyd, Monica. 2017. "Closing the Open Door? Canada's Changing Policy for Migrant Caregivers." In *Gender, Migration, and the Work of Care: A Multi-Scalar Approach to the Pacific Rim*, edited by Sonya Michel and Ito Peng, 167–90. Cham, Switzerland: Palgrave Macmillan.

Boyer, Robert. 1987. "Labour Flexibilities: Many Forms, Uncertain Effects." *Labour and Society* 121: 107–29.

Braverman, Harry. 1974. *Labor and Monopoly Capital: The Degradation of Work in the Twentieth Century*. New York: Monthly Review Press.

Brenner, Chris, Laura Leete, and Manuel Pastor. 2007. *Staircases or Treadmills? Labor Market Intermediaries and Economic Opportunity in a Changing Economy*. New York: Russell Sage.

Briskin, Linda. 2011. "Union Renewal, Postheroic Leadership and Women's Organizing: Crossing Discourses, Reframing Debates." *Labor Studies Journal* 36 (4): 508–37.

Brook, Paul. 2009. "In Critical Defence of 'Emotional Labour': Refuting Bolton's Critique of Hochschild's Concept." *Work, Employment and Society* 23 (3): 531–48.

Burawoy, Michael. 1978. "Toward a Marxist Theory of the Labor Process: Braverman and Beyond." *Politics and Society* 8 (3–4): 247–312.

Burawoy, Michael. 1979. *Manufacturing Consent: Changes in the Labor Process under Monopoly Capitalism.* Chicago: University of Chicago Press.

Camfield, David. 2013. "Renewing Public Sector Unions." In *Public Sector Unions in the Age of Austerity,* edited by Stephanie Ross and Larry Savage, 69–77. Halifax: Fernwood.

Campbell, Alexia Fernández. 2019. "Kamala Harris Just Introduced a Bill to Give Housekeepers Overtime Pay and Meal Breaks." *Vox,* July 15, 2019. https://www.vox.com/2019/7/15/20694610/kamala-harris-domestic-workers-bill-of-rights-act.

Cancian, Francesca. 2000. "Paid Emotional Care." In *Care Work: Gender, Labor, and the Welfare State,* edited by Madonna Harrington Meyer, 136–48. New York: Routledge.

Cangiano, Alessio, and Isabel Shutes. 2010. "Ageing, Demand for Care and the Role of Migrant Care Workers in the UK." *Journal of Population Ageing* 3 (1–2): 39–57.

Centre for Independent Living Toronto. 2000. *Powershift: How Self-Managed, Direct Funded Attendant Services Came about in Ontario.* Toronto: Centre for Independent Living.

Charlesworth, Sara. 2017. "Partial Protection? The Regulation of Home Care Workers' Working Conditions." In *Regulating for Equitable and Job-Rich Growth,* edited by Colin F. Fenwick and Valérie van Goethem, 125–50. Northampton, Mass.: Edward Elgar.

Charlesworth, Sara, and Jenny Malone. 2017. "Re-Imagining Decent Work for Home Care Workers in Australia." *Labour and Industry* 27 (4): 284–301.

Chun, Jennifer Jihye. 2009. *Organizing at the Margins: The Symbolic Politics of Labor in South Korea and the United States.* Ithaca, N.Y.: Cornell University Press.

Chun, Jennifer Jihye, and Cynthia Cranford. 2018a. "Becoming Homecare Workers: Chinese Immigrant Women and the Changing Worlds of Work, Care and Unionism." *Critical Sociology* 44 (7–8): 1013–27.

Chun, Jennifer Jihye, and Cynthia Cranford. 2018b, July. "Negotiating Care and the Boundaries of Unionism: Chinese and Korean Immigrant Home Care Workers in California." Paper presented at the International Sociological Association Meetings, Session on Global Perspectives on Care and Care Work I: Marketization, Migration and Gender. Toronto.

Chun, Jennifer Jihye, George Lipsitz, and Young Shin. 2013. "Intersectionality as a Social Movement Strategy: Asian Immigrant Women Advocates." *Signs: Journal of Women in Culture and Society* 38 (4): 917–40.

Clawson, Dan. 2003. *The Next Upsurge: Labor and the New Social Movements.* Ithaca, N.Y.: Cornell University Press.

Cobble, Dorothy Sue. 2010. "More Intimate Unions." In *Intimate Labors: Cultures, Technologies and the Politics of Care,* edited by Eileen Boris and Rhacel Salazar Parreñas, 280–96. Stanford, Calif.: Stanford University Press.

Collins, Patricia Hill. 2002. *Black Feminist Thought: Knowledge, Consciousness, and the Politics of Empowerment.* 2nd ed. London: Routledge.

Connolly, Amy. 2014. "Stories and Strategies of Resistance: Multi-Stakeholder Advocacy Efforts in Publicly-Provided Home Support Services in Ontario." Major research paper, Ryerson University.

Constable, Nicole. 2014. *Born Out of Place: Migrant Mothers and the Politics of International Labor.* Berkeley: University of California Press.

Cranford, Cynthia. 2005a. "From Precarious Workers to Unionized Employees and Back Again? The Challenges of Organizing Personal-Care Workers in Ontario." In *Self Employed Workers Organize: Law, Policy and Unions,* by Cynthia Cranford, Judy Fudge, Eric Tucker and Leah Vosko, 96–135. Montreal: McGill–Queens University Press.

Cranford, Cynthia, 2005b. "Networks of Exploitation: Immigrant Labor and the Restructuring of the Los Angeles Janitorial Industry." *Social Problems* 52 (3): 379–97.

Cranford, Cynthia. 2007. "'It's Time to Leave Machismo Behind': Challenging Gender Inequality in an Immigrant Union." *Gender and Society* 21 (3): 409–38.

Cranford, Cynthia. 2013, November. "Flexibility for Whom and at What Cost? Migrant Workers, Racialization and the Struggle for Security in Personal Home Care Work." Paper presented at the annual meeting of the Social Science History Association, Chicago.

Cranford, Cynthia. 2014a. "Toward Flexibility with Security for Migrant Care Workers: A Comparative Analysis of Personal Home Care in Toronto and Los Angeles." In *Migration and Care Labour: Theory, Policy and Politics*, edited by Bridget Anderson and Isabel Shutes, 173–91. Basingstoke, UK: Palgrave.

Cranford, Cynthia. 2014b. "Toward Particularism with Security: Immigration, Race, and the Organization of Personal Support Services in Los Angeles." In *When Care Work Goes Global: Locating the Social Relations of Domestic Work*, edited by Mary Romero, Valerie Preston, and Wenona Giles, 203–26. Farnham, UK: Ashgate.

Cranford, Cynthia, and Jennifer Chun. 2017. "Immigrant Women and Home-based Elder Care in Oakland, California's Chinatown." In *Gender, Migration, and the Work of Care: A Multi-Scalar Approach to the Pacific Rim*, edited by Sonya Michel and Ito Peng, 41–66. New York: Palgrave Macmillan.

Cranford, Cynthia, Tania Das Gupta, Deena Ladd, and Leah F. Vosko. 2006. "Thinking through Community Unionism." In *Precarious Employment: Understanding Labour Market Insecurity*, edited by Leah F. Vosko, 353–78. Montreal: McGill–Queens University Press.

Cranford, Cynthia, Angela Hick, and Louise Birdsell Bauer. 2018. "Lived Experiences of Social Unionism: Toronto Homecare Workers in the Late 2000s." *Labor Studies Journal* 43 (1): 74–96.

Cranford, Cynthia, and Deena Ladd. 2003. "Community Unionism: Organising for Fair Employment in Canada." *Just Labour: A Canadian Journal of Work and Society* 3: 46–59.

Cranford, Cynthia, and Diana Miller. 2013. "Emotion Management from the Client's Perspective: The Case of Personal Home Care." *Work, Employment and Society* 27 (5): 785–801.

Crawley, Mike. 2017. "New Plan Will See Ontario Government Employees Deliver Homecare." CBC News, November 6, 2017. http://www.cbc.ca/news/canada/toronto/ontario-home-care-personal-support-workers-psw-wynne-1.4385797.

DeJong, Gerbon. 1979. "Independent Living: From Social Movement to Analytic Paradigm." *Archives of Physical Medicine and Rehabilitation* 60 (10): 435–46.

Delp, Linda, and Katie Quan. 2002. "Homecare Worker Organizing in California: An Analysis of a Successful Strategy." *Labor Studies Journal* 27 (1): 1–23.

De Nanteuil-Miribel, Matthieu, and Mohamed Nachi. 2004. "Flexibility and Security: What Forms of Political Regulation?" *European Review of Labour and Research* 10 (2): 300–320.

Dhingra, Pawan, and Robyn Magalit Rodriguez. 2014. *Asian America: Sociological and Interdisciplinary Perspectives*. Cambridge: Polity Press.

Diamond, Timothy. 1992. *Making Grey Gold: Narratives of Nursing Home Care*. Chicago: University of Chicago Press.

Doellgast, Virginia. 2012. *Disintegrating Democracy at Work: Labor Unions and the Future of Good Jobs in the Service Economy*. Ithaca, N.Y.: Cornell University Press.

Doty, Pamela, A. E. Benjamin, Ruth E. Matthias, and Todd M. Franke. 1999. "In-Home Supportive Services for the Elderly and Disabled: A Comparison of Client-Directed and Professional Management Models of Service Delivery. Non-Technical Summary Report." U.S. Department of Health and Human Services and the University of California, Los Angeles. In Office of the Assistant Secretary for Planning and Evaluation, U.S. Department of Health and Human Services.

Doty, Pamela, Kevin J. Mahoney, and Lori Simon-Rusinowitz. 2007. "Designing the Cash and Counseling Demonstration and Evaluation." *Health Services Research* 42 (1): 378–96.

Draaisma, Muriel. 2019. "Ontario Minister Says Cutting Jobs Is Not Intent of New Health-Care Legislation." CBC News, February 27, 2019. https://www.cbc.ca/news/canada/toronto/ontario-health-minister-legislation-super-agency-jobs-agency-consolidation-1.5035203.

Duffy, Mignon. 2010. "'We Are the Union': Care Work, Unions, and Social Movements." *Humanity and Society* 34 (2): 125–40.

Duffy, Mignon. 2011. *Making Care Count: A Century of Gender, Race, and Paid Care Work*. New Brunswick, N.J.: Rutgers University Press.

Duffy, Mignon, Amy Armenia, and Clare Stacey, eds. 2012. *Caring on the Clock: The Complexities and Contradictions of Paid Care Work*. New Brunswick, N.J.: Rutgers University Press.

DuRivage, Virginia L., Francoise J. Carré, and Chris Tilly. 1998. "Making Labor Law Work for Part-Time and Contingent Workers." In *Contingent Work: American Employment Relations in Transition*, edited by Kathleen Barker, and Kathleen Christensen, 263–80. Ithaca, N.Y.: Cornell University Press.

Early, Steve. 2012. "Bidding Adieu to SEIU: Lessons for Young Labor Organizers?" *HuffPost*, December 7, 2012, updated February 6, 2013. https://www.huffpost.com/entry/bidding-adieu-to-seiu-les_b_2258963.

England, Paula, Michelle Budig, and Nancy Folbre. 2002. "The Wages of Virtue: The Relative Pay of Care Work." *Social Problems* 49 (4): 455–73.

Engman, Athena, and Cynthia Cranford. 2016. "Habit and the Body: Lessons for Social Theories of Habit from the Experiences of People with Physical Disabilities." *Sociological Theory* 34 (1): 27–44.

Erickson, Rebecca J., and Clare L. Stacey. 2013. "Attending to Mind and Body: Engaging the Complexity of Emotion Practice among Caring Professionals." In *Emotional Labor in the 21st Century: Diverse Perspectives on the Psychology of Emotion Regulation at Work*, edited by Alicia A. Grandey, James M. Diefendorff, and Deborah E. Rupp, 175–96. New York: Routledge.

Espiritu, Yen Le. 1992. *Home Bound: Filipino American Lives across Cultures, Communities, and Countries*. Berkeley: University of California Press.

Fine, Janice. 2006. *Worker Centers: Organizing Communities at the Edge of the Dream*. Ithaca, N.Y.: Cornell University Press.

Fine, Michael, and Caroline Glendinning. 2005. "Dependence, Independence or Interdependence? Revisiting the Concepts of 'Care' and 'Dependency.'" *Ageing and Society* 25: 601–21.

Fischer, Bernice, and Joan Tronto. 1990. "Toward a Feminist Theory of Caring." In *Circles of Care: Work and Identity in Women's Lives*, edited by Emily K. Abel and Margaret K. Nelson, 35–62. Albany: State University of New York Press.

Fish, Jennifer. 2017. *Domestic Workers of the World Unite: A Global Movement for Dignity and Human Rights*. New York: New York University Press.

Folbre, Nancy. 2006. "Demanding Quality: Worker/Consumer Coalitions and 'High Road' Strategies in the Care Sector." *Politics and Society* 34 (1): 11–31.

Folbre, Nancy, ed. 2012. *For Love and Money: Care Provision in the United States*. New York: Russell Sage.

Foner, Nancy. 1995. *The Caregiving Dilemma: Work in an American Nursing Home*. Berkeley: University of California Press.

Foner, Nancy. 2013. "Immigration Past and Present." *Daedalus* 142 (3): 16–25.

Fraser, Nancy. 1987. "Women, Welfare and the Politics of Need Interpretation." *Hypatia* 2 (1): 103–21.

Fudge, Judy. 1993. "The Gendered Dimension of Labour Law: Why Women Need Inclusive Unionism and Broader-Based Bargaining." In *Women Challenging Unions: Feminism, Democracy and Militancy*, edited by Linda Briskin and Patricia McDermott, 139–62. Toronto: University of Toronto Press.

Fudge, Judy. 2012. "Blurring Legal Boundaries: Regulating for Decent Work." In *Challenging the Legal Boundaries of Work Regulation*, edited by Judy Fudge, Shae McCrystal, and Kamala Sankaran, 1–26. Oxford: Hart.

Fudge, Judy, and Kendra Strauss, eds. 2014. *Temporary Work, Agencies and Unfree Labour: Insecurity in the New World of Work*. London: Routledge.

Fudge, Judy, Eric Tucker, and Leah Vosko. 2003. "Employee or Independent Contractor? Charting the Legal Significance of the Distinction in Canada." *Canadian Journal of Labour and Employment Law* 10 (2): 193–230.

Fudge, Judy, and Leah F. Vosko. 2001a. "Gender, Segmentation and the Standard Employment Relationship in Canadian Labour Law, Legislation and Policy." *Economic and Industrial Democracy* 22 (2): 271–310.

Fudge, Judy, and Leah F. Vosko. 2001b. "By Whose Standards? Re-regulating the Canadian Labour Market." *Economic and Industrial Democracy* 22 (3): 327–56.

Fuller, Linda, and Vicki Smith. 1991. "Consumers' Reports: Management by Customers in a Changing Economy." *Work, Employment and Society* 5 (1): 1–16.

Gantert, Thomas W., Carol L. McWilliam, Catherine Ward-Griffin, and Natalie J. Allen. 2008. "Key to Me: Seniors' Perceptions of Relationship-Building with In-Home Service Providers." *Canadian Journal on Aging* 27 (1): 23–34.

Garland-Thomson, Rosemarie. 2002. "Integrating Disability, Transforming Feminist Theory." *NWSA Journal* 14 (3): 1–32.

Gibson, Barbara E., Dina Brooks, Dale DeMatteo, and Audrey King. 2009. "Consumer-Directed Personal Assistance and 'Care': Perspectives of Workers and Ventilator Users." *Disability and Society* 24: 317–30.

Giles, Wenona. 2002. *Portuguese Women in Toronto: Gender, Immigration, and Nationalism*. Toronto: University of Toronto Press.

Glendinning, Caroline, and Peter Kemp, eds. 2006. *Cash and Care: Policy Challenges in the Welfare State*. Bristol, UK: Policy Press.

Glenn, Evelyn Nakano. 2010. *Forced to Care: Coercion and Caregiving in America*. Cambridge, Mass.: Harvard University Press.

Goldring, Luin, Carolina Bernstein, and Judith K. Bernhard. 2009. "Institutionalizing Precarious Migratory Status in Canada." *Citizenship Studies* 13 (3): 239–65.

Goldring, Luin, and Patricia Landolt. 2011. "Caught in the Work-Citizenship Matrix: The Lasting Effects of Precarious Legal Status on Work for Toronto Immigrants." *Globalizations* 8 (3): 325–41.

Gottfried, Heidi. 1992. "In the Margins: Flexibility as a Mode of Regulation in the Temporary Help Service Industry." *Work, Employment and Society* 6 (3): 443–60.

Gottfried, Heidi. 2017. "Regulating for Equality: Modalities of Regulation and Gender Gaps." In *Women, Labor Segmentation and Regulation: Varieties of Gender Gaps*, edited by David Peetz and Georgina Murray, 41–60. New York: Palgrave Macmillan.

Goulet, Alix. 1994. "Vulnerable Employee . . . Vulnerable Employer: The Self-Managed Attendant Service Direct Funding Pilot Project: An Examination of the Labour Issues." Unpublished paper.

Grant, Karen R., Carol Amaratunga, Pat Armstrong, Madeline Boscoe, Ann Pederson, and Kay Wilson, eds. 2004. *Caring For/Caring About: Women, Home Care and Unpaid Caregiving.* Aurora, Ont.: Garamond Press.

Guevarra, Anna Romina. 2014. "Supermaids: The Racial Branding of Global Filipino Care Labour." In *Migration and Care Labour: Theory, Policy and Politics*, edited by Bridget Andersen and Isabel Shutes, 130–50. New York: Palgrave Macmillan.

Guevarra, Anna Romina, and Lolita Andrada Lledo. 2013. "Formalizing the Informal: Highly Skilled Filipina Caregivers and the Pilipino Workers Center." In *Immigrant Women Workers in the Neoliberal Age*, edited by Nilda Flores-Gonzalez, Anna Romina Guevarra, Maura Toro-Morn, and Grace Chang, 247–61. Urbana: University of Illinois Press.

Hayes, Lydia. 2017. *Eight Good Reasons Why Adult Social Care Needs Sectoral Collective Bargaining.* Liverpool: Institute of Employment Rights. http://orca.cf.ac.uk/112754.

Hebson, Gail, Jill Rubery, and Damien Grimshaw. 2015. "Rethinking Job Satisfaction in Care Work: Looking Beyond the Care Debates." *Work, Employment and Society* 29 (2): 314–30.

Herrera, Lucero, Saba Waheed, Jessica Lehman, Linday Imai Hong, Melissa Crisp-Cooper, Reyna Orellana, and Aquilina Soriano Versoza. 2017. *Struggles and Support: Home Care Employers.* Los Angeles: UCLA Labor Center, Hand in Hand: The Domestic Employers Network, Senior and Disability Action, Pilipino Workers Center, and Caring across the Generations: Faith Based Los Angeles Alliance. https://www.labor.ucla.edu/publication/cahomecareemployers.

Heshusius, Lous. 2013. *Inside Chronic Pain: An Intimate and Critical Account.* Ithaca, N.Y.: Cornell University Press.

Hickey, Robert. 2012. "End-Users, Public Services, and Industrial Relations: The Restructuring of Social Services in Ontario." *Industrial Relations/Relations Industrielles* 67 (4): 590–611.

Hochschild, Arlie. 2012. *The Managed Heart: The Commercialization of Human Feeling.* 3rd ed. Berkeley: University of California Press.

Hondagneu-Sotelo, Pierrette. 2007. *Doméstica: Immigrant Workers Cleaning and Caring in the Shadows of Affluence.* 2nd ed. Berkeley: University of California Press.

Howes, Candace. 2005. "Living Wages and Retention of Home Care Workers in San Francisco." *Industrial Relations* 44 (1): 139–63.

Hughes, Bill, and Kevin Patterson. 1997. "The Social Model of Disability and the Disappearing Body: Toward a Sociology of Impairment." *Disability and Society* 12 (3): 325–40.

Iacovetta, Franca. 1992. *Such Hardworking People: Italian Immigrants in Post-War Toronto.* Toronto: University of Toronto Press.

Ibarra, María de la Luz. 2010. "My Reward Is Not Money: Deep Alliances and the End of Life Care among Mexicana Workers and Their Wards." In *Intimate Labors: Cultures, Technologies, and the Politics of Care*, edited by Eileen Boris and Rhacel Salazar Parreñas. Stanford, Calif.: Stanford University Press.

Johnston, Paul. 1994. *Success While Others Fail: Social Movement Unionism and the Public Workplace.* Ithaca, N.Y.: Cornell University Press.

Kafer, Alison. 2013. *Feminist, Queer, Crip.* Bloomington: Indiana University Press.

Kalleberg, Arne. 2011. *Good Jobs, Bad Jobs: The Rise of Polarized and Precarious Employment Systems in the United States, 1970s to 2000s.* New York: Russell Sage.

Kang, Millian. 2010. *The Managed Hand: Race, Gender, and the Body in Beauty Service Work*. Berkeley: University of California Press.

Karner, Tracy. 1998. "Professional Caring: Homecare Workers as Fictive Kin." *Journal of Aging Studies* 12: 69–82.

Kelly, Christine. 2016. *Disability Politics and Care: The Challenge of Direct Funding*. Vancouver: University of British Columbia Press.

Kimura, Jennifer, and Colette V. Browne. 2009. "Eldercare in a Filipino Community: Older Women's Attitudes toward Caregiving and Service Use." *Journal of Women and Aging* 21: 229–43.

Krogh, Kerri. 2004. "Redefining Home Care for Women with Disabilities: A Call for Citizenship." In *Caring For/Caring About: Women, Home Care and Unpaid Caregiving*, edited by Karen R. Grant, Carol Amaratunga, Pat Armstrong, Madeline Boscoe, Ann Pederson, and Kay Wilson, 115–46. Aurora, Ont.: Garamond Press.

Kumar, Pradeep, and Chris Schenk. 2006. "Union Renewal and Organizational Change." In *Paths to Union Renewal: Canadian Experiences*, edited by Pradeep Kumar and Chris Schenk, 29–60. Toronto: Broadview Press.

Laher, Nazeefah. 2017. *Diversity, Aging and Intersectionality in Ontario Home Care: Why We Need an Intersectional Approach to Respond to Home Care Needs*. Toronto: Wellesley Institute. https://www.wellesleyinstitute.com/wp-content/uploads/2017/05/Diversity-and-Aging.pdf.

Lan, Pei-Chia. 2002. "Subcontracting Filial Piety: Elder Care in Ethic Chinese Immigrant Families in California." *Journal of Family Issues* 23 (7): 812–35.

Leidner, Robin. 1993. *Fast Food, Fast Talk: Service Work and the Routinization of Everyday Life*. Berkeley: University of California Press.

Little, Deborah. 2015. "Building a Movement of Caring Selves: Organizing Direct Care Workers." In *Caring on the Clock: The Complexities and Contradictions of Paid Care Work*, edited by Mignon Duffy, Amy Armenia, and Clare Stacey, 251–62. New Brunswick, N.J.: Rutgers University Press.

Lopez, Steven. 2004. *Reorganizing the Rust Belt: An Inside Study of the American Labor Movement*. Berkeley: University of California Press.

Lopez, Steven. 2006. "Emotional Labor and Organized Emotional Care." *Work and Occupations* 33 (2): 133–60.

Lord, John. 2010. *Impact: Changing the Way We View Disability: The History, Perspective, and Vision of the Independent Living Movement in Canada*. Ottawa: Independent Living Canada.

Lord, John, and Peggy Hutchinson. 2003. "Individualized Support and Funding: Building Blocks for Capacity Building and Inclusion." *Disability and Society* 18 (1): 71–86.

Lowell, Lindsay, Susan Martin, and Robyn Stone. 2010. "Ageing and Care Giving in the United States: Policy Contexts and the Immigrant Workforce." *Journal of Population Ageing* 3 (1–2): 59–82.

MacDonald, Cameron. 2015. "Ethnic Logics: Race and Ethnicity in Nanny Employment." In *Caring on the Clock: The Complexities and Contradictions of Paid Care Work*, edited by Mignon Duffy, Amy Armenia, and Clare Stacey, 153–64. New Brunswick, N.J.: Rutgers University Press.

Macdonald, Fiona, and Sara Charlesworth. 2016. "Cash for Care under the NDIS: Shaping Care Workers' Working Conditions?" *Journal of Industrial Relations* 58 (5): 627–46.

Mahon, Rianne, and Fiona Robinson, eds. 2011. *Feminist Ethics and Social Policy: Towards a New Global Political Economy of Care*. Vancouver: University of British Columbia Press.

Mareschal, Patrice M. 2006. "Innovation and Adaptation: Contrasting Efforts to Organize Homecare Workers in Four States." *Labor Studies Journal* 31 (1): 25–49.

Martin-Matthews, Anne, Joanie Sims-Gould, and John Naslund. 2010. "Ethno-cultural Diversity in Homecare Work in Canada: Issues Confronted, Strategies Employed." *International Journal of Ageing and Later Life* 5 (2): 77–101.

Martin-Matthews, Anne, Joanie Sims-Gould, and Catherine E. Tong. 2012. "Canada's Complex and Fractionalized Home Care Context: Perspectives of Workers, Elderly Clients, Family Carers, and Home Care Managers." *Canadian Review of Social Policy* 68–69: 55–74.

McCann, Deirdre, and Jill Murray. 2014. "Prompting Formalisation through Labour Market Regulation: A 'Framed Flexibility' Model for Domestic Work." *Industrial Law Journal* 43 (3): 319–48.

Meyer, Michelle, Michelle Donelly, and Patricia Weerakoon. 2007. "'They're Taking the Place of My Hands': Perspectives of People Using Personal Care." *Disability and Society* 22: 595–608.

Michel, Sonya, and Ito Peng. 2012. "All in the Family? Migrants, Nationhood, and Care Regimes in Asia and North America." *Journal of European Social Policy* 4: 406–18.

Milkman, Ruth. 2010. Introduction to *Working for Justice: The LA Model of Organizing and Advocacy*, edited by Ruth Milkman, Joshua Bloom, and Victor Narro, 1–19. Ithaca, N.Y.: Cornell University Press.

Milkman, Ruth, and Ed Ott, eds. 2014. *New Labor in New York: Precarious Workers and the Future of the Labor Movement*. Ithaca, N.Y.: Cornell University Press.

Moore, Lisa. 2018. "Transformative Organizing in Precarious Times." *Critical Sociology* 44 (7–8): 1225–34.

Morris, Jenny. 2001. "Impairment and Disability: Constructing an Ethics of Care That Promotes Human Rights." *Hypatia* 16 (4): 1–16.

Nazareno, Jennifer. 2015. "The Outsourced State: The Retraction of Public Caregiving in America." Ph.D. diss., University of California, San Francisco.

Nazareno, Jennifer, Rhacel Salazar Parreñas, and Yu-Kang Fan. 2014. *Can I Ever Retire? The Plight of Migrant Filipino Caregivers in Los Angeles*. University of California, Los Angeles: Institute for Research on Labor and Employment. https://escholarship.org/uc/item/0zj455z5.

Ness, Immanuel. 1999. "Organizing Home Health Workers: A New York City Case Study." *Working USA* 3 (4): 59–95.

O'Conner, James. 1964a. "Towards a Theory of Community Unions." *Studies on the Left* 4 (2): 143–48.

O'Conner, James. 1964b. "Towards a Theory of Community Unions II." *Studies on the Left* 4 (3): 99–101.

Omi, Michael, and Howard Winant. 2015. *Racial Formation in the United States*. 3rd ed. London: Routledge.

Ong, Paul M., Jordan Rickles, Ruth Matthias, and A. E. Benjamin. 2002. *California Caregivers: Final Labor Market Analysis*. Los Angeles: UCLA School of Public Policy and Social Research. https://escholarship.org/uc/item/31r540qv.

Parreñas, Rhacel Salazar. 2015. *Servants of Globalization: Women, Migration, and Domestic Work*. 2nd ed. Stanford, Calif.: Stanford University Press.

Piercy, Kathleen. 2001. "'We Couldn't Do without Them': The Value of Close Relationships between Older Adults and Their Nonfamily Caregivers." *Generations* 25 (2): 41–47.

Poo, Ai-Jen. 2015. *The Age of Dignity: Preparing for the Elder Boom in a Changing America*. New York: New Press.

Price, Margaret. 2010. *Mad at School: Rhetorics of Mental Disability and Academic Life.* Ann Arbor: University of Michigan Press.

Pringle, Paul, and Hailey Branson-Potts. 2013. "Ex-SEIU Local Exec Convicted of Stealing from Low-Income Members." *Los Angeles Times*, January 28, 2013. https://www.latimes.com/world/la-xpm-2013-jan-28-la-me-tyrone-freeman-20130129-story.html.

Reitz, Jeffrey G., Josh Curtis, and Jennifer Elrick. 2014. "Immigrant Skill Utilization: Trends and Policy Issues." *Journal of International Migration and Integration* 15 (1): 1–26.

Rhee, Nari, and Carol Zabin. 2009. "Aggregating Dispersed Workers: Union Organizing in the 'Care' Industries." *Geoforum* 40 (6): 969–79.

Rivas, Lynn. 2003. "Invisible Labors: Caring for the Independent Person." In *Global Woman: Nannies, Maids and Sex Workers in the New Economy*, edited by Barbara Ehrenreich and Arlie Hochschild. London: Granta Books.

Rivas, Lynn 2007. "Built to Last: Preventing Coalition Breakdowns." Ph.D. diss., University of California Berkeley.

Roberts, Dorothy. 1997. "Spiritual and Menial Housework." *Yale Journal of Law and Feminism* 9 (1): 51–80.

Rodgers, Gerry, and Janine Rodgers, eds. 1989. *Precarious Jobs in Labour Market Regulation: The Growth of Atypical Employment in Western Europe.* Geneva: International Institute for Labour Studies.

Rodriguez, Jason. 2014. *Labors of Love: Nursing Homes and the Structures of Care Work.* New York: New York University Press.

Rodriguez, Robyn Magalit. 2010. *Migrants for Export: How the Philippine State Brokers Labor to the World.* Minneapolis: University of Minnesota Press.

Roeher Institute. 1997. *Self-Managed Attendant Services in Ontario: Direct Funding Pilot Project, Final Evaluation Report.* North York, Ont.: Roeher Institute.

Rollins, Judith. 1987. *Between Women: Domestics and Their Employers.* Philadelphia: Temple University Press.

Romero, Mary. 2002. *Maid in the U.S.A.* Tenth anniversary ed. London: Routledge.

Romero, Mary. 2011. *The Maid's Daughter.* New York: New York University Press.

Romero, Mary. 2018. *Introducing Intersectionality.* Cambridge: Polity Press.

Roosevelt, Margo. 2017. "The Fight to Deduct Union Fees from Paychecks Will Be Fought in Santa Ana's Federal Court." *Orange County Register*, July 7, 2017. https://www.ocregister.com/2017/07/07/lawsuit-challenges-a-california-home-care-union.

Ross, Stephanie. 2013. "Social Unionism and Union Power in Public Sector Unions." In *Public Sector Unions in the Age of Austerity*, edited by Stephanie Ross and Larry Savage, 57–64. Halifax: Fernwood.

Salzinger, Leslie. 1991. "A Maid by Any Other Name: The Transformation of 'Dirty Work' by Central American Immigrants." In *Ethnography Unbound: Power and Resistance in the Modern Metropolis*, edited by Michael Burawoy, Alice Burton, Ann Ferguson, Katherine Fox, Joshua Gamson. Nadine Gartrell, Leslie Hurst, et al., 139–60. Berkeley: University of California Press.

Schwiter, Karin, Kendra Strauss, and Kim England. 2017. "At Home with the Boss: Migrant Live-in Caregivers, Social Reproduction and Constrained Agency in the UK, Canada, Austria and Switzerland." *Transactions of the Institute of British Geographers* 43 (3): 1–15.

Shakespeare, Tom. 2000. *Help.* Birmingham, UK: Venture Press.

Sharma, Nandita. 2012. "The 'Difference' That Borders Make: 'Temporary Foreign Workers' and the Social Organization of Unfreedom in Canada." In *Legislated Inequality: Temporary Labour Migration in Canada*, edited by Patti Tamara

Lenard and Christine Straehle, 26–47. Montreal: McGill–Queens University Press.

Sherman, Rachael. 2007. *Class Acts: Service and Inequality in Luxury Hotels*. Berkeley: University of California Press.

Shutes, Isabel, and Carlos Chiatti. 2012. "Migrant Labour and the Marketisation of Care of Older People: The Employment of Migrant Care Workers by Families and Service Providers." *Journal of European Social Policy* 22 (4): 392–405.

Silvers, Anita. 1995. "Reconciling People with Disabilities." *Hypatia* 10 (1): 30–55.

Smith, Vicki. 1998. "The Fractured World of the Temporary Worker: Power, Participation, and Fragmentation in the Contemporary Workplace." *Social Problems* 4 (1): 411–30.

Smith, Vicki, and Esther Neuwirth. 2008. *The Good Temp*. Ithaca, N.Y.: Cornell University Press.

Stacey, Clare. 2011. *The Caring Self: The Work Experiences of Home Care Aides*. Ithaca, N.Y.: Cornell University Press.

Stacey, Clare, and Linsey Ayers. 2012. "Caught between Love and Money: The Experiences of Paid Family Caregivers." *Qualitative Sociology* 35 (1): 47–64.

Standing, Guy. 2011. *The Precariat: The New Dangerous Class*. London: A&C Black.

Stasiulis, Daiva, and Abigail Bakan. 2005. *Negotiating Citizenship: Migrant Women in Canada and the Global System*. Toronto: University of Toronto Press.

Stone, Deborah. 2000. "Why We Need a Care Movement." *Nation*, February 23, 2000. https://www.thenation.com/article/why-we-need-care-movement.

Takeyama, Akiko. 2016. *Staged Seduction: Selling Dreams in a Tokyo Host Club*. Stanford, Calif.: Stanford University Press.

Tattersall, Amanda, 2010. *Power in Coalition: Strategies for Strong Unions and Social Change*. Ithaca, N.Y.: Cornell University Press.

Theodosis, Catherine. 2006. "Recovering Emotion from Emotion Management." *Sociology* 40 (5): 893–910.

Trnka, Susanna. 2017. *One Blue Child: Asthma, Responsibility, and the Politics of Global Health*. Stanford, Calif.: University of Stanford Press.

Tronto, Joan. 2013. *Caring Democracy: Markets, Equality and Justice*. New York: New York University Press.

Tungohan, Ethel, Rupa Banerjee, Wayne Chu, Petronila Cleto, Conely de Leon, Mila Garcia, Philip Kelly, Marco Luciano, Cynthia Palmaria, and Christopher Sorio. 2015. "After the Live-In Caregiver Program: Filipina Caregivers' Experiences of Graduated and Uneven Citizenship." *Canadian Ethnic Studies* 47 (1): 87–105.

Twigg, Julia. 2000. *Bathing: The Body and Community Care*. London: Routledge.

Um, Seong-gee, and Naomi Lightman. 2016. *Ensuring Healthy Aging for All: Home Care Access for Diverse Senior Populations in the GTA*. Toronto: Wellesley Institute. https://www.wellesleyinstitute.com/wp-content/uploads/2016/07/Ensuring-Healthy-Aging-For-All_Wellesley-Institute.pdf.

Ungerson, Clare. 1999. "Personal Assistants and Disabled People: An Examination of a Hybrid Form of Work and Care." *Work, Employment and Society* 13 (4): 583–99.

Ungerson, Clare. 2004. "Whose Empowerment and Independence? A Cross-National Perspective on 'Cash for Care' Schemes." *Ageing and Society* 24 (2): 189–212.

Ungerson, Clare, and Sue Yeandle. 2007. *Cash for Care in Developed Welfare States*. New York: Palgrave Macmillan.

Valentine, Fraser. 1994. *The Canadian Independent Living Movement: An Historical Overview*. Ottawa: Canadian Association of Independent Living Centres.

Vosko, Leah. F. 2000. *Temporary Work: The Gendered Rise of a Precarious Employment Relationship*. Toronto: University of Toronto Press.

Vosko, Leah. F. 2011. *Managing the Margins: Gender, Citizenship and the International Regulation of Precarious Employment*. Oxford: Oxford University Press.

Walsh, Jess. 2001. "Creating Unions, Creating Employers: A Los Angeles Home-Care Campaign." In *Care Work: The Quest for Security*, edited by Mary Daly, 219–33. Geneva: Internal Labour Organization.

Walsh, Kieran, and Eamon O'Shea. 2010. "Marginalised Care: Migrant Workers Caring for Older People in Ireland." *Journal of Population Ageing* 3 (1–2): 17–37.

Watson, Nick, Linda McKie, Bill Hughes, Debra Hopkins, and Sue Gregory. 2004. "(Inter)dependence, Needs and Care: The Potential for Disability and Feminist Theorists to Develop an Emancipatory Framework Model." *Sociology* 38: 331–50.

Wilder, Esther Isabelle. 2006. *Wheeling and Dealing: Living with Spinal Cord Injury*. Nashville: Vanderbilt University Press.

Williams, A. P., J. Barnsley, S. Leggat, R. Deber, and P. Baranek. 1999. "Long-term Care Goes to Market: Managed Competition and Ontario's Reform of Community-based Services." *Canadian Journal on Aging* 18: 125–53.

Williams, Fiona. 2001. "In and Beyond New Labour: Towards a New Political Ethics of Care." *Critical Social Policy* 21 (4): 467–93.

Williams, Fiona. 2012. "Converging Variations in Migrant Care in Europe." *Journal of European Social Policy* 22 (4): 363–76.

Williams, Fiona. 2018, October. "Expert Panel on Care and Carework in an Uncaring World." Presented at the Gender, Migration and Work of Care Project Conference, University of Toronto.

Williams, Fiona, and Deborah Brennan. 2012. "Care, Markets and Migration in a Globalising World: Introduction to the Special Issue." *Journal of European Social Policy* 22 (4): 355–62.

Wilton, Robert. 2004. "From Flexibility to Accommodation? Disabled People and the Reinvention of Paid Work." *Transactions of the Institute of British Geographers* 29 (4): 420–32.

Yamaki, Chikako K., and Yoshihiko Yamazaki. 2004. "'Instruments', 'Employees', 'Companions', 'Social Assets': Understanding Relationships between Persons with Disabilities and Their Assistants in Japan." *Disability and Society* 19: 595–608.

Yelson, Rich. 2017. "At Labor's Crossroads." *Nation*, March 8, 2017. https://www.the nation.com/article/at-labors-crossroads.

Yoshida, Karen, Vic Willi, Ian Parker, and David Locker. 2000. *A Case Study Analysis of the Ontario Self-Managed Attendant Services Direct Funding Attendant Service Pilot: Independent Living in Action*. A Partnership between Department of Physical Therapy, Faculty of Medicine, University of Toronto, and Centre for Independent Living Toronto.

Young, Iris Marion. 1989. *Justice and the Politics of Difference*. Princeton, N.J.: Princeton University Press.

Zelizer, Viviana. 2010. "Caring Everywhere." In *Intimate Labors: Cultures, Technologies and the Politics of Care*, edited by Eileen Boris and Rhacel Salazar Parreñas, 267–79. Stanford, Calif.: Stanford University Press.

Zelizer, Viviana. 2011. *Economic Lives: How Culture Shapes the Economy*. Princeton, N.J.: Princeton University Press.

Zlomislic, Diana. 2016. "Report Revealed Major Gaps in Ontario Personal Support Worker Registry." *Toronto Star*, October 6, 2016. https://www.thestar.com/news/canada/2016/10/06/report-revealed-major-gaps-in-ontario-personal-support-worker-registry.html.

Index

Page numbers in *italics* refer to figures and tables.

women: elder care and, 28; emotional skills and, 52–53; as personal support workers, 21–27, 73–78, 90–91 (*see also* family care economies; immigrant women workers); unpaid domestic work by, 22, 24, 28, 35–36, 48–49, 52, 55, 87, 93, 98, 104, 156. *See also* gendered inequalities; immigrant women
worker centers, 171–72, 199n67, 199n74
worker cooperatives, 168
workers, 20–39; as able-bodied people, 153; class and (*see* class inequalities); collective supports (*see* collective representation; social unionism; unions); degrading treatment of, 34–35; as domestic servants, 7 (*see also* domestic workers); gender and (*see* gendered inequalities); health and safety risks, 114–18, 139, 155; multiple

jobs and, 33, 89, 157; nationality of, 7; objectification of, 138; personalities of, 67–70; quitting by, 75–76, 137; race and, 7–8 (*see also* racialization; workers of color); security for (*see* security); as self-employed, 7; services performed by (*see* tasks); skills, 35–38, 51–53; social locations of, 16, 19, 58; turnover, 87; use of term, 6
Workers Action Centre (WAC), 171
workers of color, 8, 130, 143–45. *See also* immigrant women workers; Pilipina immigrant workers; racialization
Workplace Safety and Insurance Board (WSIB), 61–62

Zelizer, Viviana, 181n52, 191n75

www.ingramcontent.com/pod-product-compliance
Lightning Source LLC
Chambersburg PA
CBHW030314270326
41926CB00010B/1366